McDonnell Douglas A-4 Skyhawk

probe and buddy-store refuelling capability; the A-4C brought with it an expanded ordnance capability and, perhaps most important, terrain clearance radar that gave the Scooter its first, albeit limited, all-weather attack capability. With the A-4E came the addition of two more weapons pylons, making a total of five; the aft avionics package of the A-4F, called by many the 'hump', brought much-needed electronic countermeasures systems with which to meet the developing threat in

The TA-4J served with the Navy's training command from the late 1960s until 1999 and trained thousands of naval and Marine Corps pilots. This Skyhawk from CTW-1'sVT-7 at NAF El Centro presents an inspiring head-on view.
Ted Carlson

CHAPTER ONE

'Heinemann's Hot Rod' – The Development of the A-4

No words can say more about an aeroplane than those by people who have flown it, both in peace and in battle. One such person is Capt Otto E. Krueger who flew the A-4 on two cruises over the hostile skies of North Vietnam:

The aircraft was simply wonderful to fly. We loved the Scooter! We always knew what it was going to do and it always did what it was supposed to do. It was the last of the real pilots' airplanes, and by that I mean there was no help from a lot of gadgets. We used iron sites and DR (dead-reckoning) navigation. There were few redundant systems. This was driven home to me one nasty dark night as I sat on the port cat aboard *Shangri-La* in the Med. Next to me was an F-4D Skyray, 'all weather fighter'. They had two gyros; a primary, which was about the size of a basketball, and a secondary, which was more like a baseball. Our gyro was about the size of a silver dollar. Later models were a bit better, but not much.

As I'm getting ready to launch, the pilot – squadron CO – reports that his plane is down, the 'Ford's' standby gyro isn't working. And, BOOM, here I go off into the night with my A-4, which wasn't really designed for 'all weather' usage, and I'm thinking, we don't even have a standby gyro![1]

A-4A to TA-4F, this late 1960s VA-125 photo depicts all A-4 Skyhawk models made by Douglas to date. The VA-125 'Rough Raiders' were responsible for training all west coast A-4 pilots following their graduation from the training wings. Harry Gann

The Douglas Aircraft Company

The Douglas Aircraft Company was founded in 1920 by Donald Wills Douglas, following his brief tenure with aircraft mogul Glenn L. Martin (responsible for the Martin PBM and B-26) from 1916–20. With the financial backing of sportsman David R. Davis, Douglas began his company in 1920 as the Davis-Douglas Aircraft Company. Douglas's first venture, a sturdy biplane dubbed the 'Cloudster', was ordered by Davis for his use. Ironically, the Cloudster bore a remarkable semblance to the requirements issued by the US Navy for a new torpedo bomber.

With new financing, the Davis name was dropped, thereby becoming the Douglas Aircraft Company, and was issued with a contract to produce the Cloudster as the DT-1 – signifying that it was the first type of Douglas-built Torpedo aircraft. While only one DT-1 was built, subsequent production of a variant known as the DT-2 began, with forty examples built for the US Navy and another forty-six built under licensing agreements.

The Douglas affiliation with the Navy continued throughout the 1930s, with production of the TBD Devastator and later, the SBD Dauntless dive-bomber/scout made famous in the 1942 Battle of Midway. Douglas sought a follow-on to the Dauntless, developing the Destroyer. However, real fame came through the AD Skyraider series. Designed too late for World War II operations, the Skyraider saw action in Korea and Vietnam, operating from both carriers and shore-based Marine installations. Skyraiders flew hundreds of sorties in Vietnam until they were withdrawn from carrier service in late 1968. Other Douglas designs, including the A3D Skywarrior and the F4D Skyray, carried on the company's tradition of excellence in the attack and fighter roles respectively. The Skyray is regarded as one of the best fighters of its time. Moreover, the A3D served with Navy units until the mid-1980s, as an electronic surveillance aircraft, tanker, and electronic aggressor.

These short comments say it all when talking about the Skyhawk, from its ruggedness to the simplicity of its design.

The Setting

During the late 1940s and early 1950s, the US Navy saw a remarkable transition in both naval strategy and assets, as the Navy moved from a vast blue-water fleet dominated by propeller-driven aircraft to the atomic age and jet-power. Indeed, following the end of World War II, many were questioning whether carriers had any role to play given the development of the new long-range, atomic-armed strategic bombers.

In 1945, the Navy had ninety-eight carriers, twenty-three of which were of the newer 27,000 ton 'Essex' class. Three other large carriers of the 45,000 ton 'Midway' class were also nearing completion, and would soon join the fleet. In less than a year, however, carrier forces would be slashed to twenty-three carriers, with naval combat aircraft down to just 14,125 aircraft

Two historic planes, the XA4D-1 and its big brother, the Douglas A3D-1, sit side-by-side at Mines Field (LAX), California, in June 1954, just prior to the Skyhawk's first flight. Boeing Historical Archives via Harry Gann

from the 29,125 of a year earlier. Events such as the Bikini Atoll test in 1946, which destroyed numerous surface ships, including aircraft carriers, left many questioning the vulnerability of any surface ship to nuclear weapons. Carrier forces were also troubled by their inability to carry the large atomic weapons of the day, some of which weighed up to 10,000lb (4,530kg), and measured nearly 11ft (3.4m) in length. Without an atomic delivery capability, some wished to relegate the Navy to transport and anti-submarine roles.

To make matters worse, the Navy itself was experiencing growing pains as it attempted to accommodate the newer jet aircraft into carrier service. Landing in bad weather was difficult enough for slower, conventionally powered propeller aircraft, let alone the newer jets, with their higher approach speeds. Naval aviation was in a state of flux, a force in transition, caught between two eras. Even as late as 1950, much of the carrier deck was occupied by propeller-driven aircraft, namely the F4U Corsair and the AD Skyraider. Most of the carriers were too small for jets, and the proposed 58,000 ton supercarrier, USS *United States* (CVB 58) had been cancelled, as it was considered unnecessary in light of the carrier's overall mission and the Air Force's developing Strategic Air Command.

Naval aviation's role was soon clarified, however, when the North Koreans crossed the 38th Parallel on 25 June 1950, marking the start of the Korean War in which carrier forces would play a vital part in containing Communist advances. Contrary to the predictions of military planners of the day, the atomic weapons, and, therefore, the entire fleet of strategic bombers, played no role. Tactical air power dominated the scene, with close air support and interdiction being the primary missions. Particularly in the early days of the war, and during MacArthur's famed Inchon landings, much of this air power was supplied by carrier aviation. Indeed, 41 per cent of all sorties were flown by Navy and Marine Corps aircraft, including over half of the total interdiction sorties.

While carrier aviation made its mark in the Korean War, it became clear that the days of the propeller plane as a mainstay of naval aviation were over. Attack planes were far too vulnerable to jet interceptors and needed the added boost of jet power to aid ingress and egress. Even the American jet planes of the day, namely, the Grumman F9F Panther, would have been no match for the MiGs had the North Korean pilots been better trained.

It was against this backdrop that the Skyhawk emerged.

Origins of the A-4

Development of the A-4 Skyhawk stemmed from the convergence of several factors. The Navy needed a jet-powered replacement for the propeller-driven Douglas AD Skyraider series attack aircraft, and internal events within the Douglas Aircraft Company had focused attention on reducing overall aircraft weight and complexity – something that had become a growing trend in the aviation industry since the 1940s.

Since 1946, the carrier-based AD Skyraider had been operating with fleet units as the air wing's light attack and close-support aircraft. However, the Navy was beginning to hear complaints from AD pilots about flying the relatively slow (as compared to its jet-powered brethren, the Grumman F9F Panthers/Cougars and McDonnell F2H Banshees) propeller-driven, Skyraiders on long-range missions, which could last from eight to twelve hours and lead to problems associated with aircrew fatigue. AD pilots also voiced concern over the Skyraider's effectiveness when pitted against the sleeker and more nimble jet-powered Soviet-built fighters of the day, such as the Soviet-built MiG-15 'Fagot'.

Also at the forefront of the Navy's collective mind was the need to be closely involved with the growing strategic arm of the US military. With the US Air Force's B-47 Stratojet and the introduction of the B-52 Stratofortress, the Navy was keen to protect its role of delivering nuclear weapons deep into the heart of enemy territory. Both the North American AJ-1 and the Douglas A3D served this purpose, but were recognized as large airframes unsuitable for close air support and conventional, non-nuclear attack carrier operations. What was needed was a smaller aircraft, with nuclear strike capability, incorporating recent advances in weapon's miniaturization, that could equally fill the conventional role. With these concerns in mind, the Navy began looking for an alternative to the AD series that would feature a more manoeuvrable and smaller jet-powered aircraft, with the load-carrying capabilities of the AD and the added capability for delivering nuclear weapons.

At the same time as the Navy was looking for a jet-powered AD series replacement, Ed Heinemann, chief engineer, and his team at Douglas, El Segundo were pursuing a high-performance, lightweight fighter design with thrust/weight

---

Ed Heinemann – Father of the Skyhawk

Born Gustave Henry Heinemann on 14 March 1908, Ed Heinemann began his association with the Douglas Aircraft Company in 1926 as a draftsman where he prepared tracings and drawings for early model Douglas aircraft and later, at the age of twenty-five, worked on Douglas's successor to the TD-1, the T2D-1. During this time, Heinemann worked in close association with John K. Northrop who would later leave Douglas to form Northrop. Although he lacked formal training as an engineer, Heinemann learned quickly and gained valuable experience taking night courses in aircraft design from Don Berlin, a Douglas engineer.

Heinemann's hard work and expertise were rewarded when he was promoted to chief engineer of the Northrop Division in 1937, which was renamed El Segundo in 1938. There, Heinemann designed such famous planes as the US Navy's Devastator and Dauntless, the DB-7/A-20 Boston/Havoc and A-26 Invader used by the Army Air Corps.

Perhaps Heinemann's biggest success, aside from the A4D, was the propeller-driven AD series Skyraider, of which over 3,000 were produced in all-weather attack, airborne early warning, and electronic warfare variants. Serving in Korea and Vietnam, Skyraiders were seldom outmatched in their ability to deliver mass destruction.

Heinemann's success was not limited to propeller aircraft. Following the end of World War II, two jet designs emerged from Heinemann's Douglas design team to fill the growing need for carrier-based jet-powered fighter aircraft. The first was the all-weather F3D Skynight, serving as a two-seat night fighter/interdiction aircraft. This capable aircraft was later adapted by the US Marines as an electronic warfare platform, where it performed well until the entry of the Grumman EA-6 Electric Intruder and later the EA-6B Prowler. Also designed by Heinemann was the supersonic delta-winged shaped fighter, the Douglas F4D Skyray, which served with frontline Navy

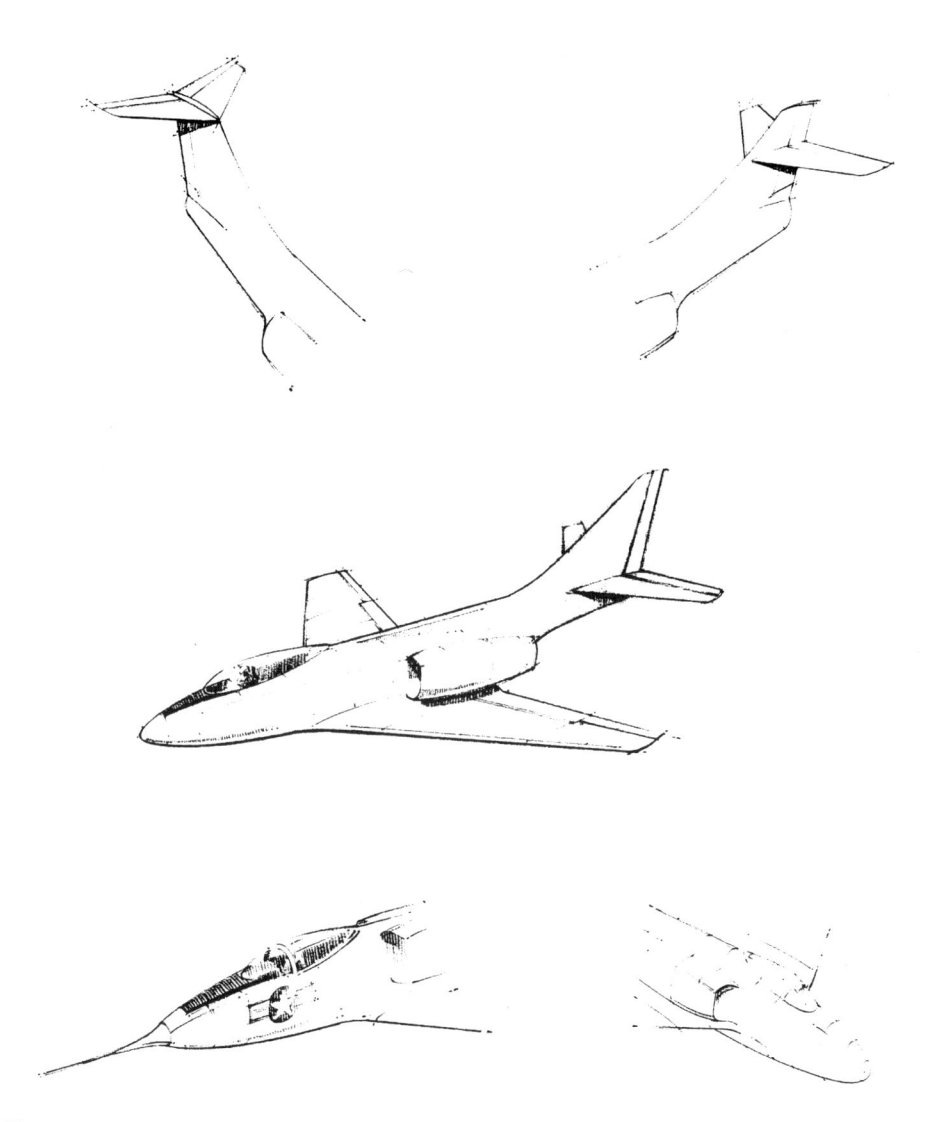

These drawings depict the first rough sketches of the A4D aerodynamic shapes. Notable are the tailless arrangement and the high tailplane configuration. Sketch via Harry Gann Collection

the probable requirements for future military aircraft. At the heart of this study were concerns over the growing complexity, weight, and cost of new aircraft and how those factors would ultimately impact upon the shape and strength of the US military. This trend dated back to World War II and was labelled by Douglas engineers as the 'growth-factor', a term referring to the additional weight likely to be added to a new aircraft design after it becomes operational. The study noted that, once the growth-factor exceeds the aircraft's original design weight by more than 12 to 15 per cent, the aircraft suffers a significant degradation in speed and performance. The report further pointed out that for every pound of weight added to a design, overall weight was increased by a factor of ten due to the addition of support equipment.

Heinemann himself had tried to guard against this trend when he designed the successful AD Skyraider series in 1944. Mandating that engineers justify every nut and bolt, the first AD was produced for the Navy a full 1,000lb (455kg) below the design specifications. Even this advantage, however, fell by the wayside as new upgrades and variants (radars, electronic radomes, and refuelling stores) were continually fielded. Indeed, over the course of its career, the Skyraider would be produced in seven variants ending with the AD-7 (A-1J) in 1957. When the AD series was phased out from the fleet during the Vietnam War, the empty weight had grown from 18,300lb (8,300kg) to 25,000lb (11,350kg). Other aircraft of the day were weighty too; the Panther weighed 18,700lb (8,490kg) and the Banshee 23,300lb (10,580kg). However none approached the awesome weight of the A3D Skywarrior, coming in at 82,000lb (37,250kg). Heinemann concluded that most combat aircraft were vastly overweight for the task assigned and that additional weight was never matched by a concurrent growth in power.

Heinemann Introduces the Lightweight Design

In January 1952, Heinemann and Robert Canady of Douglas' Washington office met with Rear-Admiral Apollo Soucek in Washington DC to discuss how to contain both the weight and cost of the next-generation jet-powered fighters then entering fleet service. (Soucek, a

ratio exceeding one-to-one. Remarkably, other fighters of the day, the F-86 Sabre and F9F-2 Panther, while noted for their agility and superior handling characteristics, touted ratios of a mere 0.36:1 and 0.39:1 respectively. Heinemann sought to beat that ratio, in part, through a simpler, more streamlined design.

It is interesting to note that while Heinemann was pursuing a lightweight fighter design, US naval commanders in Korea were already calling for a new generation of jet fighters capable of operating on a par with MiG-15 type jets. This was highlighted in the Navy's first Korean War evaluation report, which stated: '... at high priority provide a carrier fighter capable of combating contemporary developments of the MiG-15. The F9F had inadequate performance for fully effective defense against MiG-15 type jet fighters'.[2] This, too, was the general feeling of the carrier commanders, as the *Valley Forge* action reports commented: '... it is believed that if they [North Korea] had been manned by pilots as aggressive and well trained as ours that own pilot and plane losses would have been great'.[3]

The Rule of Ten

During the early 1950s, Douglas engineers had embarked on a comprehensive study of

former Commander of Task Force 77 during the Korean War, was sitting in for Rear-Admiral Thomas S. Combs, Chief of the Bureau of Aeronautics, who was unavailable.)

At this meeting Heinemann presented Soucek with an unsolicited outline of his lightweight fighter design, which he believed would reverse the trend towards heavier and more expensive aircraft. Soucek quickly informed Heinemann that, although the design was intriguing, the Navy was not currently interested in new jet-based fighter designs. At that time, development was underway of the Chance Vought F8U-1 Crusader, which was authorized in 1953 and later saw action in Vietnam. Nevertheless, Soucek asked Heinemann to see if the design concepts could be applied to procure a new jet-powered attack design in the 30,000lb weight class, which would be capable of delivering a nuclear bomb.

Within a matter of weeks, Heinemann's team was back in Washington with a proposal surpassing all of the Navy's essential criteria. Measuring approximately 38ft 4in (11.7m) in length with a wing span of 27ft 6in (8.4m), Heinemann's design would provide a top speed of over 600mph (970km/h) a combat radius of nearly 460 miles (740km), and still come in at less than half of the specified weight load. Although doubts were expressed by BuAer staff, Soucek was sufficiently impressed to authorize Douglas to conduct additional design work.

The Basic Skyhawk Takes Shape

With this in hand, Heinemann and his team returned to El Segundo and began converting their paper ideas into reality. The design pursued by Douglas concentrated on a cropped delta-wing configuration, to which Heinemann was first introduced while working with John Northrop during the 1930s. This design was also to some extent derived from the Douglas F4D-1 Skyray's delta wing, although modified with a low aspect ratio and a quarter-chord sweep of 33 degrees. With this design, the wings could be shortened to 27ft 6in (8.3m), saving some 200lb (90kg) in metal. Moreover, the reduced wing size permitted designers to forego traditional and bulky wing-folding mechanisms, since the A4D could now fit neatly

The XA2D Skyshark represented the initial attempt by Douglas at an AD Skyraider successor. This design was powered by a 5,332shp Allison XT40-A-6 turboprop engine driving two four-bladed contra-rotating propellers and armed with four 20mm cannons. Problems with the engines simply could not be worked out and the project was cancelled, with approximately $41 million in funding diverted to what became the A-4D programme. Harry Gann

Indicative of the originally planned Skyhawk mission, this group of Marines at MCAS Cherry Point load a special 'shape' on an A4D-2N/A-4C for what was undoubtedly a trial nuclear weapons delivery hop. US Navy via Harry Gann

'HEINEMANN'S HOT ROD' – THE DEVELOPMENT OF THE A-4

This production line photo of Kuwaiti A-4KUs being built during the 1970s demonstrates how the engineers who travelled to Korea in 1952 incorporated what they saw into the final Skyhawk design. The two fuselages 'break' in the middle affording maintenance personnel easy access to the engine. Boeing Historical Archives via Harry Gann

Ejection Seats

When Ed Heinemann set out to design the Skyhawk, he left no system untouched, including the ejection seat. To save weight, Douglas designed its own ejection seat, called the NAMC Type II ballistic seat, which saved some 40lb (18kg) over the standard Navy design. Modifications soon followed, as well as a redesignation to Escapac 1. By the 1970s, the Escapac 1G-3 offered a zero/zero configuration for safe ejection even at a stand-still on the ground and inverted above certain altitudes. This seat was installed in all TA-4J, A-4M and 'Blue Angel' A-4F models.

This Navy Lt (jg) demonstrates the Skyhawk's lightweight seat design. Boeing Historical Archives via Harry Gann

'HEINEMANN'S HOT ROD' – THE DEVELOPMENT OF THE A-4

An assortment of planes from the early to mid-1950s flying in formation at NAS Patuxent River, Maryland. From the top down are the Douglas A3D Skywarrior, McDonnell F3H Demon, Douglas F4D Skyray, North American FJ-4 Fury, Grumman F-11F-1 Tiger and the Douglas A4D Skyhawk. US Navy via Lt Cdr Rick Burgess, USN Retd

'HEINEMANN'S HOT ROD' – THE DEVELOPMENT OF THE A-4

This now-famous front-on publicity photograph shows the A4D as it looked upon roll-out of the Douglas plant. The long probe on the nose is for flight test equipment. Douglas Aircraft Co. via author

Test pilot Bob Rahn pauses for a photo just before the historic first flight of BuNo. 137812 on 22 June 1954. The Skyhawk's maiden voyage took place at the Muroc Dry Lake. Rahn described the flight, which lasted only forty minutes, as 'uneventful'. During the test flight the XA4D reached an altitude of 15,000ft (4,572m). Douglas Aircraft Co. via author

137812 lifts off! Test pilot Rahn commented after the flight that the Skyhawk 'handled excellent'. Rahn would go on to conduct spin tests in this same aircraft fitted with a special parachute pod. Rahn had this to say about the first such test on 4 January 1955:

> ... entry into spin made at 32,000ft – to left in glide configuration ... recovery started promptly after one-quarter turn ... no tendency for plane to go off into right spin ... nature of spin consisted of definite yaw and oscillation – recovery quite effective using right rudder ... termination of spinning (autorotation) found in vertical dive – somewhat inverted.

Following a total of twelve spins that day, Rahn concluded that the aircraft exhibited 'excellent recovery characteristics ... in all cases'. Boeing Historical Archives via Harry Gann

'HEINEMANN'S HOT ROD' – THE DEVELOPMENT OF THE A-4

The Skyhawk's rudder had to be redesigned as a result of the flight tests. Originally a conventional, smooth-skinned one piece unit with internal ribs, the new design featured a single aluminium skin cut to shape with a one-piece metal frame on the outside of the rudder. While not incorporated into the A-4A production, it became a part of all future variants, such as this A-4M from VMAT-102, and is commonly referred to as the 'tab-pole' rudder. *Rick Morgan*

bombing, interdiction and close air support missions'. The contract further mandated that the plane be capable of both delivering 'conventional or special weapons' and 'attacking sea and land targets with or without fighter escort where control of the air has not been established'.

Translating that into workable numbers, the contract called for a maximum speed of 500mph (800km/h), a 460 mile (740km) operating radius, and a 1,000lb, later increasing to 2,000lb, bomb carriage capacity. The aircraft would also have to use JP type jet fuel, a complicating factor since it weighed approximately a half a pound per gallon more than conventional aviation fuel. In addition, this all had to be accomplished at an absolute maximum cost of $1,000,000 per aircraft.

Concurrent with the design paperwork, engineers began to construct a quarter-scale precision model. Constructed from wood, the model was waxed and polished before undergoing critical low-speed wind tunnel testing at the California Institute of Technology in Pasadena. A machined one-tenth scale steel model was also constructed and tested in Cal-Tech's high-speed tunnel, with similar tests performed at Cornell University, New York. A full-size mock-up was later produced by Douglas, complete with a wooden Wright J65 jet engine, and made available for tolerance testing and inspection by naval maintenance personnel.

One of the keys to the Skyhawk's success was Douglas's willingness to listen to pilots in the field. During the summer and autumn of 1952, a group of Douglas engineers (Leo Devlin, Russ Cocks, Harry Nichols, and Len Quick) led by Cdr John Brown, the Navy's attack requirements officer, travelled to Korea to observe operational and maintenance problems encountered by fleet carrier air units and Marine Corps units ashore. Douglas engineers hoped to incorporate these observations into the A4D's design to reduce or eliminate the more common problems associated with maintenance, overhaul, repair, refuelling, and arming aircraft during combat operations.

Heinemann was not alone in his insistence on weight reduction and compartmentalization. In an effort then unmatched in the aviation industry, many component suppliers also endeavoured to produce lightweight systems – the A4D's air conditioning unit, manufactured by the AirResearch Company of Los

A 'wing drop' problem – a phenomenon where the wing slowly moves down as if pushed – was discovered during flight testing. Engineers resolved this by adding a row of small metal tabs, called vortex generators, to the upper wing surfaces. Clearly visible on this later model A-4M, these would become standard in all production models although the vortex generators would cover only a portion of the upper wing and slat. John W. Binford

The Skyhawk's three-spar wing design can be easily seen here in this January 1954 assembly photo. The entire upper and lower wings are formed from a single sheet of aluminium measuring 0.064in (1.62mm) thick. Apparent also are the fifty-eight access holes, which allow for assembly, maintenance, and repair. Just ten bolts connect the wing unit to the main fuselage. US Navy via Aerospace Publishing

Skyhawk BuNo. 137814, the second production model, first flew on 23 September 1956, a full two weeks ahead of schedule. This aircraft was later flown by test pilot Cal Shoemaker of the Douglas Test Division for stability testing. Douglas Aircraft Co. via author

The clean lines of the early A-4 models are shown to good effect in this picture of an A-4B flown by Chuck Scott. R. S. DeGroat

This April 1956 photo shows the pen-nib fairings (referred to as the 'sugar scoop') that were added during the flight testing segment to resolve a buffeting problem caused by flow separation at the base of the vertical tail. The dark smear trailing from the hole mid-fuselage is an oil stain, a trademark of all early Skyhawks. Boeing Historical Archives via Harry Gann

Angeles, reduced weight by nearly one-third. The standard ejection seat, itself weighing nearly 98lb (45kg), was completely redesigned by Douglas to shed another 40lb (18kg). Electronic 'black boxes' containing navigational and communications equipment, formerly scattered about the fuselage, were condensed into a single, cylindrical package, and bolted to the forward end of the fuselage, saving another 50lb (23kg) and significantly reducing manufacturing costs. A new gun-sight, made by Douglas, also matched AirResearch's one-third weight savings, without compromising on quality or performance.

In October 1952, and after further evaluations by the Navy's mock-up board, two contracts were issued authorizing the manufacture of nineteen pre-production aircraft. Contrary to other contracts of the day, and probably due to Douglas's track record with carrier-based aircraft, the Navy waived its usual requirement calling for the construction of two experimental and one static test aircraft, thereby leaving only the single XA4D-1 Skyhawk, (BuNo. 137812) prototype. Douglas immediately moved forward with a fixed production rate using regular tooling, something that would ultimately allow the company to turn out the first ten planes in the time it would have normally taken to produce just one experimental aircraft.

Of course, no production goes as planned. Douglas did encounter delays, first from teething problems in the special machines developed to build the one-piece wing-spars. That alone created a delay of fifteen weeks. Other delays arose as a result of difficulties in drilling small, high-tolerance holes in strengthened aluminium, and with Wright's deliveries of the J65 engines.

A second mock-up inspection took place in February 1953. Several hundred naval aviators were brought in to comment on the cockpit design. Most were pleased and little was added, although a subsequent rearrangement of gauges and dials to improve instrument scan resulted from their suggestions. Later in 1953, one of the A4D airframes was removed from the production line and used for static tests to confirm the projected strength and structural integrity of the airframe and landing gear.

Finally, in February 1954, the first A4D, BuNo. 137812, was rolled out of the El Segundo factory and was given the official name of 'Skyhawk,' following company practice of naming all aircraft some variation on 'sky'. As produced, the XA4D-1 carried no armament and was fitted with a large test probe on its nose. It also lacked the two wing pylons and a tailhook assembly. What resulted from Heinemann's efforts was nothing less than astonishing. The A4D had a radar signature equal to 1/100th of the Navy specifications, contained one-third fewer parts than were typically required for a 30,000lb class aircraft, and had a combat ceiling of nearly 50,000ft (15,000m). Maintenance was reduced by nearly 40 per cent and overhaul time was cut by nearly half.

Also, with its three hardpoints, a total of 5,500lb (2,500kg) of external bombs or fuel could be carried, including a nuclear weapon of up to 3,500lb (1,590kg) on its centreline station. Moreover, all of this was achieved at a cost of $860,000 per copy for the first 500 aircraft.

The XA4D Flies

On 22 June 1954, two years and one day after the contract was signed, Douglas test pilot Bob O. Rahn, a former pilot with the US Army Air Corps (changed to the US Air Force in 1947), piloted the XA4D-1 on its first flight at Edwards AFB in California. Lasting approximately 40 minutes, Rahn's flight reached 15,000ft (4,500m) before settling into the pattern and coming to rest on the lake bed after a rather uneventful landing. Rahn described the flight as 'excellent'. Despite the production delays, Rahn's flight was only four weeks behind schedule.

These delays, however, were soon overcome. The initial production A4D, BuNo. 134813 made its first flight on schedule; the second, BuNo. 134814, flew on 23 September 1954, a full two weeks ahead of schedule. In early January 1955, spin testing began at Edwards, with test pilot Rahn noting 'excellent recovery characteristics . . . in all cases'.[4]

Soon after the test flights began, pilots began to notice a vibration in the tail at speeds in excess of 345mph (560km/h). In an attempt to identify the cause, short tufts of wool were attached to various areas of the Skyhawk's aft fuselage and tail. Films were then taken to isolate the

Bob Rahn, the man who first took the Skyhawk to the skies, at the ceremony commemorating the withdrawal of the last Skyhawk (BuNo. 160024) from US Marine reserve duty in August 1994. Behind Rahn is the last Skyhawk, an A-4M from VMA-131. John W. Binford

problem but the solution was not readily apparent. A series of vibration tests were also performed at the El Segundo plant where an A4D was taken from the production line and suspended gear-up from a height of 5ft (1.5m). Engineers used electro-magnetic vibrators, oscilloscopes, and recording devices to search for weaknesses, but to no avail. A flightline report from Edwards AFB eventually led to the discovery of the cause. It noted skin cracks under the rivets at the trailing edge of the rudder and structural engineers soon discovered that the rudder was simply not strong enough to withstand the loads associated with the higher speeds.

To cure this problem, the rudder was redesigned 'inside-out' in a similar fashion to the North American FJ-4 Fury's rudder. Instead of the conventional internal ribs and doubler covered by outer skins and sealed with rivets, a single aluminium skin was cut to the desired shape and a one-piece metal frame placed on each side. These were then bonded together with an adhesive – no rivets were used. The 'tadpole rudder', as it was called, was later incorporated into and became standard for the A4D-2 (later designated the A-4B). While this was supposed to be temporary, designers never did modify it.

Other problems developed during the flight testing. At high altitudes and at certain speeds, the aircraft would experience a phenomenon known as 'wing-drop,' where the wing slowly moves downward as if pushed. Wing-drop is caused by air twisting and turning over and off the wing surfaces. Although mild and definitely controllable, a solution was needed and quickly found by adding a small network of eleven metal tabs, known as 'vortex generators', over the upper surfaces of each outboard wing-tip near the tip of the leading edge flap and ahead of the ailerons. These tabs then became a standard part of the A4D design.

A related buffeting problem caused by flow separation at the base of the vertical tail was cured by the addition of pen-nib fairings, referred to as a 'sugar scoop' fairing, above and behind the engine exhaust to smooth the airflow. This, too, became part of the standard A4D package. Not specifically linked to any problem, a new three-piece windshield was installed in August 1955, replacing the original one-piece design. The flat centre piece not only improved visibility in bad weather, but was also bullet-proof.

Twelve Skyhawks were selected for the flight test programme, including BuNo. 137820, referred to as the '820', which set the world's speed record on 15 October 1955. In total, over 1,544 flights were conducted by Douglas test pilots. The second aircraft, Skyhawk BuNo. 137813, bore the work-horse load of these flights, flying 319 hours testing primarily aerodynamic characteristics and aircraft systems. Following the flight test phase, 137813 was sent to the Naval Parachute Facility at NAAS El Centro, California where it served until withdrawn from service in 1969.

One of the most significant early events for the A-4, at least from a public relations perspective, was the Skyhawk's capture of the 500 kilometre closed-course record, previously held by the Air Force's F-86H Sabre fighter. For this record attempt, a twelve-pylon course was set up at the Rosamond Dry Lake, north of Lancaster, California. Test members were located at each pylon and carried a mirror to reflect light at the test pilot to assist him in spotting the pylons. The main pylon was also marked with smoke

The last Reserve Skyhawk, an A-4M from VMA-131, is shown here at the squadron's August 1994 disestablishment ceremony. The A-4M, once flown by frontline Marine Corps squadrons, was passed on to the Reserve, once the AV-8B Harrier and F/A-18 Hornet began entering service in the 1980s. John W. Binford

grenades and smoke-producing fire fuelled with old car tyres.

Four preliminary flights were made, beginning on 13 October, in order to identify any problems associated with the low-level, high-speed flight. During one flight, Rahn's A4D hit an unofficial 703mph (1,131km/h), but then suffered a rudder failure. The 820 was immediately fitted with the modified 'tad-pole' design and, on 15 October, Lt Gordon Gray set the official speed record by flying at 695.163mph (1,118.7km/h) at an altitude of 100 metres.

These flight tests were followed by a series of tests at the Navy's Air Test Center (NATC) at NAS Patuxent River, Maryland, including launch and recovery tests on the facility's simulated flight deck. Initial carrier qualifications were conducted aboard USS *Ticonderoga* (CVA 14) from 12–19 September 1955. US Navy flight evaluations continued through the autumn, with weapons testing beginning on 31 October 1955. Bureau of Inspections and Survey (BIS) trials were then completed in March 1956 to ensure that the Skyhawk satisfied all contract obligations.

Final qualifying trials, designated as the Flight Indoctrination Program (FIP-Trials), were conducted at NAS Quonset Point, Rhode Island, by Navy Attack Squadron VA-72 'Blue Hawks'. Under the command of Cdr M. E. Stewart, VA-72 logged over 600 flight hours in its six A4Ds in an effort to become familiarized with the A4D and to ready it for operational fleet duty. The pilots flew the Skyhawk virtually day and night, looking for any weaknesses in the aircraft's design. The first factory-to-fleet delivery of a production A4D-1 (BuNo. 139935) was made during October 1956 to VA-72 and the aircraft was declared operational on 26 October, only seven weeks after initial delivery. According to reports, the A4D achieved the best availability rating of any new design ever tested to that date.

At the same time as VA-72 took deliveries on the East Coast, VF (AW)-3 at NAS Moffit Field, California, served as a transitional training and FIP squadron and a precursor to the modern Fleet Replacement Squadron (FRS). NAS Lemoore's VA-125 'Rough Raiders', the West Coast Replacement Air Group (RAG), became the first operational West Coast A-4 squadron, while VA-93 'Mighty Shrikes', became the first Pacific Fleet squadron. VMA-224 'Bengals' was the first Marine Corps squadron to transition to the A-4.

CHAPTER TWO

The Scooter Comes to Life

Following the success of the XA4D, contracts were immediately issued for the A4D-1 Skyhawk, with production beginning in late 1954. Officially, the Skyhawk was described as 'a jet-propelled, single-place monoplane with a modified delta-planform wing' designed as a 'high-performance, lightweight day-attack plane' capable of operating either from a carrier or a shore base. Pilots who flew the Scooter say it was one of the most remarkable planes ever to fly '... the last true pilot's aircraft. Its simplistic design and lack of redundant systems forced you to be alert and to make the aircraft fly'.[5]

A4D-1/A-4A

Basic Fuselage Design

The Skyhawk's design was based entirely on the concept of simplification. Overall, the basic airframe was conventional and was divided into three main assemblies – forward fuselage, wing, and rear fuselage. In a somewhat innovative manner, all mission equipment, including flight controls and wiring, were installed in each section before final assembly.

The Skyhawk's forward fuselage contained the cockpit, avionics pack, and engine. A self-sealing fuel tank was positioned just behind the cockpit between the air inlet ducts. The forward fuselage was an all-metal semi-monocoque construction, with heavy skin 0.10in/2.5mm used in the cockpit area. Stiffners were not used to conserve space. All other surfaces were continuous skinned with 0.64in (1.62mm) steel.

Power for the A4D-1 was provided by using the slightly more powerful J65-W-4B engine, with its 7,800lb (3,540kg) 'MIL' thrust rating at sea-level static conditions. The W-2, used in the XA4D, proved to be somewhat underpowered, and was replaced

A lone A4D-1 from VA-113 wearing the marking of Air Group 11 'NH' sits on the tarmac at NAS Lemoore. The 'Stingers' received their first A4Ds on 29 April 1957. During their first Skyhawk cruise aboard USS Shangri-La (CVA 38) they provided support to the Republic of China during the Communist Chinese shelling of the Quenoy Islands in late summer of 1958. US Navy via author

THE SCOOTER COMES TO LIFE

The A4D-1 production line at El Segundo in 1956 shows Skyhawks in various stages of construction. At the far right, tail units await assembly with forward fuselage sections, while at centre right, a wing section and forward fuselage await assembly. The Skyhawks on the centre and left rows have been spliced and are receiving final touches. Boeing Historical Archives via Harry Gann

A gentle bank by this A4D-1 allows a good look at its underside and the three external hardpoints. When designing the Skyhawk, Heinemann rejected the idea of an internal bomb-bay in order to save weight. It is estimated that this decision saved nearly 5,000lb (2,270kg). Boeing Co. via author

29

The A4D-1 cockpit continues the simplicity sought by its designer, Ed Heinemann. Some, including the Navy, criticized the design as being too small, but Douglas' offer to remedy the situation met with no response. US Navy via author

for production models. Interestingly, the replacement consisted of the re-manufactured engine from the Republic F-84F Thunderstreak. Given the Skyhawk's modular construction, changing an engine was a fairly easy procedure. Maintenance crews could simply 'break' the fuselage in two, permitting unobstructed access to the engine for repair and easy removal. This, apparently, was a result of the lessons learned by the Douglas engineers who travelled to Korea during mid-1952 to observe maintenance problems.

The wing section was fixed to the forward fuselage with only ten bolts, yet more evidence of Heinemann's simplistic design. The flight control surfaces were of conventional design, with both leading and trailing edge flaps, the latter evenly divided between split flaps and ailerons. A trim tab was provided on only the left aileron. The leading edge slats comprised about 70 per cent of the wing and were designed to improve airflow characteristics over the wings at high angles of attack, specifically during take-off and approach. These slats opened and closed automatically, depending on aerodynamic forces, at speeds below 230mph (375km/h) and were fully opened at stall speed. Apart from adversary aircraft or those used by the 'Blue Angels' flight demonstration team which had the slats locked in the 'up' position to ensure they would not improperly deploy when in low-level or formation flight, the slats were always plainly visible on static A-4s. Split wing flaps, located on the trailing edges, were hydraulically controlled and could extend through 50 degrees.

A tricycle undercarriage was used, with the main gear retracting forward and through 90 degrees into a recess just below the cockpit. The brake system was of a single-disc, spot type, and was operated by applying pressure to the upper part of the rudder pedals.

The tail or rear fuselage contained the engine tailpipe and a triangular rudder, with a fully adjustable, electronically operated horizontal stabilizer. A standard rudder was used and was the only flight control surface not to feature a constant chord. A pair of flush-mounted speed brakes were affixed to the aft fuselage for deceleration, to which Rocket/Jet Assisted Take-Off (R/JATO) bottles would later be attached for short-field take-offs. These units would later prove indispensable for Marine Corps Skyhawks operating out of Chu Lai in South Vietnam during 1965, where a full-length landing field was not operational until 1966.

The rear fuselage was constructed on three major frames: one connected to the rear wing spar; a second supported the arresting gear loads; and the third connected to the fin spar and housed the variable incidence tailplane connections. Only six bolts were used to connect the two fuselage sections at the wing spar. All rear fuselage skin surfaces used a stiffened skin consisting of light channels with two Z-section vertical stiffners spaced between them.

Cockpit

Reflecting its 1950s design, the Skyhawk's cockpit consisted mainly of conventional gauge instrumentation for airspeed, altitude, attitude, and rate-of-climb. The left console contained the navigation, gear controls, and throttle controls and the right console contained the communications, and lighting controls. The arresting gear was released from a small handle on the right side. Located immediately below the main instrumentation panel was the armament panel, which provided a seven-position selector switch, and station and gunsight controls. This arrangement proved awkward as it forced the pilot to look down into the cockpit to change switches and was subsequently modified in the -M model, where the panel was moved directly under the HUD. 'Special weapons' were controlled from the left console.

The 'throttle and stick' design was very straightforward. Located on the pilot's left, the throttle contained a radio microphone and speed brake switch on the inboard side and master exterior lights on the outboard. Four fuel flow positions were marked, designating 'off', 'idle', 'normal', and 'military'. Tension on the throttle could be manipulated by a small knob. The 'stick' contained only three controls – trim control, bomb release, and a gun/rocket trigger. A 'select' switch was provided to prevent rockets from firing while operating the guns.

The cockpit enclosure was a fixed, three-piece windshield with a hinged 'clamshell' canopy. The two side windshield panels were constructed of moulded plastic, while the flat portion was made of alternate layers of glass and vinyl, thereby providing the

A section of Alphas from VA-34 fly in this 1957 photo. The 'Blue Blasters', based at NAS Cecil Field, transitioned to the A4D-1 in January 1957 from the Vought F7U-3 Cutlass. The squadron did cross-deck operations with the HMS Ark Royal in 1958 before flying missions in support of Operation Bluebat off Lebanon. VA-34 operated from USS Essex (CVA 9) during the Bay of Pigs invasion and from USS Enterprise (CVAN 65) during the Cuban Missile Crisis and Cuban quarantine. US Navy via author

The Nuclear Mission

The Skyhawk's first mission was to be a long-range, low-level nuclear delivery platform operating from a carrier base. For this mission, A-4 pilots trained constantly, both as new pilots going through the Replacement Air Group (RAG), and in Fleet squadrons. Capt Otto Krueger, Commander of VA-125, the Pacific Fleet RAG 1969–1970, discussed the nuclear role and how it was taught:

> The nuclear mission was viewed as the Skyhawk's primary mission in the late 1950s and early 1960s. Skyhawk pilots trained on this both in the RAGs and in their respective squadrons. RAG students practiced flying simulated nuclear strike profiles. For pilots of VA-44 on the east coast, a typical flight might see them launch from NAS Cecil Field in Florida then fly north-east to a point off of the coast. Once there, the Skyhawks would turn around and cross the beach, perhaps in the Carolinas or Georgia, flying the rest of the mission at low altitude, which for the A-4 was around 50ft. Pilots would then head to the Pine Castle Range and drop their practice load. For graduation, student pilots would fly similar, but longer, missions with a 'shape' representing the nuclear weapon. Typical low-level nav hops for west coast RAG pilots would fly from NAS Lemoore out to sea, crossing the beach inbound around Ukia in northern California, over the Sierra Nevadas and a lot of desert country in Nevada or Utah before hitting their target at NAS Fallon. Because of the low altitudes flown for these missions, pilots considered them to be 'legalized flat-handing', and great fun![6]

On these missions, pilots relied on dead-reckoning navigation using strip maps. Missions were flown at precise airspeeds and heading from one checkpoint to the next, using a stopwatch to determine the time to turn to the next leg. 'You would basically fly at X speed for X minutes, then turn X degrees'. Interestingly, at the appropriate speed, which was between 489–517mph (792–837km/h) pilots could trace around the edge of a nickel on their maps and match the Skyhawk's turning radius precisely. When the Charlies arrived, limited radar usage allowed pilots to locate significant landmarks. Krueger noted that determining where you were was hard at

For its nuclear role, the Skyhawk included a canopy thermal shield designed to protect pilots from the effects of a nuclear blast while they left the target area. When using the shield, pilots flew their A-4s on instruments only. The shields were eventually phased out in the mid-1960s as the Skyhawk abandoned the nuclear mission for its conventional one. US Navy via Lt Cdr Rick Burgess USN Retd

A-4 Possible Weapons Carriage

Bombs		
Mk 81	250lb	LDGP
Mk 81	250lb	Snakeye I
Mk 82	500lb	LDGP/LGB
Mk 82	500lb	Snakeye II
Mk 83	1000lb	LDGP/LGB
Mk 84	1000lb	LDGP/LGB

Guided bombs/missiles
AGM-12 Bullpup (a/g)
AGM-62 Walleye (a/g)
AGM-65 Maverick (a/g)
AGM-45 Shrike (ARM)
AGM-78 Standard (ARM)
AIM-9 Sidewinder (a/g)
Aero 14/B smoke

Guns
Mk 12 20mm (2) internal
Mk 4 gun pod   Mk-40
Mk 11 gun pod   Mk-41

Practice
Mk 76
Mk 106
ATM-45
ATM-65
AIM-9/MDU-26/A

Other Munitions
Mk 77 napalm
Mk 79
Mk 20 Rockeye II
CBU-72/B FAE
CBU-59/A APAM

Rockets	
LAU-10/A	5.00in Zuni
LAU-61/A	19 x 2.75in FFAR
LAU-68/A	7 x 2.75in FFAR
LAU-69/A	19 x 2.75in FFAR
Aero 6D	

Non-combat stores
Aero 1D 150, 300, 400 US gallon tanks
D-704 refuelling store
SUU-40/44 flare dispenser
Mk 24/25 paraflare
LB-18A camera pod
Mk-12 spray tank

Mines – Destructor Series
Mk-36

Special Weapons
B-43
B-57
B-61

Ejection racks/launches
Aero 7A (wing station)
Aero 10D
Aero 20
TER (Triple Ejection Rack)
MER (Multiple Ejection Racks)
LAU-7/A (AIM-9 launch rail)
LUU-]2B/B (rocket launcher)

---

radio. Operating in the 225 to 399 megacycle frequency range, the ARC-27A could transmit or receive using the same antenna on any of 1,750 channels. A total of twenty channels could be preset. A 'guard' preset was added beginning with BuNo. 137832. Manual frequency selection was accomplished by three dials, with the outer dial controlling the first two digits, the middle dial controlling the third digit, and the innermost dial selecting the digits to the right of the decimal point. VHF radio communications using the ARN-14E omni-range radio could be attained by adding an external navigation package (NavPac) mounted on the centre pylon.

Navigation equipment included the AN/ARA-25 automatic direction finder and the S-2 gyrosyn compass system. The ARN-12 marker beacon, which allowed a pilot to check the aircraft's relative position by referencing a specified beacon station, could also be carried in the externally mounted NavPac. A five-position IFF ('off', 'stdby', 'low', 'norm', 'emergency') was provided by the APX-6B IFF transponder and APA-89 identification coder and operated on a simple 'challenge and reply' basis. All navigation and communications equipment were limited to line-of-sight range.

Armament was simple. Two forward-firing Colt Mk 12 Mod 0 20mm cannons were nestled in each wing-root complete with 100 rounds of ammunition for each gun housed in rotating drums to ease feeding and minimize potential for gun jams. The Mk 12 guns, although limited in their ammunition capacity, could fire simultaneously at the rate of 1,000 rounds per minute in short bursts. Of all the Skyhawk's systems, few have received as much criticizm as the cannons. Some have commented that the guns were an afterthought and this seems to be borne out by company documents which show that it was not until BuNos 137817, 137832 and subsequent aircraft that guns were installed. Installation of the guns also reduced the overall maximum external load by 450lb (204kg). The guns were not reliable and the ammunition store too small. 'The A-4's 20mm guns were basically an afterthought added early on and they simply didn't carry enough ammunition. This was due, of course, to the guns' location in the nose and the limited space for the ammo boxes.'[10] Space requirements for subsequent ECM gear installed during the Vietnam War reduced the 100 round load even further.

As to their accuracy, Krueger explained, 'while the 20mms were good for strafing, they were not very accurate, especially with the iron sight. We had no lead computing sights; those were added by the foreign purchasers. That doesn't mean we didn't get proficient with the sight, but it was definitely a learned technique'.[11] Krueger further commented, 'I think the problem with the gun is best highlighted by the fact that most of the foreign users, especially the Israelis and others, immediately put in their own gun and lead-computing sight'.[12]

The three hardpoints allowed carriage of a variety of weapons, including Mk 80 series iron bombs, mines, rockets, and special weapons of the Mk 7, -8, and -12 class. Some sources also list the Mk 91 nuclear weapon. The centreline pylon, rated at 3,575lb (1,625kg), contained a four-hook type bomb rack capable of using either 14in (35cm) or 30in (75cm) suspension. The wing pylons, numbers one and three, were rated at 1,200lb (545kg) each, and featured two-hook ejection racks limited to 14in (35cm) suspension.

A total of 165 A4D-1s were built with the model seeing service in eighteen US Navy and Marine Corps squadrons. The VA-72 'Blue Hawks', an East Coast squadron that previously operated F9F Panthers, were the first Navy squadron to receive the A4D-1 was VA-72 'Blue Hawks'; and VMA-211 'Wake Island Avengers' became the first US Marine Corps unit. The first West Coast squadron to receive the aircraft was VA-93 'Blue Blazers' who also made the A4D-1's first cruise aboard USS *Ticonderoga* in September 1957. When the AD-1s were phased out of fleet operations, some used for replacement training were redesignated as TA-4As, a move which some have proposed occurred to reduce the apparent attack inventory so that more aircraft could be procured for the war in Vietnam.

MCAS El Toro's VMA-224 'Bengals' were the first US Marine Corps squadron to transition to the A4D-1. The 'Bengals' flew the Skyhawk for nearly ten years before transitioning to the all-weather Grumman A-6A Intruder. US Navy via author

A4D-2/A-4B

Even before deliveries of the A4D-1 were completed, plans were being drawn for the follow-on A4D-2 that would improve the Skyhawk's range and upgrade its navigational systems. In fact, production of the AD4-2 began parallel with that of the A4D-1. The two principal modifications affecting range were the addition of an in-flight refuelling capability, and increasing the external fuel carriage by the addition of 300 US gallon (1,135 litre) Aero-1 drop tanks. This factor was significant, because with all three pylons sporting 300 US gallon tanks, a total of 1,695 US gallons (6,410 litres) of usable fuel could be carried.

Externally, the A4D-2 differed from its predecessor by the installation of the refuelling probe and the incorporation of the so-called 'inside-out' or 'tad-pole' rudder design. At first, the engineers experimented by adding the refuelling probe beneath the starboard wing just outboard of the undercarriage fairing. That location was subsequently changed to the starboard fuselage nose for production models, with the probe adding less than a foot to the aircraft's overall length.

At about the same time as the refuelling probe experiments, Ed Heinemann developed the D-704 buddy-store which, when mounted to the Skyhawk's centreline station, allowed for the refuelling of other aircraft at the off-load transfer rate of 200 US gallons (755 litres) per minute. This system was developed in response to the Navy's suggestion that Douglas explore modifying both the Skywarrior and Skyhawk to add in-flight refuelling capabilities. The Navy fully appreciated the fact that a replacement was needed as the fleet's primary tanker, the A J Savage, was nearing the end of its operational career. While the A3D was large and sufficient room remained for the hose and reel, the Skyhawk's diminutive size made internal incorporation of such a system impossible without ruining its most precious attributes. Heinemann's solution was to add the capability externally; hence, the D-704. Rumour holds that this design was sketched by Heinemann on a napkin.

Using a hose and drogue assembly and itself carrying 300 US gallons (1,135 litres) of fuel, the Skyhawk could now serve in the tanker role for other aircraft. The D-704 permitted the A-4 to transfer all external fuel and half of its internal fuel load for a total off-load capability of 1,300 US gallons (4,920 litres). By using a small impeller, the D-704 provided its own power source independent of the aircraft for the pump and hose reel line. According to reports, an A-4 with this

An early production A4D-1 modified for in-flight refuelling takes on fuel from an AD Skyraider. Notice the location of the Skyhawk's refuelling probe stemming from the right wing-root. This location was initially tried, but the fuselage mount proved more practical. Boeing Historical Archives via Harry Gann

buddy-store system 'saved' its first fellow aircraft during the D-704's maiden deployment with VA-12. This capability would later prove significant during the Vietnam War when A-4s frequently provided emergency tanking.

From a performance standpoint, the A4D-2 received the slightly improved -16 version of the Wright J65, providing 7,700lb (3,500kg) of thrust. This version was later up-rated to the W-18 standard of 8,500lb (3,860kg) thrust in some A-4s. These benefits were somewhat lost, however, as the additional equipment added to the variant increased empty weight from 8,400lb (3,810kg) to 9,140lb (4,145kg). Surprisingly, this resulted in a loss in maximum speed of only 3mph (5km/h).

Most of the other major modifications were internal. For example, fully powered flight control systems were added and the rear undercarriage strengthened to allow the Skyhawk to increase its maximum manoeuvre limit to 7g at maximum speed. To give the flight control systems proper 'feel', bungee springs were used in parallel with the pilot's controls. The cockpit was likewise modified to improve pilot scan and to the readability of certain instruments and gauges which were too small and, therefore, hard to see. Some of these deficiencies were discovered during night flights by units operating the A4D-1.

Other changes were prompted to cure deficiencies in the Alpha. For example, on the original model the tailpipe temperature gauge only registered temperatures of 450–550°C. This led to a false impression of a flame-out when the engine was in 'idle'. Also problematic were the overly simplistic 'go/no go' indicators for oil temperature and oil pressure, which were replaced by dials.

Communications were enhanced through the installation of an angled UHF aerial slightly behind the cockpit canopy, an AN/ASN-19A dead reckoning computer system, and an AN/ARN-21 TACAN. A single point pressurized fuelling system was also added, as was a dual hydraulic system, in part to correct perceived deficiencies with the A4D-1's original design. The addition of the TACAN was welcomed for marine operations but sometimes led to difficulties when Skyhawks operated over land. Land-based facilities had yet to adopt TACAN stations and relied instead on Omni, so any cross-country flight had to use visual navigation. Eventually, Omni and

TACAN became compatible in frequency and the problem disappeared.

Armaments were enhanced by the installation of an improved bomb sight and the incorporation of the Martin Company's AGM-12 Bullpup rocket-powered, radio-guided missile. The AGM-12, which could be carried by all three stations, now allowed Skyhawk pilots to have a limited stand-off capability against surface targets on land and at sea. Introduced to the fleet on 25 April 1959 as the AGM-12A, the Bullpup was originally made with a 250lb warhead. Its stand-off range was approximately 7 miles (11km). The Bullpup-B, which became available in 1965, had a larger, 1,000lb warhead and a slightly longer range. Both missiles suffered one drawback – the pilot had to maintain a steady dive trajectory from altitudes up to 10,000ft (3,000m) after release in order to guide the missile, thus making himself a target. This became even more of a concern with the discovery of North Vietnamese SA-2 SAM sites in 1965.

An air-to-air capability was also added for carrying the AIM-9 Sidewinder. This would later prove valuable as A-4Bs, and later A-4Cs, would provide a limited air defence capability for the Navy's Anti-Submarine Carriers (CVS) during the middle 1960s. These Skyhawks served primarily with VSF-1 and VSF-3 and with some VA and VMA squadrons as four-plane Dets.

USS *Essex* (CVS 9) would become the first CVS to deploy with Skyhawks in the air defence role. In 1961, twelve A4D-2Ns from VA-34 squadron joined *Essex*'s CVSG-60 for a nineteen-day deployment that saw A-4s, in a tribute to their versatility, amass a total of 768 flight hours and 512 traps. VSF squadrons generally consisted of four A-4s and were to serve in a limited strike and air defence role. Although VSF-1 and -3 deployed with several carrier units, only VSF-3 saw combat during the Vietnam War with Air Wing 10 aboard USS *Intrepid* (CVS 11) during 1967. VA-113 Det. Q saw combat during its stint aboard USS *Bennington* (CVS 20) during 1965 as did VA-153 Det. R aboard USS *Kearsage* (CVS 33), and VMA-223 Det. T aboard USS *Yorktown* (CVS 10). H&MS-15 Det. N served aboard USS *Hornet* (CVS 12). These units, and the need to provide air defence for the ASW carriers soon passed, when, in 1972, the carrier air wing (CV) concept

This A4D-1 has a Douglas-designed D-704 refuelling store on its centreline. The feature was later added to the A4D-2. Douglas Aircraft Co. via Aerospace Publications

A-4 Fuel Quantity Data (US gallons)

Fuel Tanks	Usable Fuel	Unusable Fuel – level flight	Expansion Space	Total Volume
Integral wing tank	570	6	9	585
Fuselage tank	240	0	0	240
LH/RH wing (external tank)				
150 US gallon	147	2	1	150
300 US gallon	147	2	1	150
Centreline tank (external)				
150 US gallon	147	2	1	150
300 US gallon & refuelling store	147	2	1	150

Usable Fuel Total Combination (US gallons)

Tanks	Total Fuel
Fuselage, wing	810
Fuselage, wing, (150) centre drop	957
Fuselage, wing, (300) centre drop	1105
Fuselage, wing, (300) air refuelling store	1105
Fuselage, wing, two (150) wing rack drop	1104
Fuselage, wing, (150) centre, two (150) wing rack drop	1251
Fuselage, wing, (300) centre, two (150) wing rack drop	1399
Fuselage, wing, (300) air refuelling store	1399
Fuselage, wing, two (300) wing rack drop	1400
Fuselage, wing, (150) centre, two (300) wing rack drop	1547
Fuselage, wing, (300) centre, two (300) wing rack drop	1695
Fuselage, wing, (300) air refuelling store, two (300) wing rack drop	1695

THE SCOOTER COMES TO LIFE

An early A-4B without squadron marking or the refuelling probe. Notice the 'tad-pole' rudder, which became standard in all future models. Boeing Co. via author

This TA-4 aboard USS Lexington (CV 16) demonstrates how the refuelling probe permits crews to 'hot refuel' a Skyhawk. Harry Gann

The A-4 as a Tanker

When the A-4B was in its early production, Douglas was approached by the Navy about the possibility of adding an in-flight refuelling capability to the Skyhawk so that it could serve an auxiliary role as a fleet tanker. The Navy had realized that its fleet tanker, the A J Savage, was quickly ageing and that a replacement was needed. Douglas, particularly Ed Heinemann, initially scoffed at the idea because it meant possibly altering the aircraft's weight or performance envelope. Unlike the A3D Skywarrior, which was large enough to house an internal reel and drogue system, the Skyhawk was short on space and if an internal design was sought, something would have to be sacrificed.

Douglas eventually came up with an external refuelling mount, called the Aero 1D, or D-704, that could be suspended from the centreline pylon. Using an aerodynamic shape and a self-powered impeller, the D-704 store contained a 300 US gallon (1,136 litre) fuel cell, a constant speed ram air-driven hydraulic pump, and a hydraulically operated nose reel. 50ft (15.2m) of hose was also provided, with a collapsible drogue. The D-704 off-loaded fuel at a rate of 200 US gallons (756 litres) per minute. With the Skyhawk carrying two 300 US gallon tanks, plus the store, a total of 1,300 US gallons (4,920 litres) could be transferred, basically one half of the A-4's total fuel.

The D-704-equipped A-4 gave air wing commanders more flexibility in composing strike packages as the tanking element could now fly a similar profile to the rest of the strike force. In the late 1950s and early 1960s, it was common for D-704-totting Skyhawks to fly along with strike groups, refuel the Skyhawks, then return to the carrier, with another tanker A-4 meeting the strike group on the in-bound leg. During the Vietnam War, tanker operations for A-4s were more limited, with much of the mission tanking performed by AD Skyraiders, A-3 Skywarriors, and KA-6D Intruders.

The A-4 was a good, but limited tanker. We used it around the boat a lot for emergency tanking or for launch/recovery operations or when the Whales (A-3s) were either busy or down. On Ranger and Enterprise, we typically kept a Skyhawk with a store ready in case we needed something. In the early 1960s, for nuclear strike profiles, we routinely used an A-4 tanker which would accompany the strike aircraft. As far out on the profile as possible, maximum fuel would be transferred to the strike aircraft, leaving the tanker just enough gas to get back to the boat, and the strike bird would proceed on its mission. Sometimes another tanker would catch us on the egress and top us off for our home stretch. But that couldn't be counted on and wasn't built into the mission profile.

But the Skyhawk had its limitations as a tanker. It simply couldn't give enough fuel for the gas-guzzling F-4 and F-8 aircraft that operated with afterburners and also burned a lot of fuel at lower altitudes. An A-4 could only give these birds enough for one or two extra passes at the boat before they'd need another drink.

Sometimes we'd launch an A-4 if the A-3 tanker needed to come aboard. The A-4 would launch and take up position overhead until the A-3 was ready. Then after the Whale was airborne, the Skyhawk would transfer the balance of its fuel before landing so that the Whale was topped off and ready to go.[13]

Overall, having the ability to use the A-4 as a tanker was a convenient option for air wing commanders.

Here, an A-4C from VA-216 refuels a VF-31 F-4B overhead USS Saratoga (CV 60) while she steams in the Mediterranean Sea. US Navy via Lt Cdr Rick Burgess USN Retd

THE SCOOTER COMES TO LIFE

A ground view of A4D-2 BuNo. 175538 displaying its straight refuelling probe. Two 150 US gallon (568 litre) fuel tanks hang from stations one and three and a navigation package (NAVPAC) hangs from the centreline station. The NAVPAC contained an AN/ARN-14E omni-range receiver for directional homing and an AN/ARN-12 marker beacon receiver. Both were helpful for cross-country flights where TACAN navigation was unavailable. Boeing Historical Archives via Harry Gann

This A-4B, seen at Lakehurst in 1972, has a '7Z' tail code, which means it belongs to a Reserve Air Wing.
Stephen H. Miller via Lt Cdr Rick Burgess USN Retd

Only two squadrons flew the A-4B in Vietnam; VA-15 and VA-95 aboard USS Intrepid **(CV 11). These two Bravos, piloted by Lt Cdr G. L. Sagehorn USN, and Lt Bill Iams USNR, are en route to the Thanh Hoa Bridge in September 1966.** Capt Walter Ohlrich USN Ret

An A-4B from VA-12 aboard USS Essex **(CV 9) sits with a 'shape' on the tarmac at a gunnery meeting at NAF El Centro. Its fighter counterpart, the Douglas F4D Skyray sits off behind the Skyhawk's nose.** Boeing Historical Archives via Harry Gann

THE SCOOTER COMES TO LIFE

A-4Bs flew with many of the anti-submarine carriers, such as the Skyhawk pictured here belonging to USS Kearsage (CVS 33). Armed with AIM-9 Sidewinder air-to-air missiles, these Skyhawks provided combat air patrol for the air group's Trackers and Tracers. Featured here is a VA-23 A-4B from CVSG-53.
US Navy via Boeing Historical Archives via Harry Gann

Navy and Marine Corps Skyhawks are parked on the ramp at MCAS Yuma, Arizona during the Fourth Annual Naval Air Weapons Meet in December 1959. In addition to the Skyhawks, a squadron of Chance Vought F-8 Crusaders appear in the back row. Boeing Historical Archives via Harry Gann

44

The Mk 11 pod-mounted gun became operational in 1959 and offered Skyhawk pilots a step-up from their internal Mk 12 cannons. Developed by industrialist/flier Howard Hughes, the Mk 11 fired 4,000 rounds per minute and was used primarily for ground-attack missions. US Navy via Lt Cdr Rick Burgess USN Retd

was introduced and the ASW mission was consolidated with the large deck carrier.

First flown by Douglas test pilot Drury Wood on 26 March 1956, service deliveries of the A4D-2 to the Marine Corps (VMA-211) began in September 1957, and to the Navy (VA-12) at NAS Cecil Field, Florida in February 1958. VA-12 flew the initial squadron test flights with the new 300 US gallon (1,135 litre) external fuel tanks and also pioneered night-time air-to-air refuelling using the D-704.

Over its production run, a total of 542 were built. As with the A4D-1s, many of the A4D-2s were relegated to training roles with the Reserve squadrons and redesignated TA-4Bs, although no physical changes were made to the aircraft. Although some TA-4As did serve with the Reserves, the programme did not really gather steam until the TA-4B was introduced into the reserve ranks.

A4D-3

The A4D-3 represented a Douglas design intended to satisfy a 1957 Navy requirement for a new 'state-of-the-art' light attack aircraft capable of travelling greater distances through adverse weather and terrain. Douglas proposed the addition of new avionics to meet the all-weather requirements and substitution of the more efficient Pratt & Whitney J52 engine in place of the Wright J65 (being developed for the Grumman A-6A Intruder).

Unfortunately for the Navy, the design never made it past the mock-up stage. While orders were let for development of four of these variants and BuNos reserved for six more, rising costs associated with the new avionics and the new engine ultimately led to its cancellation. What resulted from this, however, was a compromise, the A4D-2N (A-4C), which, while adding a sophisticated autopilot, a Low-Altitude Bombing System (LABS), a terrain clearance radar, and an angle-of-attack indicating system, still retained the less powerful J65 engine.

A4D-2N/A-4C

The introduction of the A4D-2N, later redesignated the A-4C in 1962, saw some of the most significant upgrades to the baseline Skyhawk, complete with the revamping of approximately 15 per cent of the aircraft's structures. A primary impetus for the A-4C was the Navy's late 1950s requirement for greater range and an all-weather, adverse terrain capability, which had led Douglas to pursue the A4D-3 variant in the first instance.

Many of the technologies supporting the A4D-3 were adopted by the A4D-2N/A-4C design, and, together with improved avionics, gave the Skyhawk its first, albeit

THE SCOOTER COMES TO LIFE

A member of VA-46 squadron from NAS Cecil Field poses with typical Skyhawk ordnance. Included in this arsenal are standard 20mm ammunition, Mk 80 series 250lb, 500lb, and 1,000lb bombs, Zuni rockets, AGM-12 Bullpups, AIM-9 Sidewinders, 2.75in rockets, and Mk 84 2,000lb bombs. On the Skyhawk are 300 US gallon (1,135 litre) fuel tanks and a buddy-store. US Navy via Aerospace Publications

JATO bottles, shown here being readied by a US Marine, were used frequently at the Marine base in Chu Lai, Vietnam. The bottles provided added thrust to enable the Skyhawk to take off from a shortened runway.
Boeing Historical Archives via Harry Gann

jet, which delivered 8,300lb (3,768kg) thrust at 'MIL' (102 per cent) and 7,400lb (3,360kg) thrust at 100 per cent. This provided more than enough power to compensate for the increased weight of the upgrades. Indeed, weight was now becoming less significant with the advent of refuelling brought on by the A4D-2 and as engines became more powerful and efficient. The W-20 increased the Skyhawk's rate-of-climb to nearly 7,500ft (2,330m) per minute and overall range to 1,139 miles (1,845km). Although this engine hailed a significant improvement over the W-16, it was still considered by Vietnam pilots to be an under-powered airframe. Lt John G. Kuchinski, assigned to VA-94 aboard USS *Hancock* in 1967 observed:

> Since we had A-4Cs, we would climb to 20–23,000 feet and then descend coming in to keep our speed up. The A-4C engine could not keep us, with a full bomb load and maneuvering at 350 knots plus, straight and level.[17]
>
> ... the drawback to the A-4C was the under-powered engine and the fact that we had to carry two 300-gallon drop tanks along with the bombs, usually four Mk. 82s.[18]

This power problem was later cured by the -E and -F models.

The A-4C was produced in the largest numbers, with some 638 eventually produced for the Navy and Marine Corps, and, at its high point, equipped some twenty-three Navy and nine Marine Corps squadrons. Initial fleet deliveries were made to Marine Squadron VMA-225 at MCAS Cherry Point, South Carolina, in March 1960, and to VA-192 in May, replacing their older FJ-4B Furies. Interestingly, the A-4C was the first Skyhawk model to be built at the new Douglas factory at Long Beach, and was the model in production when the DoD announced its aircraft redesignation system in 1962. A-4Cs saw the bulk of the early action in Vietnam, serving with twenty-nine Navy attack and eleven Marine Corps VMA squadrons over the course of the war. Two squadrons, VA-12 and VA-72 aboard USS *Shangri-La*, continued to fly the A-4C as late as 1970.

The Army Looks at the 'Hawk'

Of particular interest to the -C model was Douglas's promotion of a modified A4D-2N for the US Army's 1961 close air support contract, called the Model 840. Due to a growing lack of interest by the USAF, now separated from the Army, in the close air support role, the Army was looking for its own aircraft to fill that slot, and one that could perform the job in unimproved forward-operating areas. Douglas quickly responded to that need by taking two A4D-2Ns, BuNos 148483 and 148490, and modifying them to Army requirements. These modifications, undertaken at the El Segundo factory, included revising the landing gear to add twin main wheels for better handling on rough ground, constructing modified underwing fairings, and the installation of a 24ft (7.3m) diameter drag chute taken from the Douglas A3D Skywarrior. These revisions were accomplished in just two weeks.

Illustrative of the differences between the variants, an A-4C (left) sits next to an A-4E on the NAS Oceana flight line with the markings of VA-81 squadron. The immense carriage potential of the five-station Echo is highlighted when it sits next to the three-station Charlie. In what was probably a disappointment to squadron members, VA-81 transitioned back to the A-4C from the more capable A-4E in September 1967 before transitioning again to the Chance Vought A-7 Corsair II in May 1970. The 'Sunliners' took the Charlie on two cruises to the Mediterranean, the first aboard USS Shangri-La **(CV 38) and the second aboard the USS** John F. Kennedy **(CV 67)**. US Navy via author

Two A-4s from VMA-332 of the Second Marine Air Wing (MAW) refuel en route to Rota, Spain. The two made a non-stop trans-Atlantic crossing. US Marine Corps via Lt Cdr Rick Burgess USN Retd

An artist's impression of the A-4C Skyhawk proposed for US Army operations from front-line, unimproved fields.

Marine Corps A-4 Carrier Deployments (courtesy Mike Weeks)

Squadron	Aircraft	Modex	Carrier/Air Wing	Cruise	Deployment Dates
VMA-225	A4D-2	AK5xx	CVA-9/CVG-10	MED	08/07/59 – 02/26/60
VMA-224	A4D-2	WK8x	CVA-62/CVG-7	MED[2]	08/04/60 – 03/03/61
VMA-121	A4D-2	VK88xx	CVA-43/CVG-15	WESTPAC[3]	09/19/60 – 05/27/61
VMA-324	A4D-2	DX6xx	CVA-43/CVG-15	WESTPAC[4]	09/19/60 – 05/27/61
VMA-225	A4D-2N	AK6xx	CVA-38/CVG-10	MED	02/02/61 – 05/15/61
VMA-311	A4D-2	WL8x	CVA-41/CVG2	WESTPAC	02/15/61 – 09/28/61
VMA-225	A-4C	CExx	CVAN-65/CVG-6	CARIBBEAN[5]	10/18/62 – 12/08/62
VMA-324	A-4B	AG5xx	CVA-62/CVG-7	MED	08/06/63 – 03/04/64
H&MS-32	A-4B	DA40x Det.1	CVS-9/CVSG-60	MED	10/01/63 – 12/23/63
VMA-214	A-4B	WK8x Det. N	CVS-12/CVSG-57	WESTPAC	10/09/63 – 04/15/64
VMA-331	A-4E	AJ5xx	CVA-59/CVW-8	MED	07/10/64 – 03/13/65
VMA-223	A-4C	WP8x Det. T	CVS-10/CVSG-55	WP/SEA	10/23/64 – 05/17/65
H&MS-15	A-4C	YV8x Det. N	CVS-12/CVSG-57	WP/SEA	08/12/65 – 03/23/66
VMA-324	A-4E	AG3xx	CVA-62/CVW-7	MED	06/13/66 – 02/01/71
VMA-331	A-4E	AG3xx	CVA-62/CVW-7	MED	06/23/70 – 01/31/71

Competitors for this contract included the Northrop N-156 (predecessor to the F-5) and the Fiat G-91. Neither of these competing proposals was specially modified for the fly-off.

After a nine and a half week, Army-sponsored evaluation, some of which took place near Pensacola and NAS Jacksonville, no contracts were issued, in part due to the Army's decision to refocus its efforts on attack helicopters and the Air Force's agreement to re-evaluate its position on close air support. During these tests, the Skyhawk performed well, defeating both competitors in the landing competition, and scoring a 'tie' in the take-off phase, despite the N-156's afterburner. Interestingly, this decision by the Air Force to review the close air support role ultimately led to the development of the A-10 Thunderbolt II, which rose to fame in the 1991 Gulf War.

Douglas also proposed an A4D-4, which would have had folding wings, a larger fuselage, and seven hardpoints. Boeing Historical Archives via Harry Gann

The Replacement Air Group (RAG)

Two VA squadrons provided the bulk of Skyhawk pilots for the fleet. VA-44, located at NAS Cecil Field, Florida, trained all east coast A-4 pilots and VA-125, at NAS Lemoore, California, trained the west coast pilots. In the early years, the Grumman TF-9 filled this role. As more A-4s became available with the newer models entering the fleet, TA-4A/B aircraft made their way into the training command. A major impetus behind the two-seat TA-4E/F design was the need for a new weapons and tactics trainer for the Skyhawk community. Deliveries of this model, which possessed the same weapons capability as the single-seat Skyhawks, began on 19 May 1966 to VA-125. With the success of the TA-4F, orders soon came in for a new dedicated trainer version without a weapons capability, which was dubbed the TA-4J.

Without question, the methodology and substance of the RAG syllabus changed drastically with the coming of the Vietnam War in 1965:

> When the Vietnam War started we were still training the kids based on Korean War tactics. And when they got over to Vietnam, everything was a surprise. We simply weren't teaching them what they needed to know. But, as we learned, as the word came back from the war, we modified our syllabus and started doing a great deal better. We would go out and meet the guys coming home and ask them, 'what have you been doing?' and they'd tell us and we'd incorporate that into the syllabus. When 1968 and 1969 came around, the people that we were turning out knew how to do everything that the fleet units were doing on Yankee Station. These guys were much better going out than we were. Clearly, passing on what worked made us all better. And that shouldn't be a surprise. The guys in the fleet were amassing 250–300 missions as Lieutenants on their first and second cruises. There were a lot of these guys, like Tom Brown, 'Boot' Hill, Jim Busey and a number of others, who would go on to become Admirals.[19]

Capt Thomas Mariner was another Skyhawk pilot familiar with the training command and how the A-4 impacted that community:

> Principally, the Skyhawk was a Navy plane. When a flight student strapped it on, and that is what you did with the tight cockpit of a Scooter, you knew you were at last a real part of naval aviation. Not some little safe trainer like the T-34 or T-2. Men had fought and died (and were still doing so when I first flew TA-4s) from the decks of carriers in the A-4. It was a large aircraft for a trainer, sitting well off the ground as you taxied, with room enough under its wings for bombs. The aircraft excelled at Navy missions of bombing, strafing, carrier landings and air combat maneuvering. The skills learned in the Skyhawk were directly translated to one's future jobs in strike warfare.
>
> The aircraft was relatively simple, but had some characteristics which could kill you if you ignored NATOPS [Naval Aviation Training and Operational Standard]. So the A-4 was a perfect transition between the trainers of earlier stages and the Fleet aircraft in a student's future. I do not think I ever met a Navy pilot that regretted a moment he or she spent in the A-4, even the moments that scared the hell out of you.[20]

For the Marine Corps, Skyhawk pilots were trained with VMAT-101 and VMAT-102 as well as VMT-203.

VA-125 served as the west coast A-4 RAG until handing over its duties to VA-127 in 1970. US Navy via author

THE SCOOTER COMES TO LIFE

An A-4C from VA-172 'Blue Blots' refuels an RF-8A from VFP-62 over the Gulf of Tonkin in 1966. The squadron made eleven deployments with the A-4, including two Vietnam cruises. US Navy via Lt Cdr Rick Burgess USN Retd

The wing vortex generators fitted to prevent the 'wing drop' problem are clearly visible on the outer wing sections of this A-4E. Boeing Company via author.

A4D-4

In 1958, Douglas prepared a proposal for a long-range, all-weather attack variant of the Skyhawk, whose primary mission would be to deliver nuclear weapons from low altitude. This proposal, given the A4D-4 designation, replaced the cropped delta wing with a moderately swept, tapered design that featured two drag-reducing 'Whitcomb Bodies' and provided for seven external weapons stations. A longer fuselage was also designed to accommodate the additional electronics and fuel. Because of the larger wingspan, approximately 10ft (3m) greater than that of the traditional A-4, the outer wings were given a folding mechanism to allow for carrier storage. Due to funding problems within the Navy, however, this proposal never got beyond Douglas.

A4D-5/A-4E

Of all of the Skyhawks produced, none marked the shift from the original nuclear mission to one of a close air support/conventional bomber more than the A-4E. Indeed, the importance of conventional warfare had been re-emphasized to Navy officials by the 1958 crisis in Lebanon. US warplanes from the carriers USS *Saratoga* (CVA 60) and USS *Essex* (CVA 9) were called upon to support US Marines ashore when President Camille Chemoun of Lebanon requested US assistance to keep peace after Arab nationalists seized power in neighbouring Iraq. The carriers USS *Forrestal*, *Randolph*, and *Wasp* would also take up positions off Lebanon to protect US interests.

During that crisis, US Navy planners quickly realized that much of the naval aviation inventory – the A-2, A-3 and A-4 – had been designed largely for nuclear missions and that conventional warfare capabilities were sorely lacking. Ironically, this was the same lesson taught by the Korean War, but apparently forgotten, where carriers provided the bulk of close air support and interdiction strikes.

Of special note, the requirements for the A-4E were generated before the A-4C had even flown its maiden flight. Following discussions between the Navy and Douglas, a formal proposal was submitted in February 1959, with authorization to proceed given on 30 July. The existing A-4C contract was then modified to allow for the last two -Cs to be built in the -E configuration.

Approximately 30 per cent of the A-4E's airframe was modified from the previous model. However, the greatest changes

This A-4E shows its stuff with a full load of Bullpup, Walleye, and Mk 80 series bombs. The more powerful engine and additional two hardpoints allow it to carry a theoretical load of 9,155lb (4,155kg) of ordnance and still have enough thrust to get pilots out of jams. Boeing Historical Archives via Harry Gann

VA-144 went to Vietnam in October 1969 with CVW-5 aboard USS Bon Homme Richard (CVA 31) and, together with its two sister squadrons VA-22 and VA-94, spent ninety-seven days on the line. During that time, the squadron lost one aircraft to combat. The 'Roadrunners' returned to the Gulf of Tonkin in 1970, this time flying the A-4F, and spent 101 days on the line with no combat losses. US Navy via author

were to the engine and avionics – the -E saw the introduction of the 8,500lb (3,860kg) thrust Pratt & Whitney J52-P-6 twin-spool turbojet originally planned for the cancelled A4D-3. This required some redesign of the forward fuselage to allow it to accept the new engine and a modified inlet face. The J52, the same core engine as found in the Grumman A-6A, was tested in two A4D-2Ns (BuNos 148613 and 148614) that had been converted while still on the production line to serve as YA-4E prototypes. This engine was not only lighter than the J65, it was significantly more fuel-efficient. Moreover, unlike the J65, which had already reached its design limitations, the J52 had plenty of room for growth, and, indeed, would eventually see its thrust upgraded by 800lb (365kg) – nearly 30 per cent. Thrust-to-weight ratio of this engine would come in at a respectable 1.2:1, comparable to many of the fighters of the day. The A-4E's rate-of-climb was an impressive 8,750ft (2,710m) per minute and its combat radius/mission time increased to 610 miles (988km) and 2½ hours.

Taken together, these two factors served to increase overall range by nearly 27 per cent to approximately 1,400 miles (2,270km) with one ton of ordnance, and to allow the addition of two additional outboard wing pylons, numbers one and five, and rated at 570lb (258kg) carriage. These additional hardpoints came at some cost, however, as the wing structures had to be reinforced. Yet, the added flexibility and the total payload capability of 8,200lb (3,725kg) of the five pylons dramatically increased the Skyhawk's potency as a conventional platform.

Internally, the avionics package was again upgraded by the addition of the Mk 9 toss bombing system, AN/ARN-52(V) TACAN, and AN/APN-153(V) Doppler radar navigation system. The LABS was also upgraded to AJB-3A standards. An improved ejection seat, the Escapac 1A-1, was also added, which permitted ejection at zero airspeed/ground level (zero-zero), ground level at 103.5mph (167km/h) with a 45 degree roll, inverted flight escape at heights above 320ft (99m) and speeds over 103.5mph, and wings-level ejection impact at speeds where the rate of descent was less than 2,000ft (620m) per minute. The 'zero-zero' capability greatly enhanced a pilot's chances of a safe ejection during launch malfunctions.

Not commonly reported, some A-4Es were re-engined with the J52-P-8A, 9,300lb (4,225kg) thrust engine and referred to unofficially as the 'Super Echo', although no official redesignation occurred.

All but eight of the 499 A-4Es were built under the pre-1962 A4D-5 designation system, with production continuing until April 1966. Although 500 were actu-

This comparison diagram shows the relative size difference between the A-4E (A4D-5) and the proposed A4D-6 VAL competition aircraft. Boeing via the author

Aerial refuelling from a tanker's perspective. Here, an A-4M loaded with AIM-9 Sidewinders and a centreline tank approaches a KC-10 for aerial refuelling. Gary Campbell

The JATO clips on the speed breaks of an A-4M. The small triangular-shaped opening represents the JATO igniter. Note the repair patches on the corners of the speed brakes. Gary Campbell.

The beautiful artwork on this VMA-131 A-4M was painted by Harry Campbell. John W. Binford

THE SCOOTER COMES TO LIFE

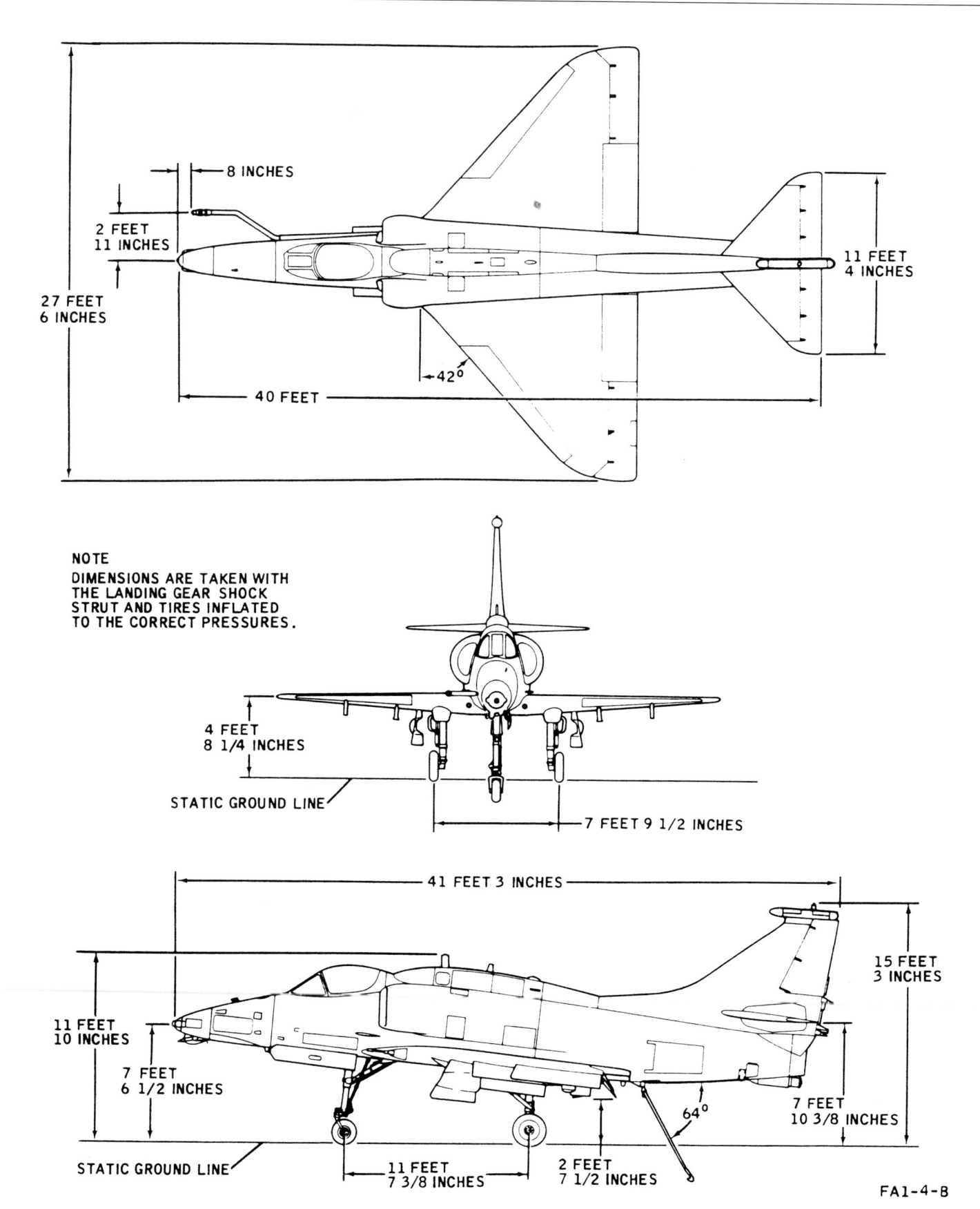

NOTE
DIMENSIONS ARE TAKEN WITH THE LANDING GEAR SHOCK STRUT AND TIRES INFLATED TO THE CORRECT PRESSURES.

FA1-4-B

The dimensions of the A-4M are shown in this company diagram.

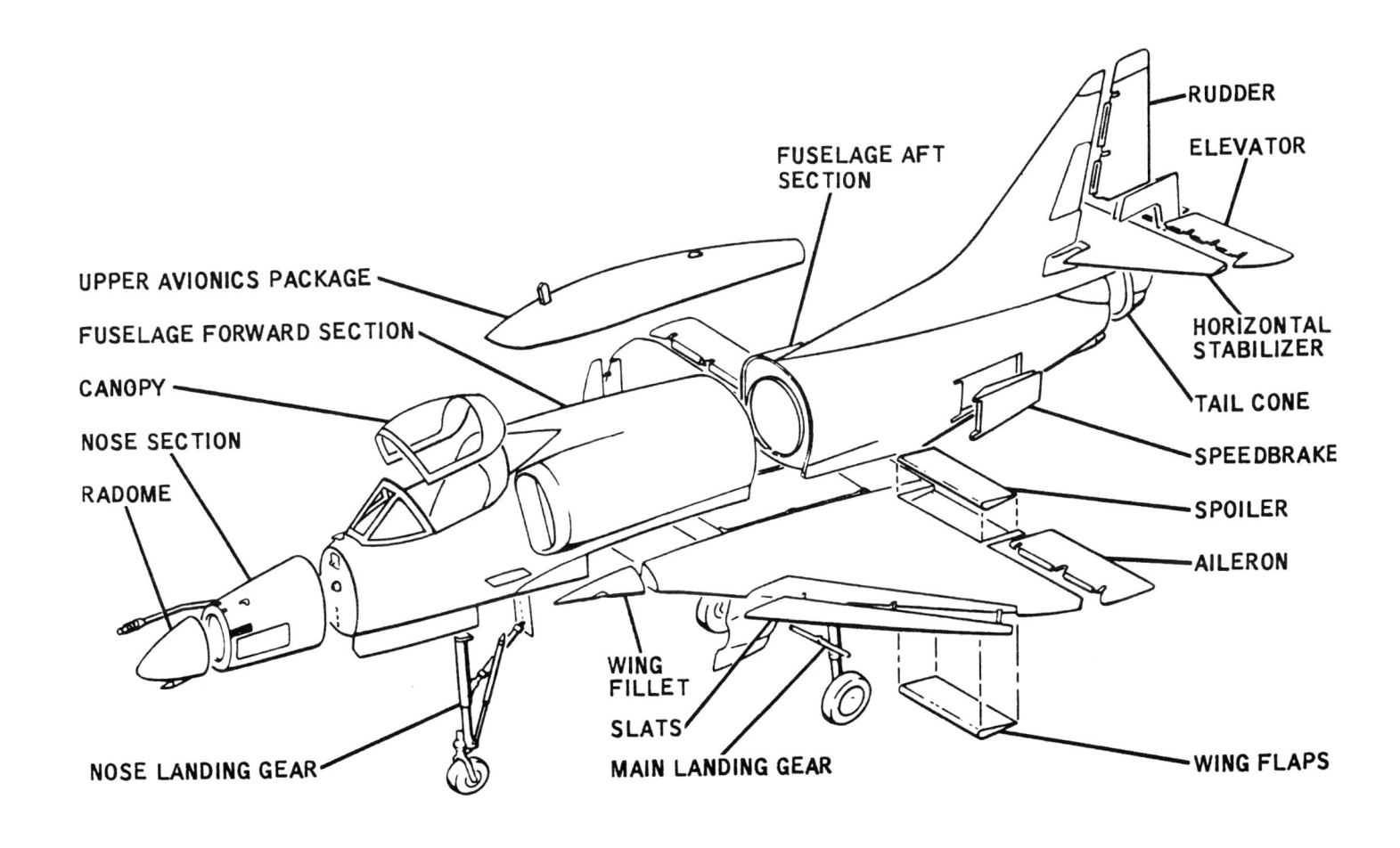

This diagram from the A-YM NATOPS highlights the Skyhawk's major airframe components.

These two photos of a VT-7 TA-4J reveal the Skyhawk's forward edge slats (left) and spoilers (right).

THE SCOOTER COMES TO LIFE

Multiple Carriage Bomb Racks (MCBRs) were conceived and developed by Navy Cdr Dale Cox, Marine Corps Maj K. P. Rice, and Capt H. W. Fitch of VX-5. Boeing Historical Archives via Harry Gann

An artist's rendition of the Douglas VAL competition entrant, the A4D-6, internally called the A-4F. It was through this contest that the Navy sought a successor to the A-4. The A4D-6 was considerably larger than the standard Skyhawk, but maintained the basic and familiar shape. LVT, later the Chance Vought A-7 Corsair II eventually won the competition and was awarded the VAL contract. Boeing Historical Archives via Harry Gann

Control Sticks

In contrast to the control stick of the A-4A, which featured a centre-mounted trim control switch, a gun trigger, and a bomb release switch the A-4C/L stick (right) adds a missile guidance switch and an autopilot override button.

On the left is the A-4M throttle control, looking more like a modern HOTAS (Hands On Throttle And Stick) system from an F-15 Eagle or F/A-18 Hornet. Featured are a tracker slew and tracker stabilization switch for the ARBS, a stadiametric range control, speed brake control, and an air-to-air/air-to-ground selector switch. The stadiametric range control allows the pilot to adjust the linear range from 557–2,624ft (170–800m) into the range solution, which controls the aiming sight in the A/A gun mode and aiming circle in the HUD missile mode. The range increases as the control is rotated forward.

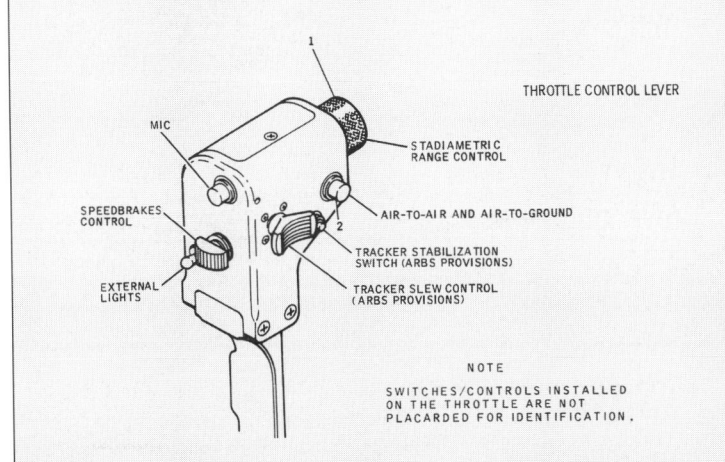

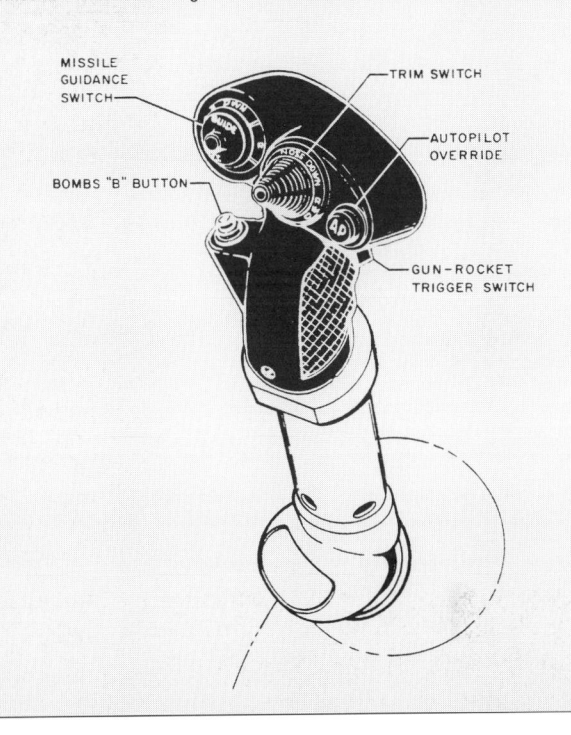

A VMA-211 Echo does a 'dirty' fly-by at NAS Cubi Point, Philippines, in November 1974 carrying a full load of Zuni rockets.
US Navy via Tailhook Association via author

US Navy Operational History

Skyhawk entry into US Navy service began in September 1956 with VA-72 squadron, based at NAS Quonset Point, Rhode Island, receiving the first batch of A4D-1s for an initial operational work-up. Prior to that, the 'Hawks' had operated the F9F Cougar. The VA-93 'Blue Blazers' based on the West Coast, became the second A4D-1 operator in November that same year and the first Pacific Fleet squadron. By the end of 1957, seven more Navy squadrons had converted to the A4D-1. Both VA-44 and VA-125, the two Skyhawk RAGs, received their first A4D-1s in 1958. By the end of production, fourteen squadrons had flown the Alpha model and four had taken it on cruise.

However, even before full transition could be completed, the new A4D-2 emerged and began entering service with the fleet. The vast majority of A4D-2 conversions took place between 1958 and 1960, with a total of thirty-eight squadrons flying the A4D-2 at some point in their operational history. VA-12 squadron, the 'Flying Ubangis' made the first transition, having transferred to the A4D-1 just the preceding April. The A4D-2, later designated the A-4B, made a total of sixty-six squadron cruises, with three to Vietnam.

Of all the Navy Skyhawks, the A4D-2N (A-4C) saw the most use; thirty-seven squadrons operated this variant, making 124 squadron cruises, forty-two of which were to Vietnam. The first two squadrons to operate the A-4C were RAGs. VA-44 and VA-125 received their A-4Cs in February and March 1960, followed by VA-195 in May and VA-192 in June. Most squadron conversions to the Charlie took place between 1960 and 1962, although four squadrons waited until the 1966–68 timeframe. VA-152 made its transition to the A-4B and -C at approximately the same time, having traded in its A-1Js in February 1968.

The Echo was used almost as frequently as the A-4C, although it equipped only twenty-eight squadrons and made only fifty cruises. As testament to its functionality, thirty-eight of these cruises were to Vietnam.

VA-125 received the first -Es in December 1962, and VA-81 and VA-83 at NAS Cecil Field transitioned the following April and May. VA-55 and VA-56 of NAS Lemoore followed in July 1963.

Reflecting the overall lower level of production, the A-4F saw service with only fourteen Navy squadrons, all with the Pacific Fleet. VA-192, the 'Golden Dragons' were the first to convert in July 1967. As the war in Vietnam progressed into its final years and the A-4 was phased out of carrier light attack squadrons and replaced by the A-7 Corsair II, most carrier deployments were made by the Foxtrot with two or three A-4F-equipped squadrons per air wing. The -F marked the last Skyhawk used by frontline Navy squadrons.

Over the years, the Navy operated several Reserve squadrons who, before 1970, operated a limited number of TA-4A and TA-4B models. Indeed, at that time Reserve squadrons were not assigned their own aircraft and instead relied on those based at their home air station. This changed with the 1970 reorganization and all became stand-alone squadrons with the older A-4s. Many of these were replaced with the uprated A-4L – a Charlie brought up to Foxtrot standards – and operated with four Atlantic Fleet Reserve squadrons, VAs-203, -204, -205, and -209, beginning in mid-1970. VAs- 303, -304, and -305 on the west coast received A-4Cs and -E (VA-305 only). Three other Reserve units operated Skyhawks, VA-776 (A-4B and -E), VA-831 (A-4B), and VA-873 (A-4B and -C). These three squadrons were activated on 27 January 1968 in response to the North Korean seizure of USS *Pueblo* (AGER 2). All returned to reserve status on 12 October 1968.

Six other Reserve units (Reserve Air Wings) operated early model and A-4L Skyhawks at various Naval Air Stations across the county: RAW-67 (NAS Atlanta, '7B' tail code); RAW-70 (NAS Dallas, '7D' tail code); RAW-74 (NAS Jacksonville, '6E' tail code); RAW-81 (NAS Minneapolis, '7E' tail code); RAW-82 (NAS New Orleans, '7X' tail code); RAW-87 (NAS Alameda, '6G' tail code).

A-4Fs served admirably during the later years of the Vietnam War and were often selected for the dangerous Iron Hand anti-SAM missions because of their superior ECM equipment. Most of this equipment was housed in the aft avionics package, called the 'hump'. This hump distinguished the Foxtrot from other models, but only for a short time, as it was quickly added to many Echoes and was later incorporated into the Charlie through the A-4L modifications. Loaded on this Scooter are two Bullpups, one Walleye, and several larger Mk 80 series LDGP bombs. US Navy via Tailhook Associatioin via author

THE SCOOTER COMES TO LIFE

Seen here at Andrews AFB in February 1973, this VA-164 A-4F wears the markings of the Air Wing Commander or 'CAG'. The '00' modex aircraft from each squadron in the air wing are regarded as the squadron CAG-bird. Modex '01' belongs to the squadrons' skippers. Stephen H. Miller via Lt Cdr Rick Burgess, USN Ret

ally ordered, the last (BuNo. 152101) was used as the A-4F prototype. In all, nearly thirty Navy and Marine Corps squadrons operated the A-4E, with many serving in Vietnam and some continuing to serve with Reserve units into the middle 1970s. VA-23 then serving with CVW-2 aboard USS *Midway*, was the first squadron to receive the new A-4E variant in November 1962. The -E's first flight took place on 12 July 1961.

A4D-6

Douglas proposed constructing a Skyhawk with an enlarged airframe, powered by the 11,500lb (5,220kg) thrust Pratt & Whitney TF30 turbofan. This competed directly with the Chance Vought A-7 Corsair II in the Navy's carrier light attack (VAL) design competition, which had been authorized by the Navy's 1963 Request for Proposal. The VAL was supposed to find an interim aircraft, of which 100 would be produced, to fill the gap until the planned VAX programme came to fruition. It would later turn out, however, that between 500 and 1,000 VALs would be needed. Moreover, the VAX programme was experiencing delays and could not be expected to come online for some time.

Douglas had already submitted an unsolicited proposal for an improved Skyhawk, which it called the A4D-6 or A-4F (not the A-4F that Douglas would subsequently develop). This proposal was later reworked to fit the VAL requirements. Other designs in the competition included variants of the North American FJ-4 Fury, a stripped-down (single-seat) variant of the Grumman A-6A, and the Chance Vought F-8 Crusader.

In February 1964, the A-7 was declared the winner and was selected to replace the A-4 as the fleet light attack aircraft. With its first flight taking place on 27 September 1965, the A-7A began to enter service in December 1967 and had completely replaced the A-4 in frontline Navy service by 1973.

A-4F

A highly capable Skyhawk, the A-4F would be the last single-seat production model to enter service with the US Navy. Indeed, the -F was produced especially for the Navy's needs in the Vietnam War, although only 146 were produced. Unlike earlier Skyhawk variants, the A-4F would bring about a new look for the Skyhawk. According to reports, Ed Heinemann did not necessarily approve of this addition, complaining that it ruined the A-4's aesthetics. Although the first A-4F was outwardly identical to the A-4E, all subsequent production models were fitted with a large aft avionics 'hump'. Running from the rear of the cockpit to the base of the vertical tail, the hump housed mostly electronic gear, including the ALQ-45 (V) homing warning system, the ALQ-55(V) radar receiving system, and the ALQ-100 ECM system. Skyhawk pilots would sometimes refer to A-4s with these humps as 'camels'. This aft hump was later retrofitted to many A-4Es and to the 100 A-4Cs converted to the 'F' standard under the A-4L designation programme.

The impetus for the addition of the avionics hump is almost a story in and of itself. As the war in Vietnam progressed, the US military became increasingly aware of the sophistication of North Vietnam's air defences, particularly their Anti-Air Artillery (AAA) and Surface-to-Air Missile (SAM) sites and the increasing use of ground radar. To foil these measures, electronic devices were developed specifically to confuse enemy

The A-4L resulted from modifications to the A-4C airframe and included the addition of the avionics 'hump' and other features of the Foxtrot. The Lima, however, retained the J65 engine and the three-station configuration. This A-4L flew many hours with VA-204 before it was transferred to the Marine Reserves.
Lt Cdr Rick Burgess USN Retd

search and fire-control and/or reduce their effectiveness. Indeed, modern electronic warfare was born in Vietnam. With the Skyhawk, installation of these electronic devices posed a problem due to the minimal internal space available. Douglas developed a solution to this problem, however, by locating the necessary electronics equipment externally, but within the new aft avionics hump.

While waiting for the A-4Fs to be delivered, the Navy established two small groups, one in the Philippines officially called Project *Shoe Horn*, and one at MCAS El Toro, to perform what were essentially field retrofits of the aft equipment for existing A-4Es. Both groups were closed once the retrofits were completed and factory production could keep pace on its own. According to sources, at least a few A-4E and A-4F models were not fitted with the aft package.

Demonstrating their ingenuity, Navy maintenance personnel adopted a makeshift solution to the ECM problem by replacing the Skyhawk's port cannon with electronic countermeasure gear. Because vibrations from the starboard cannon easily damaged the electronics, crews loaded the Hughes Mk-4 gun pod for use against ground targets. The Mk-4 was widely used in Vietnam by A-4 Marine squadrons.

One of the drawbacks of the *Shoe Horn* modifications was that it meant A-4 pilots had less ammunition for the gun:

We normally carried a full load of 200 rounds, 100 per gun. When they did the *Shoe Horn* modifications, they put some of the electronic gear in the ammo storage area and had to cut us down to 75 rounds per gun . . . [at first] they even disconnected the wiring for the guns . . . They hadn't told us the guns were disconnected . . . One of the guys was on a strike and pulled up with a MiG right in front of him. He squeezed the trigger and nothing happened. When he got back to the boat, maintenance said they had disconnected the leads to the guns.

Although these were later reconnected, the ammunition quantity remained the same at seventy-five rounds, which, 'at the Mk 12's rate-of-fire of 1,000 per minute, didn't last very long'.[21]

In some squadrons, the lack of adequate ammunition was made even worse, as the vibrations caused by the cannon's firing often damaged the sensitive electronics, forcing maintenance staff to remove the gun entirely from the port side, leaving only seventy-five rounds in total.

Many internal changes and modifications were ushered in under the A-4F designation. For enhanced communications, the ARC-51A UHF radio and an ARR-69 auxiliary receiver were installed. Navigation was further enhanced by the addition of the ARA-50 direction finder, ARN-52 (V) TACAN, and the ARA-63 Instrument Landing System (ILS). Other improvements included the addition of an upgraded AIMS transponder system, with five modes, including two IFF and one secured IFF, the AN/ASN-41 navigation computer, and the ALE-29A chaff unit.

While armaments remained basically the same as the A-4E, a Battle Damage Assessment (BDA) capability was added by modifying a centreline bomb rack pylon to carry the LB-18A camera pod. The LB-18A could carry either a DBM-4A 16mm motion picture camera or the KB-10A still picture camera. The DBM-4A was a high-speed precision camera with a frame rate from two to 400 frames per second. 200ft (62m) of this film would contain forty frames per foot for a total of 8,000 frames. The KB-10A took a maximum of five frames per second and could photograph with an f/2 8 lens with shutter speeds of 1/2000, 1/1000, and 1/500 seconds. Film was carried in 15ft (4.6m) and 50ft (15.5m) spools, producing either seventy or 230 pictures.

Avionics were modernized in the -F model, with total package weight rising to 744lb (340kg), contributing to the overall empty weight of 10,448lb (4,740kg). Cockpit armour was also added as were several improvements to enhance the aircraft's handling characteristics, especially during cross-wind landings. For example, a hydraulically controlled steerable nose gear was added, as were lift spoilers and low-pressure tyres. Again, these changes were all originally part of the TA-4E design.

In the late 1960s, 100 A-4Fs were modified with the up-rated J52-P-408 11,200lb (5,085kg) thrust engines, and were unofficially dubbed the 'Super F', reflecting their increased thrust. To accommodate the increased airflow of the -408s, the Skyhawk's air inlets were slightly enlarged. With the Super F's new lift spoilers, take-off distances could be shortened by 1,000ft (310m).

Completed at the Palmdale factory on 3 August 1966, the first A-4F flew on 31 August with fleet deliveries beginning in June 1967 to VA-23 and VA-192 from CVW-19. Its combat debut came on 26 January 1968, when these squadrons launched strikes from the carrier USS *Ticonderoga*. Three more A-4F squadrons joined less than a month later, when VA-22 and VA-94 began strikes against North Vietnam. Most 'Essex' class carriers operated at least one -F squadron towards the end of the war, with USS *Hancock*'s last three cruises seeing all three VA squadrons with A-4Fs. Indeed, all A-4Fs would see assignment with Pacific Fleet squadrons. No new-built A4-Fs were given to Marine Corps units – they began to replace older A-4s in the Marine VMA squadrons only after they were replaced in Navy units by the A-7.

Some of these A-4Fs would go on to serve with the US Navy's 'Blue Angels' flight demonstration team from 1974–87 and with several adversary squadrons including VF-126, the prestigious Top Gun, and VF-127 at NAS Fallon's Strike U. A-4Fs flown in these roles were typically stripped of all unessential equipment, such as armament and the aft avionics hump, to provide for the lightest possible airframe.

The 'Blue Angels' Get the Scooter

From 1969, the 'Blue Angels' had flown the McDonnell Douglas F-4J Phantom II during their flight demonstration performances. However, in the autumn of 1973, they decided to switch to the diminutive Skyhawk. This decision was due in part to financial concerns that were threatening the continued viability of the flight demonstration programme but was also influenced by the aftermath of an August

The 'Blue Angels' began flying the A-4F during their 1974 show season. The decision to go with the Skyhawk proved the right one, both in terms of maintenance costs and performance value. The A-4F was cheaper to operate and handled better than the F-4J previously flown by the team. Vice-Adm Tony Less, who commanded the 'Blue Angels' during their first two seasons with the Foxtrot, is shown here exiting his Skyhawk. US Navy via author

THE SCOOTER COMES TO LIFE

The Skyhawk's size and power (at least in its later years) made it well-suited to the adversary role. VF-171, the East Coast F-4 RAG, established a detachment at NAS Key West to provide its own adversary training. In 1994, Det. KW stood down and transferred its three A-4Es to VF-45. US Navy via author

mid-air F-4J collision that had claimed the lives of three team members. The A-4F presented a more affordable option, with its lower maintenance costs, and better specific fuel consumption. Moreover, its lighter airframe, agility and high roll rate at moderate speeds (300 degrees per second), made it better suited to demonstration purposes.

Vice-Adm Anthony A. Less, then Cdr Less, the CO of the 'Blue Angels' during their two years with the A-4F, made the following observation of the Skyhawk's impact on the team:

The A-4F was simply the right aircraft, at the right time for the 'Blue Angels'. Its maneuverability allowed us to keep the show in front of the audience, which is where you want to be when your performance is only thirty-five to forty minutes long.[22]

A good example of this, Vice-Adm Less explained, is the altitude at which the A-4 would go 'over the top':

With the F-4, they would go 'over the top' in a loop at 10,000 to 12,000 feet. With the smaller A-4F, we could top out at 7,000, sometimes 8,000 feet. Again, this kept the show closer to the crowd. The A-4F also allowed us to shorten our reversals to be back in front of the center point in a shorter time.[23]

This decision could not have come at a better time – hordes of A-4Fs were now becoming available as the Navy completed the switch from A-4Fs to A-7s in 1973. Moreover, approximately 100 of these models were of the so-called 'Super F' version, which featured the powerful P-408 engine. Vice-Adm Less commented:

68

'Blue Angels' Nos 5 and 6 taxi to the runway at NAS Atlanta for a show in 1981. The combination of the stripped-down Foxtrot and the J52-P-408 engine gave the 'Super Fox' a one-to-one empty thrust ratio. This added performance helped keep the 'show' in front of the audience, as pilots could perform tighter turns and did not need as much altitude to go 'over the top'. Frank Mirande

. . . the Super Fs were slicked by removing the two outboard racks on each wing. We kept the centerline for cross-country flights. With the P-408, we had a lot of power available. The Foxtrot's empty weight was about 11,300lb and with the P-408 we were looking at a near 1:1 thrust to weight ratio without fuel. One drawback, however, was that it had no burner, which prevented us from going over the top 'dirty' in formation.[24]

Interestingly, when an alternative for the F-4 was being considered, the A-4 was not alone. The Grumman F-14 Tomcat, Rockwell T-2 Buckeye, and LTV Corsair II were all considered, but rejected for various reasons. With the decision made to go ahead with the Skyhawk, eight A-4Fs were selected and sent to Long Beach for reworking to 'Blue Angel' standards. This work included deletion of the hump avionics package, the addition of a drag chute, and incorporation of a smoke system. The smoke-producing system featured a 30 US gallon (113 litre) tank of a lightweight, biodegradable paraffin-based oil pressurized by engine bleed air. Sprayed from a small tube near the exhaust pipe, the oil mixed with the hot exhaust gases and created smoke. To facilitate control of the smoke system, it could be activated by a switch on the control stick.

To help improve the aerobatic performance of the A-4, an inverted fuel system was added. Vice-Adm Less described this in more detail:

When we were testing the A-4Fs, NAVAIR test pilots discovered that prolonged inverted flight could cause a flame-out. Of course, inverted flight is an absolute given in aerobatic flight, so they had to look for a solution. The problem was caused by the inverted stand pipe in the main fuselage fuel tank. The pipe ended about four to five inches from the bottom of the cell and when the Skyhawk went inverted, air would get into the line and cause a flameout. The solution was to add a fuel accumulator, which used bleed air to pressurize the tank. We had a small light in the cockpit that glowed indicating that the accumulator was working and that we could go inverted. This accumulator meant that we could basically perform any negative 'g' maneuver and fly inverted for stretches of 50 to 60 seconds.[25]

Load feel bungees were also installed to provide greater demonstration stick force. The 'Blue Angels' also required the installation of a foldable ladder for entry that had its storage compartment in the port gun station. The wings were modified by bolting the leading edge wing slats in a closed position.

The latter modification eliminated the potentially fatal scenario where the slats would deploy in a non-uniform manner during low-altitude or close-formation flying, where the pilot would have little time to correct. Indeed, this was a common and predictable occurrence while flying the Scooter at slow airspeeds – particularly during aerobatics. At least a few A-4s were lost due to this phenomenon when the slat popped and the pilot was unable to recover. For the 'Blue Angels', such a problem would have been disastrous if it had occurred during their

Instructors at Top Gun, the Navy's Fighter Weapons School, chose the A-4 for their dissimilar adversary aircraft because of its MiG-like performance characteristics. This A-4E represents a 'stripped' version of those flown by the fleet and has been unofficially termed the 'Mongoose'. Rick Morgan

diamond, or delta, formation. However, the modification provided uniform and predictable flight characteristics while in tight formation, even if it made landing speeds a little faster.

One of the problems with the slicked-up Super F was the relative ease with which it would roll. Vice-Adm Less commented:

> The roll rate on the Super F was so phenomenal that our solo pilots had to be careful not to overdo it and 'blow out' the wing. In an excessive roll rate scenario, the high g-force would force the fuel out into the wing-tips and stress the wingskin. We learned this the hard way in our first year when, during a practice session, one of our solos sprung a wing leak after a high roll and we had to replace the wing. . . . Once this was discovered we quickly learned to limit the amount of stick deflection during rolls.[26]

In addition to the single-seat Foxtrots, the 'Blue Angels' also received one new TA-4J to serve in an administrative role. The Skyhawk became the official flight demonstration aircraft for the 1974 season, which began in April of that year. A total of eighteen A-4Fs would serve with the 'Blue Angels' over the Skyhawk's thirteen-year stint with the demonstration team, until they were replaced in 1987 by a modified version of the McDonnell Douglas F/A-18A. After their tour, four were reassigned to various adversary squadrons, one (BuNo. 154180, formerly *Blue Angel No. 1*) was given to the Museum of Flight in Seattle, Washington, and three were given to the Museum of Naval Aviation in Pensacola, Florida. Four of these A-4s now hang in the famous 'Blue Angel' diamond formation at the Museum's Exhibition Hall. (*Blue Angel No. 1* of that display is actually A-4E BuNo. 150076.)

A-4s at Top Gun

One of the most innovative uses of the Skyhawk was by the adversary squadrons, first at the Navy's Fighter Weapons School, also called 'Top Gun', and later by fleet adversary squadrons, such as Oceana's VF-45 and VFC-12, Miramar's VSC-13, and Key West's VF-43. Top Gun was created by the Navy in 1969 to help reverse the poor kill ratios that had been accumulated in the first part of the war – 3.5:1. To achieve this end, Top Gun created a graduate-level course in air combat manoeuvring based on the observations noted in the now-famous Ault Report. At first, there were insufficient funds around to allow Top Gun its own planes, so instructors resorted to borrowing TA-4Fs from the local instrument RAG, VF-126.

Once Top Gun became an independent command, funding became available and the quest began for an adversary aircraft. To fill that role, the A-4E was selected because of its ability to simulate the performances of Soviet-built aircraft such as the MiG-17 flown by North Korea. Stripped of all of its external store stations and its aft avionics pod, adversary pilots

Four familier aircraft from the Top Gun of the 1980s are, left to right, the Grumman E-2C Hawkeye, Grumman F-14 Tomcat, General Dynamics (now Lockheed-Martin) F-16 Falcon and McDonnell Douglas A-4 Skyhawk.
Lt Cdr Tom Twomey USN

quickly discovered that the A-4 could perform almost as well as the Navy's frontline fighters, the F-4 Phantom and the F-8 Crusader. These fighters were then given a camouflage paint scheme intended to mimic the enemy aircraft Top Gun students were likely to see if a war broke out.

The adversary role, though, was not exclusive to Top Gun, as VF-126 and VA-127 flew A-4s in support of various fleet exercises. VF-126 flew the Skyhawk until it disestablished in 1994, while VF-127, after being redesignated VFA-127, flew the A-4 until it was finally replaced by the F/A-18A in 1992. Skyhawks also flew in adversary roles for various fleet and Composite squadrons, such as VC-8 and VFC-12 and -13. Today, only VC-8 at NAS Roosevelt Roads, Puerto Rico, operates the A-4. Although other models of the Skyhawk were flown at Top Gun, the A-4F was clearly the model of choice due to its powerful -408A engine. Indeed, A-4s would go on to serve in the adversary role, especially at Top Gun, until they were replaced in 1994, by F/A-18As.

A-4L

Unlike all other variants, the -L represented a rebuilding programme that converted 100 former A-4Cs to the A-4F standard, without the J52 engine. These models also retained the A-4C's three hardpoints. All A-4Ls were assigned to Navy and Marine Corps Reserve units, with the initial deliveries made to the Naval Reserve Training Unit (NARTU) at NAS Jacksonville, Florida, in December 1969. Marine Corps -Ls were later replaced

THE SCOOTER COMES TO LIFE

An A-4 'Mongoose' from Top Gun makes an approach at NAS Miramar in January 1989. Formerly the home of Top Gun, the base has now been redesignated and the Top Gun school moved to NAS Fallon.
Lt Cdr Tom Twomey USN

by the A-4Fs, as the A-7 Corsair IIs became more abundant. Douglas converted the first A-4L (BuNo. 148307) at its Long Beach plant, but then produced a total of ninety-nine kits for the Navy to convert at its Naval Air Rework Facility (NARF) in Pensacola. The first A-4L flew on 21 August 1969, with conversions arriving in Reserve units in mid-1970, where they served until replaced by early model A-7s and were reassigned to various fleet utility (VC) squadrons. Navy Reserve squadrons operating the A-4L included VAs-203, -204, -205, and -209. VMAs-124, -142, and -543, all Reserve units, also flew this model.

No A-4Ls saw service in Vietnam. A-4Ls were outwardly identical to A-4Cs, with the exception of the avionics hump.

A-4M

When the Navy conducted the VAL competition in the early 1960s, the winner was supposed to become the standard light attack aircraft for both Navy and Marine Corps attack squadrons. While the Navy followed this course, the Corsair II was simply too expensive and too maintenance-intensive for the Marine Corps' needs and they opted instead for a further upgraded Skyhawk, the A-4M. Named the 'Skyhawk II', the A-4M was specifically designed by McDonnell Douglas to meet the Marine Corps' requirements for a low-cost, potent close-support aircraft. Costing approximately $1,500,000, the A-4M was just what the Marines were looking for to match their limited budget.

By any standard, the A-4M represented the most potent of the Skyhawk models. Central to the A-4M was installation of the improved J52-P-408A engine, which has been described as the greatest single improvement to the A-4M model. The

72

Two Reserve A-4Ls from VA-203 wait their turn on the forward starboard catapult during air operations aboard USS John F. Kennedy **(CV 67) in September 1971. Reserve Air Wing Twenty (CVWR-20) was requalifying.** US Navy via Lt Cdr Rick Burgess USN Retd

The A-4L cockpit shows the APG-53 radar screen and more conveniently located dials, as compared to the A-4A. US Navy via author

A mixed foursome of Marine Skyhawks is represented here, with an A-4M from VMA-223 on the right, an A-4F from VMA-142 on the left, and a VMA-132 A-4F in the slot, all led by a TA-4J from VMAT-102. The lead Skyhawk carries two Zuni rocket packs while the A-4M and the A-4F carry a 2,000lb laser-guided bomb. Harry Gann

An A-4M of VMAT-102 pictured at MCAS, Yuma, Arizona. Robert F. Dorr

A close-up of the right side of this Marine Corps A-4 reveals several of the plane's unique features. Visible on the top front surface of the leading-edge slats are the vortex generators added during the initial flight test period. The slats hang down when the plane is at rest and are actuated by airflow. To the aft of the wing is the aileron (closest, angling up) and spoiler (drooping). Harry Gann

Two Douglas employees work on the A-4M fuselage. This variant was produced solely for the US Marines and is regarded as the most capable of all the Skyhawk variants. Most notable are its advanced avionics, 200 rounds of ammunition per gun, and J52-P-408 11,200lb (5085kg) thrust engine. The Mike's ECM suite was also greatly enhanced. Boeing Historical Archives via Harry Gann

The A-4M cockpit is much more sophisticated than earlier models and features easy-to-read and scan gauges as well as an Elliot 546 HUD. Visible to the right is the Concentric Warning Receiver used to locate serious threats. *Harry Gann*

NWC China Lake is responsible for testing new ordnance – an A-4M readies for the first test-firing of the new AGM-65E laser Maverick. USMC Maj John P. Bland stands next to his plane conducting the pre-flight check. This version of the Maverick is heavier than that used at the time by the **US Air Force**. *US Navy via Lt Cdr Rick Burgess USN Retd*

A ribbon-type drag chute was added to the A-4M model to give Marine Skyhawks the ability to stop on the smaller runways that might be encountered in forward-deployed areas. This Skyhawk is from VMA-324 at Marine Corps auxiliary landing field, Bogue Field, North Carolina. Notice the deployed spoilers on the wings. US Navy via Boeing Historical Archives via Harry Gann

VX-5 operated a number of A-4s in its test and evaluation program. Here, an A-4M is set-up as the test aircraft for the new ARBS system. This aircraft has been called the 'Smart Hawk' because its capabilities enhanced the A-4's stand-off value. Lt Cdr Rick Morgan USN Retd

A close-up of the Angle Rate Bombing System (ARBS) nose reveals the details of the ARBS device. The large lens in the centre serves as the 'window' for the TV-like sensor and the Laser Spot Tracker (LST).
Lt Cdr Rick Morgan USN Retd

An A-4M loaded with Mk 7 dispensers and CBU-59/B APAM waits for takeoff. D August via Gary Campbell

The starboard fuselage of the last VMA-131 is shown here, marking the squadron's lineage. The port painting can be seen on page 59.
John W. Binford

An A-4K (NZ6212) of No. 75 Squadron RNZAF takes on fuel from an RAF VC10 K.4. Peter Foster

General specifications

	A-4A	A-4B	A-4C	A-4E	A-4F	A-4L	A-4M	TA-4F	TA-4J
Length	39'-1"	39'-4"	40'-1"	41'-3"	41'-3"	40'-1"	41'-3"	42'-5"	42'-5"
Wing Span	27'-6"	27'-6"	27'-6"	27'-6"	27'-6"	27'-6"	27'-6"	27'-6"	27'-6"
Height	15'	15'	15'	15'	15'	15'	15'	15'	15'
Empty Weight	8,391 lb	9,146 lb	9,619 lb	9,853 lb	10,448 lb	10,448 lb	10,800 lb	10,602 lb	10,602 lb
Max T/O Weight	22,500 lb	22,500 lb	22,500 lb	24,500 lb	24,500 lb	24,500 lb	24,500 lb	24,500 lb	24,500 lb
Max Level Speed	664	661	649	673			670	675	
Engine	J65-W-4	J65-W-16A	J65-W-16A	J52-P-6/8	J52-P-8/408	J65-W-20A	J52-P-408	J52-P-6/8	J52-P-6
Thrust lb	7,700	7,700	7,700	8,500/9,300	9,300/11,200	8,400	11,200	8,500/9,300	8,500

-408A, with its 11,200lb (5,085kg) thrust rating, almost 20 per cent more than its predecessor, brought with it significantly better manoeuvrability, acceleration, rate-of-climb, and take-off performance, with only a small reduction in overall range. Comparatively speaking, manoeuvrability at Mach 0.75 was improved by 100 per cent from 1.5g to 3.2g; acceleration in dive bombing by 23 per cent; rate-of-climb improved 50 per cent from 5,620ft (1,715m) to 8,440 ft (2,575m) per minute and take-off distance was reduced from 3,720ft (1,134m) to 2,700ft (823m), while maximum speed at sea level with 4,000lb (1,815kg) ordnance increased from 598–644mph (953–1,037km/h).

To help reduce smoke trails, something that earmarked earlier Skyhawk models, the J52-P-408A was fitted with smokeless burner cans. To accommodate the greater mass flow of the new engines, the intake areas were widened by 2½in (6.35cm) – approximately 7 per cent. Other significant additions to the A-4M consisted of increasing the ammunition for the two 20mm guns to 200 rounds each; enlarging the cockpit canopy to provide for greater forward and rearward visibility; and adding a new rectangular windshield, which increased the angle of vision downwards from 16–18 degrees and sideways from 46–55 degrees.

Externally, the A-4M differed by the addition of a canted refuelling probe in place of the standard straight probe introduced on the A-4B. This angled configuration, bending outward to the right, was necessitated by the need to prevent interference between the metal surfaces of the probe and the nose-mounted APG-53 radar, as well as other nose-mounted electronics. This 'cranked probe' was also retrofitted to certain other early model A-4s during the 1970s. A ribbon-type drag chute and an enlarged tailfin were also added, both of which were developed for the foreign Skyhawk production programme. The drag chute, located just aft of the arrest hook, helped to slow the aircraft and allow landings on shorter fields. The square-tipped tailfin, changed to accommodate additional antennas, provides another means of identifying A-4Ms from A-4Fs.

The A-4M retained the same five stores configuration of the -F. The new Skyhawk's basic operating weight came in at 12,280lb (5,575kg). Given its normal gross weight of 24,500lb (11,120kg), the A-4M could carry up to 9,155lb (4,155kg) of ordnance, leaving a maximum of 3,065lb (1,390kg) for internal fuel, or about 470 US gallons (1,775 litres).

Avionics also saw an upgrade, with the installation of the ARC-159 (V) UHF radio which could acquire up to 7,000 channels manually, the ARC-114/-114A VHF/FM radio, an additional VHF secured radio, and the improved ARN-118 (V) TACAN. The ARC-114/-114A radio allowed voice communications in the VHF range of 30.00 to 75.95 MHz, and could operate on any one of 920 channels. Additional features on the A-4M included installation of an improved electrical generator and a self-contained electrical starter, two items that also originated in the foreign Skyhawk programmes, and a new fixed gun sight.

First flight of the A-4M took place on 10 April 1970, with fleet deliveries commencing on 16 April 1971 to VMA-324 of MCAS Beaufort, NC. Test pilot Walt Smith piloted the A-4M on its first flight. Due to an operational exercise, deliveries were accepted at MCAS Yuma. At the same time as the initial deliveries were being made, four other A-4Ms were busy completing BIS trials at the NATC Patuxent River, while the fifth operational delivery, BuNo. 160245, was celebrated as the 2,500th Skyhawk produced at the 20 April 1971 ceremonies performed at NAF Washington.

Other changes followed the initial deliveries to Marine squadrons. In 1974, funding was released for the addition of the Elliot 546 HUD, with both air-to-air and air-to-ground modes, and for other cockpit improvements permitting better situational awareness. In 1977, the offensive capabilities were further enhanced by the addition of the Hughes Angle/Rate Bombing System (ARBS), which enabled the Skyhawk to operate laser-guided munitions, such as the AGM-65E Maverick, for use against hardened targets. The ARBS was installed on several new builds and retrofitted to older A-4Ms. At one point, consideration was given to renaming the ARBS-equipped Skyhawks as A-4Ys, but that idea was eventually dropped.

It was an A-4M that would be the 2,960th and last Skyhawk produced, and later delivered to Marine Corps squadron VMA-331 on 27 February 1979. To com-

The parachute housing, seen on some foreign variants, emerged on the A-4M and allowed Skyhawks to land on shorter runways. Gary Campbell

The nose-gear mechanism of the Skyhawk is shown on this A-4M. The A-4C modified for the US Army proposal was the only Skyhawk to have a dual nose-wheel system. John Binford

memorate the festivities, the last Scooter was given a non-traditional paint scheme with both Navy and Marine Corps markings and the flags of all foreign Skyhawk users painted along the fuselage.

A-4Ms served with all active-duty Marine Corps VMA squadrons until retired from frontline service on 27 February 1990, when VMA-211 transferred its last Skyhawk, BuNo. 158428, to Reserve unit MAG-42 at NAS Alameda, California. The A-4M continued to serve with Reserve units until August 1994, when Marine Air Wing-3s VMA-131 'Diamondbacks' retired its last Skyhawk at NAS Willow Grove, Pennsylvania. Lt Col George 'Eagle' Lake, Commander of VMA-131, made the final flight. In a tribute quite fitting to the Skyhawk's long career, Bob Rahn, the man who piloted the first Skyhawk to the skies in 1956, delivered the closing tribute before VMA-131's pilots and crews.

A total of 158 A-4Ms were built, plus the two A-4Fs (BuNos 155042 and 155049) reworked to the -M standards for prototype development. A-4Ms were replaced in the Marine Corps' inventory with another McDonnell Douglas product, the AV-8B Harrier II, and thirty-six would later be refurbished for sale to Argentina as the A-4AR Fightinghawks.

CHAPTER THREE

Two-Seat Skyhawks

Despite the fact that the Skyhawk had been in service since 1956, it was not until 1964 that plans for a two-seat variant gained momentum within the Navy. Douglas had long advocated a two-seater for use in advanced training and to enhance the overall mission but tight budgetary constraints delayed this proposal for some time. In 1964, however, with the US becoming more involved in the Vietnam conflict, funding became available to study a two-seat Skyhawk. The Navy asked Douglas to produce two prototypes out of the last two production A-4Es (BuNos 152102 and 152103) which could serve as operational combat trainers. These would then be designated as TA-4Es, although they were referred to in Douglas/Navy correspondence as A4D-5Ts. Playing a significant role in the Navy's decision to proceed with the two-seat variant was the need to use the single-seat A-4s currently used by the training command to replace the combat losses in Vietnam.

A total of 555 two-seat Skyhawks were produced between 1965 and 1978, with post-1969 production running parallel with the A-4M. The A-4 seemed perfect for advanced navigation, type-training, and familiarization flights, not to mention certain combat roles for which two sets of eyes would be better than one. Two-seat Cougars were already being used by the Marine Corps for observation and Forward Air Control (FAC) duties.

TA-4E/TA-4F

Douglas modified BuNos 152102 and 152103 into the new design by adding another 28in (71cm) to the fuselage to accommodate the tandem cockpit. This resulted is some loss of range, due to the loss of 136 US gallons (515 litres) of fuel, but it was not viewed as significant as the aircraft was intended as a combat trainer. In fact, Douglas offered to resolve this problem by adding a 270 US gallon (1,020 litre) faired fuel tank to the top aft fuselage, but the plan was rejected by Navy officials.

Douglas also took the opportunity to incorporate further upgrades into the two-seater that had been under development

A detachment of seven TA-4Js from VT-7 prepare for a mission at NAS Fallon, Nevada, during a February 1984 weapons Det. Rick Morgan

This TA-4F, delivered on 10 July 1967, was the 2,000th Skyhawk. It was delivered to VF-126, the West Coast instrument RAG, stationed at NAS Miramar. This squadron later provided two-seat Skyhawks for use as dissimilar aircraft during the early years of Top Gun. Douglas Aircraft Co. via Aerospace Publishing

Douglas had long pushed for a two-seat Skyhawk on the basis that it would make a perfect trainer. Douglas also suggested that a second 'set of eyes' might enhance certain missions then flown by the A-4. The Navy resisted these suggestions at first, due to lack of money, but finally made the commitment in 1964, and ordered the last two A-4Es to be converted to the new configuration. This photo shows BuNo. 152102 being flown by H. H. Knickerbocker on its maiden flight, 30 June 1965. Boeing Co. via author

The first conversion Model 'Ts', BuNos. 152102 and 152103, sit on the tarmac at Palmdale, California, following early flight tests. Both 'first flights' occurred two months ahead of schedule. The addition of lift spoilers, nose-wheel steering, and a modified ejection seat were significant modifications to the basic Skyhawk model, as was installation of the latest enhancement to the Pratt & Whitney J52 series, the 9,300lb (4,225kg) thrust P-8A engine. The fuselage was also stretched by 28in (71cm) to accommodate the second cockpit. *Douglas via Lt Cdr Rick Burgess USN Retd*

Although the Navy had been told that the Echo would be last Skyhawk model, attrition mandated that war losses be replaced and the Navy ordered the A-4F. This decision occurred at about the same time as the initial production of the TA-4E and many already on the production line were converted into the new -F model, which itself incorporated many of the changes brought to the Skyhawk programme by the TA-4E. Given this, Douglas redesignated the TA-4E to the TA-4F, reflecting its commonality with the single-seat Foxtrot. This top view of an A-4F and TA-4F shows their comparative size. The A-4F has its new lift spoilers and its speed brakes open. Both show their leading-edge slats fully deployed. *Boeing Historical Archives via Harry Gann*

TWO-SEAT SKYHAWKS

VA-125 at NAS Lemoore, California, received the first TA-4Fs for training new pilots entering the Skyhawk community. Fleet deliveries on 19 May 1966 were marked with this ceremony. Douglas Aircraft Co. via Lt Cdr Rick Burgess USN Retd

Shown here is a close up of the TA-4J's large canopy and steerable nose-wheel. The Skyhawk is from Modex '04' VC-13 and wears the 'UX' tail markings.
Lt Cdr Rick Burgess USN Retd

87

TWO-SEAT SKYHAWKS

This TA-4F hails from Marine unit H&MS-24 at MCAS Kaneohe Bay, Hawaii, where it provided adversary services for local Marine and Air Force squadrons. Bruce Trombecky

The Marines used TA-4Fs like this one from H&MS-31, for Forward Air Control (FAC) missions in Vietnam. This photo was taken in 1979 at NAS Moffit Field. Lt Cdr Rick Burgess USN Retd

The Mighty 'T' in Tracom

The TA-4J became the Navy's exclusive advanced jet trainer following the initial delivery of fifty TA-4s to VT-21 and VT-22 at NAS Kingsville on 6 June 1969. In the early 1970s, two-seaters began arriving at NAS Beeville, where Training Command Three operated VT-24 and VT-25. Advanced jet training was formerly the responsibility of the TF-9 Cougar, but it had become outdated, and the new Skyhawk was welcomed with open arms.

The training of new Navy and Marine Corps pilots was overseen by the Chief, Naval Aviation Training (CNATRA) at NAS Corpus Christi, who in turn reported to the Chief, Naval Education and Training (CNET) in Pensacola. During the 1970s and 1980s, six training commands, called Training Wings (TW), were organized under CNATRA to provide basic, intermediate, and advanced flight training for both pilots and Naval Flight Officers (NFOs). The six commands were located throughout the southern part of the US as follows: TW-1 at NAS Meridian, Mississippi; TW-2 at NAS Kingsville, Texas; TW-3 at NAS Beeville, Texas; TW-4 at NAS Corpus Christi, Texas; TW-5 at NAS Whiting Field, Florida; and TW-6 at NAS Pensacola.

TA-4Js were flown by the advanced jet training squadrons with TWs-1, -2, -3, and -6. The three pilot 'pipelines', Training Wings 1–3, oversaw VTs-7, VT-21, -22, and VTs-24, -25 respectively. Instructor pilots from these squadrons taught students who had been selected for the strike community – the A-4, A-6, A-7, S-3, and later the F/A-18 and F-14. A typical TraCom pilot syllabus covered swept-wing familiarization or FAM, all-weather instrument flight, formation flying, tactics, and advanced air-to-air/air-to-ground (usually at NAF El Centro), and Air Combat Manoeuvring (ACM). The last step was carrier qualifications, which during the 1970s and early 1980s was usually on USS *Lexington* (CV-16), the Navy's dedicated training carrier, although fleet carriers were sometimes used when *Lexington* was unavailable. To graduate, students had to complete 270 flight hours and make six landings on the carrier. TW-6 trained the NFOs and VT-86 at NAS Pensacola was the squadron responsible for running the syllabus. VT-86 students followed one of three syllabuses: Over-Water Jet Navigation (OJN) for EA-6B Prowler and A-6 Intruder crew members; Tactical Navigation (TN), for the S-3 Viking community; and Radar Intercept (RI), for the F-4 Phantom II, and later the F-14 Tomcat, community. TA-4Js were used by the RI instructor pilots to help teach prospective Radar Intercept Officers (RIOs) how to work with pilots as a team and also how to operate the radar and weapons gear while under the severe stress of high g-forces.

Towards the end of the 1980s and early 1990s, the TA-4Js started to be replaced by the Boeing T-45 Goshawk. NAS Meridian's VT-7 officially retired its TA-4Js in an elaborate ceremony at the National Museum of Naval Aviation in Pensacola, Florida, on 26 June 1999, although the last class did not complete its carrier qualifications until late September. Retd Adm Stanley R. Arthur, who commanded VA-164 from 8 July 1971 until 1 July 1972, was the guest speaker.

VT-25 was based at NAS Beeville, Texas, and flew from Chase Field. The 'Cougars' belonged to Training Wing Three.
Lt Cdr Rick Burgess USN Retd

Students with the advanced jet training squadrons take a Skyhawk aboard for carrier qualifications (CQ). Here, two TA-4Js from VT-7 sit on the elevator of USS Enterprise **during CQ off the coast of San Diego. USS** Lexington **(CV 16) served as the official training carrier, although fleet carriers were used when she was not available.** Rick Morgan

for future Skyhawk variants. A zero-zero ejection seat was installed with an expanded operational envelope and the engine was modified with the latest upgrade to the J52 series, the P-8A, with 9,300lb (4,225kg) thrust. All armament and weapons systems were retained, although some TA-4Fs later had the gun removed. However, of all the modifications the most significant involved the addition of the nose-wheel steering and wing spoilers. Since the TA-4E/F would be used as a trainer for new pilots, it was recognized that something needed to be done to improve the handling characteristics while landing in strong cross-winds. Because of the Skyhawk's unique landing gear arrangement, a strong cross-wind could cause significant handling problems for inexperienced pilots. This problem was effectively countered by the addition of lift spoilers, which in turn provided the added benefit of a reduced landing roll-out. Although initially used to transition pilots to combat tactics and instrument training (with the instrument RAGs, such as VA-43 and VA-126) the TA-4F went

VT-21 at NAS Kingsville was one of the first advanced jet training squadrons to receive the TA-4J.
Lt Cdr Rick Burgess USN Retd

Navy RAGs trained foreign Skyhawk purchasers as well as US aviators as export sales began to rise in the late 1960s and early 1970s. Here, two TA-4Js from VA-127's instrument RAG fly with two Singapore A-4S. Harry Gann

Two ex-RAN TA-4Gs are flanked by two TA-4Ks shortly after delivery to the RNZAF. RNZAF

An VMAT-102 A-4M (back) flies with its TA-4J squadron mate. VMAT-102 provided instrument training for Marine Corps pilots. *Harry Gann*

VT-22 from Training Wing Two received its model Ts on the same day as VT-21 when a mass of fifty TA-4Js were flown to Kingsville from the Palmdale Plant
Lt Cdr Rick Burgess USN Retd

VT-4 operated out of NAS Pensacola under control of Training Wing Six. They are not known to have a squadron name. Lt Cdr Rick Burgess USN Retd

on to undertake a wide range of training duties.

Piloted by H. H. Knickerbocker, the first TA-4E (BuNo. 152102) took to the air on 30 June 1965, with the second (BuNo. 152103) following shortly after on 2 August. Deliveries began on 19 May 1966 to VA-125 at NAS Lemoore, which was the west coast squadron responsible for training newly-winged pilots on the A-4, as well as transitioning A-4 pilots who were assigned to A-4 operational squadrons. Deliveries to VA-44, who shared these responsibilities, but for east coast pilots, and VMAT-102, the Marine Corps' Replacement Air Group (RAG), began shortly thereafter.

Soon after the first flight, the Navy decided to procure the A-4F, which incorporated many of the new features introduced on the TA-4E. The TA-4E was then redesignated as the TA-4F. A total of 241 TA-4Fs were produced, plus the two TA-4E prototypes. Over 100 of these were later reworked to the TA-4J standards and twenty-three were converted into OA-4Ms for the US Marine Corps. Four were made into electronic warfare models, designated as EA-4Fs and used by VAQ-33 to fill the role of surface fleet aggressors.

Interestingly, several TA-4Fs actually made their way into combat during the Vietnam War with several of the Marine Corps' Headquarters & Maintenance Squadrons (H&MS), later redesignated as Marine Aviation Logistics Squadrons (MALS). Taking advantage of the added set of eyes, TA-4Fs were used by the Marines in the Fast Forward Air Control (Fast FAC) and Tactical Air Coordinator (Airborne), or TAC (A), roles to co-ordinate air strikes, artillery, and naval gunfire in support of ground units and, by using smoke rockets, to mark targets. The TA-4F, with its high speed and modern weapons suite, seemed a natural for this role. These innovative applications would later lead to the development of the OA-4M, a FAC/TAC (A) variant of the A-4M. The TA-4F's FAC missions over South Vietnam began in late 1967 and were flown primarily from Marine Corps bases in Da Nang and Chu Lai. Replacing the two-seat TF-9J Cougar formerly used by the Marines for this role, TA-4Fs would also mark targets. Reconnaissance was also a favoured TA-4F mission. The H&MS units were selected for the Fast FAC and TAC (A) roles because no two-seaters were assigned to VMA squadrons. The H&MS units also were assigned TA-4Fs for proficiency and other administrative support flights. Records show that H&MS-11, -12, and -13 all participated in this role during the war.

Several NAS Lemoore-based squadrons also used TA-4s for short periods; VA-144 and VA-195 had at least one, and VA-164 actually took the type to sea aboard USS *Hancock* in 1974 and 1975. Their two-to-three two-seaters for use with hand-held laser designators, called the Light Weight Laser (LWL). Measuring 4½ × 4½ × 10in (11.4 × 11.4 × 25.4cm) and weighing a mere 8lb (3.6kg), the box-shaped LWL was aimed by the back-seater in the same fashion as one uses a camera. Special goggles were worn to prevent damage to the eyes from reflected laser light.

For such missions, the 'spotter' TA-4F carried two Aero-1 fuel tanks on its inboard stations. Maintenance officers typically served as the designator in the aft cockpit. The accompanying strike aircraft were then armed with Mk 82 LGBs on the outboard stations and Mk 83 bombs on the inboard, with a centre-line tank. VA-164, on its 1972 cruise aboard the *Hancock*, used this TA-4F/LWL combination in conjunction with its laser-bomb touting A-4Fs.

This Skyhawk belongs to the Chief, Naval Aviation Training (CNATRA) and carries the '000' Modex. Lt Cdr Rick Burgess USN Retd

TA-4J

The second two-seat version of the A-4 resulted from a 1968 decision by the Navy to incorporate the two-seat trainers into the advanced training command as a replacement for the ageing Grumman TF-9J Cougar and the F-11F Tigercat, both of which had been in service since the 1950s. To more reflect the training role, and also in an effort to reduce costs, the TA-4J, as it would be called, was produced without a weapons system, missile launch capability, or LABS. The ability to receive in-flight refuelling was retained, but the ability to refuel other aircraft via the buddy-store system was eliminated. These deletions resulted in a saving of approximately 230lb (104kg), thereby allowing the lower-rated P-6 engine to be used instead of the P-8A that had been used in the TA-4F. In most other respects, the TA-4J was identical to the TA-4F, although later production models saw the incorporation of the canted refuelling probe that was installed on the A-4M.

Due to the conversion of a number of former TA-4Fs, only 277 TA-4Js were newly produced. For this training role, TA-4Js were painted in a red-orange and white paint scheme to distinguish them from the gull-grey and white fleet aircraft. With its first flight taking place on 17 December 1968, deliveries to VT-21 and VT-22 began in earnest on 6 June 1969 when a mass of fifty two-seaters were flown to NAS Kingsville from the Palmdale plant. Since then, all US Navy advanced jet training squadrons have operated the TA-4J, including VT-24 and VT-25 at NAS Chase Field, Texas, VT-4 and VT-86 at NAS Pensacola, and VT-7 at NAS Meridian. All TA-4Js have been replaced in the training pipeline by the Boeing T-45 Goshawk.

TA-4Js also flew with several Navy support squadrons, namely NAS Miramar's VF-126 adversary squadron, VA-127 (later redesignated as VFA-127) at NAS Lemoore, VF-43 at NAS Oceana, and VF-45 at NAS Key West. It also served with the Composite squadrons, namely: VC-1 at Barber's Point, Hawaii; VC-2 at NAS Oceana; VC-5 at Cubi Point, Philippines; VC-7 at NAS Miramar; VC-8 at NAS Roosevelt Roads, Puerto Rico; VC-10 at Guantanamo Bay, Cuba; and RVAH-3 at NAS Key West, where it helped facilitate training and other support operations. TA-4Js were also flown by the Marine H&MS (later Maintenance and Logistics Squadrons, or MALS).

OA-4M

With the advances brought on by the A-4M, the Marines were soon looking for an aircraft with the same capabilities as the TA-4F Fast FAC platforms that had proved so successful in Vietnam. McDonnell Douglas quickly responded with the two-seat OA-4M, and authority was given by the Navy to rework some twenty-three TA-4Fs for use as high-speed reconnaissance and air control platforms. All reworks were completed by the Naval Air Rework Facility (NARF) in Pensacola.

Key to this modification, authorized by AFC 542, was the installation of new communications gear to enhance the FAC role, namely the ARC-114 VHF, ARC-139 UHF, and KY-28 secured (encrypted) voice communications systems. Additional armour-plating for the cockpit sides and a ground-controlled bombing system were also added as was a canted A-4M-style refuelling probe. The aft avionics hump, made a common sight by the A-4F model, was also included. These upgrades essentially brought the TA-4F up to A-4M standards, although the ARBS was not added because the OA-4M lacked a true direct bombing mission. Interestingly, at one point, consideration was

TWO-SEAT SKYHAWKS

Training for fleet Naval Flight Officers took place at NAS Pensacola under the care of VT-86 'Sabrehawks'. This TA-4J is being refuelled at NAS Atlanta to complete its training mission. The training command's distinctive orange-red and white paint scheme is seen here, with a black rudder. These colours enhance the TA-4's visibility. *Frank Mirande*

A freshly painted OA-4M assigned to H&MS-32 at MCAS Cherry Point. The OA-4M represents a FAC version of the A-4M and served solely with the Marines. *Rick Morgan*

This depicts the typical front TA-4J cockpit.
Ted Carlson

given to up-rating the J52-P-408A 11,200lb (5,085kg) thrust engine, but that was rejected, a decision which later led to the OA-4M's fleet reputation of being underpowered.

These modifications were first installed experimentally on TA-4F BuNo. 152856. The first OA-4M, however, was BuNo. 154294, which was outfitted at NATC Patuxent River and first flew on 23 May 1978. H&MS-32 at MCAS Cherry Point, VA, was the first squadron to receive the OA-4M in late 1979, with H&MS-12 at MCAS Iwakuni, Japan, and H&MS-13 at MCAS El Toro, California, following in subsequent years. The OA-4M could carry a maximum warload of 6,500lb (2,950kg) and achieve a maximum level speed 'clean' of 670mph (1,085km/h) at low level.

EA-4F

Yet another use for the two-seat Skyhawk came about when the US Navy surface fleet set out to create their own version of the Navy's successful Fighter Weapons School. Impressed with the NFWS's ability to train pilots to counter Soviet air forces, surface officers were anxious to create a training environment where surface ships could obtain the same experience in countering Soviet and Chinese-built anti-surface weapons, such as the Chinese Silkworm and the widely exported French Exocet.

What resulted was the creation of the Fleet Electronics Warfare Support Group (FEWSG), which featured an electronic aggressor squadron, designated VAQ-33 'Firebirds', which could electronically simulate the signals of Soviet aircraft and naval weapons systems. Fleet units would then develop tactics and electronic countermeasures designed to thwart such weapons. After VAQ-33 relocated to NAS Norfolk from Quonset Point, where it was winding down as the last fleet A-1 Skyraider squadron, it subsequently moved to NAS Key West in 1980 where it enlisted a hodge-podge of naval aircraft (the NC-121K Constellation, ERA-3B Skywarrior, EA-6A Electric Intruder, TA-7C Corsair) to serve as the airborne aggressors.

The two-seat TA-4F was chosen for one of these roles, and redesignated as the EA-4F. Three TA-4Fs (BuNos 152869, 153481, 154655) were so modified in 1970 at the McDonnell Douglas Long Beach plant, with BuNo. 152852 converted in 1973 by fleet personnel at NAS Norfolk. Externally, the EA-4Fs looked virtually identical to their TA-4F counterparts, except for the absence of the gun barrels, modified canted probes, and modified contoured nose-cones. The latter was added to accommodate the installation of an internal jammer, which was apparently never followed-up. They differed internally by the addition of wiring enabling the use of chaff and jammers, and the ability to carry external electronic stores, including the AN/AST-4 jammer pod and

This VT-7 'Marine' TA-4J, painted in the familiar orange and white scheme, hopes to beat the coming storm as it waits for the handler to remove the chocks. Frank J. Mirande

A-4s from the Marine Corps played an active role throughout the Vietnam War, flying thousands of missions from their base at Chu Lai. This A-4E from VMA-121 awaits final permission to taxi. Aerospace Publishing

The A-4F was selected by the 'Blue Angels' to replace the F-4J Phantom II in late 1973 and began performing with the Flight Demonstration Team for its 1974 season. 'Blue Angel' No. 1 (BuNo. 155033) is seen here at Andrews AFB in May 1981. Lt Cdr Rick Burgess USN Retd

Only an air show could put such dreaded foes in such close proximity without causing alarm! Pictured together at the 1990 Oshkosh Air Show, this MiG-21 'Fishbed' and A-4B Skyhawk would have had different impressions of one another had they met over the skies of Vietnam some twenty years earlier. R.S. DeGroat

VMA-311 played a significant role during the Vietnam War. Based at Chu Lai, they accumulated over 50,000 combat sorties between 1965 and 1973 and, along with VMA-211, were the last fixed-wing assets to leave Vietnam. This photo of an A-4M was taken at Randolph AFB in July 1979. A 300 US gallon (1,136litre) tank and Multiple Carriage Bomb Racks (MCBRs) are loaded on the aircraft's stations.
Rick Morgan

VMA-322's famous Revolutionary War-era Minuteman insignia is displayed on the A-4E in this photo. US Navy via author

Top Gun eventually flew the A-4M shown here.
Lt Cdr Tom Twoney USN

The first Skyhawk, BuNo. 137812, sits in front of the Douglas plant for a publicity photo, circa 1956. US Navy via author

This colourful VT-7 Skyhawk taxies for take-off at NAF El Centro, Nevada, where students conduct their air-to-ground syllabus. Ted Carlson

Four TA-4Fs were modified as electronic 'aggressors' and served with VAQ-33 at NAS Norfolk, then NAS Key West, and provided electronic support for the Fleet Electronic Warfare Support Group. This EA-4F is pictured off the coast of Puerto Rico in 1981. Only four Skyhawks were converted to this configuration. Rick Morgan

New Zealand purchased a total of fourteen Skyhawks, beginning in 1969. To commemorate the 50th Anniversary of the RZNAF, this two-seat TA-4K (NZ 6256) was painted in this unique gold finish. RNZAF via author

The Navy created two large Anti-Submarine Fighter Squadrons, VFS-1 and VFS-3, from which smaller detachments could deploy and provide the ASW carrier air groups with a basic level of fighter support. VFS-1, to which this A-4C belongs, was the parent squadron from which VFS-3 was created in 1967. This concept soon fell by the wayside as the ASW carriers were phased out and their mission taken over by the large-deck carriers as part of the 'CV' concept in the early 1970s. US Navy via author

An A-4B belonging to the Naval Missile Center sits loaded with three AGM-12 Bullpup missiles. The Bullpup capability was introduced on the A-4B, but failed to live up to its advertisement as a workable stand-off weapon. The pilot had to maintain a straight approach while the bomb was guided to its target, making him susceptible to enemy AAA and small arms fire. US Navy via author

VF-101 and VF-171 both acquired small numbers of A-4s to assist with dissimilar air combat training and established a detachment at NAS Key West where students could go for the DACM portion of their RAG syllabus. Here, an A-4E from VF-171 KW Det. taxies on the ramp in colourful camouflage. Rick Morgan

Singapore purchased forty Skyhawks for its Royal Singapore Air Force, which have since undergone two upgrades. Here, the product of the second such project, an A-4SU Super Skyhawk of No. 145 Squadron, sits at Kuantam, Malaysia. The large black VHF aerial aft of the cockpit distinguishes this from earlier -S models. Also note the lack of an avionics hump typical of US -E, -F, -L, and M models. The hump was removed and replaced with a saddle-type ADF antenna. *Peter Foster*

A pilot from VMAT-102 demonstrates his prowess by delivering two Mk 83 Snakeye retarded bombs. The Snakeye was developed to allow pilots to attack targets from a lower altitude without fear of damaging their aircraft from the bomb blast. Designed as a high-drag complement to the Mk 80 series designed by Ed Heinemann, the Snakeye's fins deployed, thereby slowing the bomb's flight and giving the pilot sufficient separation to escape. Snakeye kits have been replaced today by an air-inflated bag, known as a 'ballute', which is more reliable. *Harry Gann*

The last Marine Corps A-4 was retired from Reserve Squadron VMA-131 'Diamondbacks' in August 1994. Especially visible on this A-4M is the parachute canister just aft of the tailhook. The painting on the Skyhawk's side can be seen in detail on **pages 59 and 79.** *John W. Binford*

The A-4M's Angle Rate Bombing System (ARBS) was added in the mid-1970s to enhance the Skyhawk's weapons delivery capability. Shown here in this close-up of a VMA-131 Skyhawk is the ARBS TV sensor (centre) and LST (Laser Spot Tracker). On each side of the nose are antennae for the ALR-45 radar warning system. The two white antennae are for the ALQ-126 jamming system. *John W. Binford*

Zuni rockets are fired from a steep-diving A-4M of VMAT-102. *Harry Gann*

Five A-4s painted for delivery to the US Marine Corps are parked neatly to commemorate the 2,500th Skyhawk produced. *McDonnell Douglas via author*

Proving itself during the Vietnam War, the TV-guided AGM-62 Walleye was one of the early 'smart' weapons and brought to the fleet the ability to send one plane after one target. Here, a VMA-324 A-4M releases a Walleye over the Chocolate Mountain target range in Southern California. Close inspection shows the pilot's head is down, watching his screen. Harry Gann

This Marine Corps Reserve A-4E sits on the tarmac at NAS Key West in April 1981 and is painted in the more colourful high-viz markings that were prominent prior to the adoption of low-viz two-tone grey scheme in the mid-1980s. Rick Morgan

Catapult crews hook an A-4E from VA-212 to the bow cat near the end of USS Hancock's 1965 cruise. The Skyhawk carries Zuni rocket pods, drop fuel tanks, and a centreline-mounted Triple Ejector Rack (TER) with four Mk 80 series bombs. Robert F. Dorr

The Navy experimented with several different camouflage combinations in an effort to better protect pilots from enemy gunners. This scheme, which features a dark green colour, was tested for a short time aboard USS Enterprise (CVAN 65). US Navy via author

TWO-SEAT SKYHAWKS

The electronic aggressors, represented by this VAQ-33 EA-4F, flew out of NAS Key West. A sister unit, VAQ-34, was formed on the west coast, but was unable to secure its own EA-4Fs. McDonnell Douglas converted this Skyhawk to the electronic aggressor variant in 1970 at its Long Beach plant. This EA-4F served with VAQ-33 until 1988 and was transferred to VC-10 at Guantanamo Bay. Notice the extended nose cone, designed for jammer gear that was never added. Rick Morgan

Two-seat Skyhawks were also well-received by the experimental and test community. Here, a Skyhawk from Reserve Air Wing 81 (RAW-81) of NAS Minneapolis, Minnesota, bears the markings of the Naval Air Test Center at NAS Patuxent River. Interestingly, the TA-4J retained its '7E' tail code.
Lt Cdr Rick Burgess USN Retd

The 'Blue Angels' received one TA-4J to provide maintenance and support duties for the Flight Demonstration Team. This Skyhawk wears the markings of 'Blue Angel' No 7 and is being inspected by onlookers at the air show at NAS Patuxent River, Maryland in 1977.
Lt Cdr Rick Burgess USN Retd

Many Composite Squadrons, such as VC-8, became full adversary squadrons during the early 1980s. Based at NAS Roosevelt Roads, Puerto Rico, the 'Red Tails' first transitioned to the A-4 in 1967, receiving a batch of A-4Bs to replace their ageing FJ-4D Furies. Note the bright red star tail markings designating it as an adversary unit. Jim Winchester

ALQ-167 jammer. A target missile launcher capability was also added. A new panel was installed in the aft cockpit allowing the Naval Flight Officer (NFO) to operate the electronic equipment.

Electronic exercises with fleet units were performed on both coasts by VAQ-33 until the formation, in 1983, of a sister unit, VAQ-34, at NAS Point Mugu, California. VAQ-34 requested its own EA-4Fs, but this was rejected due to a shortage of TA-4 airframes in the jet training command. Aggressor missions would often involve the EA-4F using an AST-4 pod to simulate an incoming cruise missile. This pod produced a signal similar to that emitted by a missile seeker and provided a near-live 'threat' to locate and identify. Combining the AST-4 touting Skyhawks with other VAQ-33 aircraft created a very effective electronic training scenario for fleet EW operators. As evidence of the EA-4F's usefulness in this role, the four VAQ-33 Skyhawks (two EA-4Fs and two modified TA-4Js) flew a combined 1,142 hours (approximately 18 per cent) of the squadron's total of 6,286 flight hours during 1986.

One EA-4F, BuNo. 152869, was lost in April 1980 in Colorado following an oil system failure. The Navy later replaced this with a TA-4J, BuNo. 154343, that was modified to carry the various pods, but not redesignated. A second EA-4F, BuNo. 154655, was lost in 1985, off NAS North Island, California, due to an engine failure. It, also, was replaced by a modified TA-4, BuNo. 158136, but not redesignated.

The remaining two served with VAQ-33 until March 1988 and ended their service life with VC-8 (BuNo. 152852) and VC-10 (BuNo. 153481) on 5 and 9 October 1990, respectively. The two modified TA-4Js continued to serve – BuNo. 154343, with VF-43 at NAS Oceana, Virginia, until 1994, and BuNo. 158136, with TW-2 until 1997. While other Composite squadrons had similarly modified TA-4s, none were designated as EA-4Fs.

Composite Squadrons

Fleet Composite (VC) squadrons employed the TA-4 in a variety of roles as they attempted to support the fleet units. The primary VC function, until the advent of dissimilar adversary service in the mid-1970s and early 1980s, was fleet support, which ranged from transporting VIPs to towing or launching targets for other Navy aircraft and ships. TA-4Js frequently pulled TDU-series towed targets for strafing or missile firings, and launched BQM-34 Firebees or AQM-37A supersonic targets for fleet exercises.

Six Fleet and two Reserve Composite squadrons were active during the 1970s.

TWO-SEAT SKYHAWKS

This Skyhawk from VC-1 tows a TBU-22B target off the coast of Oahu, Hawaii. VC-1 was based at Barber's Point and provided logistics and adversary support for Pacific Fleet units. US Navy via Lt Cdr Rick Burgess USN Retd

An in-flight VT-22 'Golden Eagle' from Training Wing Two. The TA-4J played a integral role in advanced jet training for nearly twenty years until replaced by the McDonnell Douglas T-45 Goshawk. Bob Thomas via Robert F. Dorr

A VFC-13 TA-4J makes a final approach at NAF El Centro in early 1990. The squadron began at NAS New Orleans in 1973 and moved to Miramar in 1976 to augment VC-7. Many of its original members were from VSF-76 and VSF-86, which were disestablished in 1973. Later that year, the *'Saints'* traded in their A-4Ls for two-seat Skyhawks and since acquired A-4E and A-4F single-seaters as supplements. The 'Saints' continue in their adversary role today, although they traded in their A-4s for F/A-18 Hornets in 1994. Ted Carlson

Of the six Fleet squadrons, two were forward-deployed in the Pacific to assist fleet units during their WestPac cruises. VC-1 was based at NAS Barber's Point, Hawaii. With its Marine Corps brethren H&MS-31 (later MALS-31), VC-1 flew support for fleet units out of Pearl Harbour, Air Force F-15s at Hickam AFB, and Marine Corps squadrons from MCAS Kaneohe Bay. VC-5 operated out of Cubi Point in the Philippines and provided fleet support for forward-deployed units, such as USS *Midway* based in Japan and those carriers deploying to WestPac or the Persian Gulf/Indian Ocean (PG/IO). VC-1 disestablished in September 1992 and VC-5 disestablished in September 1992, when Cubi Point was closed.

Back in the States, two Composite squadrons operated in conjunction with the fighter-oriented master jet bases. VC-2 resided at NAS Oceana, while VC-7 was based at NAS Miramar. Both flew support missions for their respective coast squadrons and fleets, and were augmented in 1975–6 with the rebasing of the two Reserve VC squadrons. VC-2 was disestablished in October 1980 and VC-5 in September 1992.

Two VC squadrons served in the Caribbean; VC-8 operated out of NAS Roosevelt Roads and served Atlantic Coast fleet units and squadrons. VC-10's 'Challengers', flying out of MCAS Guantanamo Bay, Cuba, served a dual role as fleet support and air defence for the Marines based at Gitmo. Because of their air defence mission, Gitmo's TA-4Js were the last remaining US-operated two-seat Skyhawks configured to carry the AIM-9 Sidewinder. Both squadrons are operational at the time of writing and are still flying the TA-4J.

Two Reserve VC squadrons were formed on 1 September 1973; VC-12 'Fighting Omars' at NAS Detroit, Michigan, and VC-13 'Saints' at NAS New Orleans, Mississippi. The 'Saints' were formed in part with members of the then-disestablished VSF-76 and -86, the Reserve Anti-Submarine Fighter squadrons intended to supplement VSF-1 and -3. Both Reserve VC units operated the A-4L. VC-12 moved to Oceana in 1975 and took over VC-2's duties following their disestablishment. VC-13 did the same in 1976 when it went to Miramar. Both VC-2 and VC-7 were disestablished in October 1980, with the Reserve units assuming all VC duties. VC-1 and VC-5 stood down in September 1992.

How the TA-4 Impacted Top Gun and the Adversary Squadron

No true review of the two-seat Skyhawk can be complete without some discussion of its role in the establishment of Top Gun, the Navy Fighter Weapons School, or in the emphasis on dissimilar aircraft adversary training that flourished from 1973 until 1990. When Top Gun was formed in 1969 funds were short. Instructors, who still were working out of a trailer at NAS Miramar, had to look for aircraft wherever they might be found. Since Top Gun began as a part of the West Coast F-4 RAG, VF-121, finding Phantoms was not the real problem. Rather, the difficulty was finding adversary aircraft.

An interesting photo of TA-4E BuNo. 152102 with four AIM-9 Sidewinders. US Navy via Aerospace Publishing

Top Gun's founders quickly worked out an arrangement with VF-126, the west coast instrument RAG, to use some of their TA-4Fs in the adversary role. It has been reported that famed MiG-killer Randy Cunningham credits the moves he learned from Top Gun students flying the VF-126 TA-4Js as being, in part, responsible for his air combat successes in Vietnam. Top Gun would later go on to acquire its own A-4s as it became a separate command, flying stripped-down versions of the A-4E, A-4F and Super Fox, and finally the A-4M, before transitioning to the F/A-18 in 1994. At one point, the A-4, together with the F-5E, was the mainstay of Top Gun's adversary force.

Instrument Squadrons

In the late 1960s and early 1970s, four squadrons served the Navy as so-called 'instrument squadrons', each flying the TA-4J. These squadrons were responsible for providing all-weather instrument ground and flight training to naval aviators *en route* to Fleet squadrons from the training command. Two of these squadrons were located on the east coast – VA-43's 'Challengers' operated out of NAS Key West and VA-45's 'Blackbirds' flew out of NAS Oceana. VA-126, called the 'Bandits', flew at NAS Miramar and VA-127's 'Desert Bogeys' at NAS Lemoore, then at Fallon, flew on the west coast. The following summary discusses how these squadrons became involved in the adversary role.

VA/VF-43

Based at NAS Oceana, the 'Challengers' received their first Skyhawks during the early 1960s for use in the instrumentation-training role but it was not until 1970 that they began flying some limited Air Combat Manoeuvring (ACM) training. In 1973, the adversary role was added to their training mission and squadron aircraft started to receive the camouflage paint-schemes that traditionally designated this role. In 1978, VF-43 was ordered to make

Instrument RAGs helped train naval aviators en route to the Fleet squadrons and fleet-experienced aviators returning to the cockpit who need instruments refreshers. One such squadron was VA-45 based at NAS Oceana. Originally designated as a VA squadron, the 'Blackbirds' received authorization to fly dissimilar ACM missions in 1976 and later assumed the mission completely. In recognition of this, they were redesignated as VF-45 in 1985. *US Navy via author*

adversary activities their number one priority. One of the squadron's most significant innovations was the creation of the Fleet Fighter ACM Readiness Program (FFRAP), which became a standard part of the VF-101's F-14 instructional syllabus. FFRAP was a series of lectures and dissimilar ACM missions flown by RAG students against the adversary pilots. VF-43 stood down in 1994 due to budgetary constraints associated with the massive military downsizing of the early 1990s.

VA/VF-45

This squadron began as VA-45 and, as with VF-43, served as an instrument RAG. It was based at NAS Key West and began operating two-seat variants of the Skyhawk in 1967. On 16 August 1976, the 'Blackbirds' were authorized to begin providing dissimilar ACM (DACM) training and, in recognition of this role, were redesignated as VF-45 in 1985. The 'Blackbirds' flew single and two-seat A-4s, plus a mixture of F-5s and later F-16Ns, a special version of the F-16 designed for use by the Navy. VF-45 taught DACM to Hornet and Tomcat pilots alike, both as fleet units and for the community RAGs, later called Fleet Replacement Squadrons (FRS), as part of their tactics and ACM training phases. VF-45 remains today, although its Skyhawks were retired in 1994.

VA/VF-126

Again an instrumentation RAG, this squadron, located at NAS Miramar, was long noted as the premier adversary squadron. VF-126 developed a counterpart training programme for the fighter community, called Turnaround ACM Program (TAP), which was later meshed into one programme with the East Coast FFRAP. VF-126 flew A-4E, -F, -M, and TA-4J variants in the DACM role, in addition to F-5Es, and later F-16Ns. This squadron stood down in 1994.

VA/VF-127

VA-127 began as a detachment of VF-126, referred to as VF-126 Det. Alpha, providing instrument training to squadrons at NAS Lemoore. In May 1970, VF-127 took over the role of A-4 community RAG as VA-125 was stood down and VA-122 handled the new A-7s. It served in this role until July 1975. Shortly after that, the squadron was officially designated as an adversary unit. As with all other squadrons performing the adversary role, VF-127 adopted the camouflage schemes of the foreign threat nations. One VF-127 aircraft was even painted with the silhouette of a MiG-17. In 1987, with the F/A-18 taking such a prominent position in the force structure, the squadron was redesignated as VFA-127 and moved to

One of the early duties of the Composite Squadrons was target towing. Here, a VC-1 A-4E flies near Hawaii with a TDU-10 Dart target package installed. US Navy via Aerospace Publishing

NAS Fallon, where it flew adversary missions in support of the Navy's Strike Warfare Center. VFA-127 was disestablished in 1993, with VFC-13 assuming its adversary role.

Two other squadrons operated a small number of A-4s for the adversary role. VF-101, the east coast Tomcat RAG, kept three A-4Es in its VF-101 KW Det. VF-171, the RAG for the F-4 Phantom II, operated a similar detachment called VF-171 KW Det., also equipped with A-4Es. VF-171's Det. stood down in 1984.

VC Change of Mission

The idea of adversary squadrons caught on fast and by 1975 virtually all of the then-remaining VC squadrons had shed their support missions and were performing adversary work. As the original VC squadrons stood down, their DACM duties were assumed by VC-12 and VC-13, both of which were redesignated in 1987 to VFC units, to reflect their primary role as fleet adversary squadrons. Both squadrons flew their A-4s until 1994 when they were traded in for the newer F/A-18 Hornet.

CHAPTER FOUR

Skyhawks at War

Probably nothing tests the endurance capabilities of an aircraft more than combat. In this regard, the A-4 Skyhawk performed admirably, flying thousands of missions for both Navy and Marine Corps squadrons in one of the nation's darkest hours, the Vietnam War. From its beginning on 5 August 1964 to the last mission flown in January 1973, Skyhawks flew hundreds of thousands of sorties, both from aircraft carriers on Yankee and Dixie Stations and from Marine Corps bases at Da Nang, Chu Lai, and later Bien Hoa. 196 Navy and 70 Marine Corps Skyhawks were lost to enemy action in the conflict.

Skyhawks suffered from the same handicap that plagued all military operations in Vietnam, as overly burdensome political restraints unnecessarily prolonged the war and prevented military objectives from being achieved. Nevertheless, the A-4 earned a reputation as a tough, rugged, reliable war-horse, that would later go on to help drive export sales to foreign governments so impressed by the Scooter's performance that they, too, wanted the A-4 for frontline roles.

The Skyhawk Has a Few Close Calls

The 1958 Lebanon Crisis saw the Skyhawk on the verge of combat, as two carriers from the US Navy's Sixth Fleet, USS *Saratoga* (CVA 60/CVG-3) and USS *Essex* (CVA 9/ATG-201), stood offshore ready to provide air cover for the Marines who had gone ashore under Operation *Bluebat* to help keep the peace and to allow Lebanese Army units to go into the countryside to defeat leftist guerrillas. The Skyhawks aboard *Saratoga* included VA-

This VA-86 Sidewinder CAG '00' A-4E starts down the port catapult aboard USS Independence **(CVA 62) during its 1965 Vietnam cruise. 1 July 1965 marked the squadron's baptism into combat, flying raids against targets in South Vietnam from Dixie Station. Stations one and five appear to carry Mk 83 1,000lb bombs.**
US Navy via Tailhook Association

These A-4Es from the USS Oriskany **are carrying a load of Mk 83 bombs and a centreline tank as they prepare to go 'feet dry' over Vietnam. The Skyhawks belong to VA-163 'Saints'.** US Navy via author

34's A4D-1s, while VA-83 aboard *Essex* flew A4D-2s. USS *Wasp*, although it had no A-4s, also stood ready to assist.

One of the missions assigned to Skyhawk units during that crisis included providing a nuclear deterrent against any possible Soviet retaliation, for Soviet Premier Nikita Khrushchev had threatened to strike at the US carriers and turn them into 'flaming coffins'. At least one-third of the carriers' Skyhawks stood nuclear alert during the crisis, with some A-4s even loaded and on deck. American carrier aircraft paid close attention for signs of any Soviet fleet movement from ports in the Black Sea, but that never materialized.

The mainstay of the Skyhawks' missions, however, was surveillance, as described by Cdr James L. Holloway III, skipper of VA-83 aboard USS *Essex*:

> The other two-thirds of our aircraft were employed on surveillance missions, which consisted mainly of flying border patrols around the perimeter of Lebanon, the Israeli side as well as the Syrian side. We also conducted route reconnaissance, involving flying over some of the main roads leading out of the principal cities of Sidon, Tyre and Beirut and through the mountains into the Bekka Valley and from there across the border. The purpose of the border patrols was to detect the incursion of any foreign military forces, and the road recces were just to keep track of what was moving on the roads in Lebanon.[27]

For these missions, Skyhawks were typically armed with two or four pods of 2¾in (6.9cm) rockets, which could be fired singly or in salvos and would have been particularly useful against trucks or lightly armed vehicles. Full ammunition was also carried for the twin Mk 12 20mm cannons.

With two carriers on station, air coverage responsibilities were often rotated, with one air group taking responsibility for full air operations while the other stood down for replenishment. This 'stand-down' generally took place every four to five days. These carriers provided much-needed air coverage for the Marines for approximately one month, until US Air Force units could be moved into place at the NATO air base in Adana, Turkey. The entire operation ended on 25 October

A veteran of World War II, USS Essex **(CVA 9) is seen here with a complement of A-4 Skyhawks lined down her deck. The** Essex **stood ready with VA-34 to provide air cover for US Marines ashore in the 1958 Lebanon Crisis.** US Navy via author

1958, when the Marines withdrew after General Fouad Chehab, former head of the Lebanese Army, was elected President.

As the Lebanon crisis was coming to an end, US carrier forces were again sent into harm's way during the summer of 1958 when a dispute arose between Communist China and Taiwan over the islands of Quemoy and Matsu. Quickly dispatched were the Seventh Fleet carriers USS Hancock (CVA 19) and USS Lexington (CVS 10), which took up stations east of Taiwan. USS Midway (CVA 41), with its nuclear weapons arsenal, was also sent to the region and USS Essex, now freed from its duties off Lebanon, was ordered to 'chop' from the Mediterranean to the western Pacific. Despite several exchanges of shelling and the downing of four Communist China MiG-17s by ROCAF F-86Fs, the matter came to an end with a cease-fire announced on 6 October. No shots were fired by US forces. Of these named carriers, only Hancock, Essex, and Lexington operated a contingent of A-4s.

Other operations also took the Skyhawks to the brink of combat action. During the early 1960s, Skyhawks were often a part of carrier patrols off Central America, as the US attempted to contain the spread of communism to countries such as Nicaragua and Guatemala. During November 1960, for example, Skyhawks from VAs-12, -15, and -106 stood ready aboard USS Shangri-La as it steamed through the Carribean as part of the Carribean Task Force. Skyhawks aboard USS Franklin D. Roosevelt (CVA 42) performed similar missions in 1963 off the Dominican Republic.

Most notable, however, were the units sent to provide support for the disastrous

Bay of Pigs invasion in 1961 and those involved in the now-infamous Cuban Missile Crisis in October 1962. Alarmed by the activities of Fidel Castro in opposition to Cuba's Dictator Fulgencio Batista, the US government sponsored an invasion of Cuba, called Operation *Zapata*, which involved transporting US-trained Cuban refugees to a remote landing spot called the Bay of Pigs. Providing air support for those landings was a collection of US Navy ships, including USS *Essex*, with VA-106, deployed as part of CVG-10. The Skyhawks stood ready but President John F. Kennedy refused to call them into action in an effort to prevent any direct involvement. The operation was no less than a total failure, as the Cuban nationalists were quickly captured by Castro's forces.

The Cuban Missile Crisis followed in October 1962, as the US sought to remove recently-deployed Soviet SS-4 Sandal and SS-5 Skan IRBMs. Also deployed to Cuba were various Soviet-built MiG fighters and SA-2 SAM units, as well as Il-28 'Beagle' tactical bombers. In an effort to concentrate air power in the south-east of the United States to support OpPlan 312, the air strike option against the Cuban sites, approximately half of the US Marine Corps' A-4 squadrons were placed on alert starting on 22 October, with VMA-242 and VMA-533 being transferred from MCAS Cherry Point to NAS Key West and VMA-324 transferred to the same base from MCAS Beaufort. Beaufort's VMA-331 was moved to NAS Roosevelt Roads and VMA-121, the only west coast VMA unit affected, was sent to NAS Cecil Field. VMA-224 remained on alert at MCAS Cherry Point.

The alert had an equal impact on the Navy, where the carriers USS *Enterprise* (CVAN 65), USS *Essex* (CVS 9), and USS *Independence* (CVA 63) were deployed to the Caribbean. USS *Randolph* (CVS 15), an anti-submarine carrier, was also tasked into service in support of the

Skyhawks from USS Shangri-La **(CVA 38) stood ready to assist democratic nations throughout the Caribbean resisting the spread of communism during the early 1960s. Here, a formation of A4D-2s led by then Lt Cdr Otto E. Kruger, from CVG-10's VA-106 squadron fly overhead. The 'Gladiators' flew three variants of the A-4 until disestablished in November 1969.** US Navy via author

Four VA-66 Bravos pose in formation in June 1961 operations with USS Intrepid **(CVA 11). The lead and left wing are carrying AGM-12 Bullpup missiles while the remaining Skyhawks carry iron bombs.** US Navy via Tailhook Association

the two-seaters went along to provide hand-held laser designation for laser-guided munitions, as no laser designating pods were then available.

In all, thirty-six A-4 squadrons deployed on a record 112 cruises over the course of the nine-year war, with some squadrons, namely VA-55's 'Warhorses', VA-164's 'Ghostriders', and VA-212's 'Rampant Raiders', seeing as many as eight deployments. The number of A-4 losses, 196 Navy aircraft, reflects the aircraft's high rate of usage rather than its vulnerability. In fact, most pilots would agree that the Skyhawk was one of the most survivable planes in the inventory. It was also one of the most reliable aircraft of the war, with availability numbers reaching 90–100 per cent at times. Key to this was the simplicity of its design, which allowed even major damage to be repaired fairly quickly.

The Carriers

A total of twenty-one carriers fought off the shores of Vietnam as part of Task Force 77, serving some 9,178 days on the line. Of these carriers, USS *Hancock* made eight combat cruises; USS *Ranger*, *Coral Sea*, *Oriskany*, and *Constellation*; made seven combat cruises; and USS *Kitty Hawk*, *Bon Homme Richard*, and *Enterprise* made six cruises.

Skyhawks were operated from all of the carriers, although most A-4s were phased out of the large decked ships beginning in December 1967 with the introduction of the A-7 Corsair II aboard USS *Ranger*. The smaller deck carriers (USS *Essex*, *Hancock*, *Intrepid*, *Yorktown*, *Oriskany*, and *Ticonderoga*) typically operated two A-4 squadrons, with a third added in early 1968 following the exit of the A-1 Skyraider. The first three A-4 squadron cruise took place in 1966/7 aboard USS *Franklin D. Roosevelt*, when CVW-1 was stocked with VAs-12, -72, and -172. Although it would not be until mid-May of 1967 before another air wing would deploy with three A-4 squadrons, that would later become the standard for the small deck 'Essex' class carriers (USS *Hancock*, *Bon Homme Richard*, *Shangri-La*, and *Oriskany*) as the war wound down.

With an average of fourteen Skyhawks per squadron, the three-A-4 squadron air wing composition gave the small deck carriers a powerful complement of forty-two strike aircraft. These A-4s typically flew their missions with F-8 Crusaders providing escort or flak suppression. The larger carriers substituted their A-4s and A-1s with Intruders and Corsairs and the newer F-4 Phantom IIs for the Crusaders, with the A-7s taking over the *Iron Hand* missions.

Of special interest was the late 1965 cruise of USS *Enterprise*. For this, the

A VA-95 A-4 sits with an AGM-12 Bullpup. The 'AJ' markings belong to CVW-8, which cruised the Mediterranean Sea aboard USS *Shangri-La* in 1968. US Navy via author

Route Packages (RPs)

Air Force and Navy air operations over North Vietnam were controlled by two groups; the Commander, Second Air Division, in Saigon, and the Commander of Task Force 77. When the air war began, the sparse number of approved targets in the North created a 'competition' between the services as to who could strike a particular target. Service strikes were often duplicative of one another, due in part to poor communications. In an attempt to remedy this, days were divided into three-hour slots, for which control would alternate between the Navy and the Air Force. While theoretically appearing sound, this soon proved to be a problem, as weather delays continued to cause confusion about who would hit a particular target.

Co-ordination of these efforts was eventually given to the *Rolling Thunder* Armed Reconnaissance Coordinating Committee (RTARCC, later RTCC). In November 1966, the RTARCC devised a plan to divide North Vietnam into six Route Packages, the control of which would alternate between the services on a weekly basis. This also proved problematic, and control over the individual RPs was eventually permanently assigned.

Route Package I began at the DMZ and ran north to the Mu Gai Pass. Because of its proximity to the fighting in the south, command of RP I was given to Gen William C. Westmoreland, Commander, US Ground Forces, Vietnam. Route Packages II, II, and IV ran along the coast and extended to just below the Hanoi/Haiphong area, stopping at an imaginary line someway from Hanoi. These RPs were given to the Navy. RPs III and IV carried much of the traffic south, with major transportation facilities located in RP IV. The infamous Thanh Hoa Bridge and the Dong Suong and Quang Lang airfields were in that RP.

The Air Force was assigned responsibility for Route Package V, the most north-eastern part of North Vietnam. This assignment made sense, as Air Force planes based in Thailand were much closer to the targets. Route Package VI was considered the 'hot spot,' as it contained Hanoi and Haiphong. This RP was sub-divided at the north-eastern rail line into China, with RP VI-A, the northern segment, including Hanoi and the airfields at Kep, Gia Lam, and Phuc Yen. RP VI-B was to the south and included Haiphong and Hon Gai and the MiG base at Kein An. RP VI-A was assigned to the Air Force and RP VI-B assigned to the Navy.

Carrier Stations

Because the carriers steaming off the coast of Vietnam never faced any significant threat of air attack, they could generally cruise in the same location. Two stations that would become well-known terms in the life of naval aviators were Yankee Station in the north, and Dixie Station in the south.

Gen Westmoreland was so impressed with the performance of Navy and Marine aviators operating from USS *Midway* and USS *Hancock* during the early part of 1965 that he lobbied for the establishment of a permanent station off the coast of South Vietnam. This became Dixie Station and was staffed initially by USS *Oriskany* (CVA 34). Seventh Fleet carriers deploying to Task Force 77 would often begin their line periods by serving a few days or weeks at Dixie Station as a 'warm up' for operations 'up North'. Dixie Station was eventually discontinued in August 1966 as sufficient Air Force assets had been located in South Vietnam and Thailand to support ground operations in the south.

Yankee Station was the base for all operations against North Vietnam and the point from which the majority of Navy strikes were conducted during the war. Initially located due east of the DMZ, Yankee Station moved north beginning in April 1966 to a point east of Vinh, then moved south with the end of Operation *Rolling Thunder* in 1968. It moved north again during 1972 during the Operation *Linebacker* raids, at one point coming within 70 miles (113km) of Haiphong. Yankee Station was generally staffed by two to three carriers 'on the line' and was unquestionably considered more hazardous by the pilots and air crews who flew there.

Carrier Air Wings

The A-4 Skyhawk has played a vital role in the carrier air wing from its initial deployment with CVG-9 aboard USS *Ticonderoga* (CVA 14) in September 1957 to its final cruise with CVW-21 aboard USS *Hancock* (CVA 19) in 1975. Skyhawks first deployed on attack carriers and anti-submarine carriers with air groups designated as Carrier Air Groups (CVG) and Carrier ASW Groups (CVSG). On 20 December 1963, Carrier Air Groups were redesignated as Carrier Air Wings, hence the CVW abbreviation. For a time, Carrier Air Groups aboard the ASW carriers were designated ATG, for Air Task Group.

When the air war broke out over Vietnam in August 1964, all CVWs included two A-4 squadrons in the light attack role, with AD Skyraiders and A-3 Skywarriors serving in the medium and heavy attack roles respectively. Fighter squadrons were staffed with F-8 Crusaders on the small-deck carriers and the new F-4B Phantom II on the large-deck carriers. A-3s generally flew the medium attack role for the large-deck ships, with A-5 Vigilantes flying the heavy attack role. With the deployment of the A-6A Intruder in May 1965, the larger carriers began replacing the AD in their medium attack squadrons, and eventually deployed the Intruder on all large-deck carriers.

Interestingly, USS *Enterprise* (CVAN 65), on its first Vietnam cruise in late 1965 took four A-4 squadrons to sea as part of the largest air wing assembled up to that time. A Det. of A-3Bs from VAH-4 and RA-5Cs from RVAH-7 also accompanied CVW-9. This would be the only time that four A-4 squadrons would deploy on a single carrier.

In June 1966, the phasing out of the Skyraider led to many of the carriers deploying with three A-4 squadrons. USS *Franklin D. Roosevelt* (CVA 42), made the first such deployment in June 1967 with CVW-1's VAs-12, -72, and -172 on board. USS *Intrepid* (CVA 11) followed this pattern in May. December 1967, however, marked the beginning of the end for the A-4 in carrier light attack squadrons, as VA-147 aboard USS *Ranger* (CVA 61) made the Corsair II's maiden war cruise.

The A-7 eventually replaced the A-4 in all light attack squadrons aboard large-deck carriers, and, later in the war, as the newer A-7C entered service, also did so aboard many of the modified 'Essex' class carriers, such as USS *Ticonderoga*. The A-4, however, continued to serve throughout the remainder of the Vietnam War with the smaller carriers.

Several other air wing deployments were notable throughout the war. USS *Ranger* and CVW-2 deployed in both November 1967 and October 1968 with a unique combination of one squadron of A-4, A-6, and A-7 aircraft. Also, the first large-deck carrier deployment without A-4s occurred with USS *America*'s (CVA 66) departure of 10 April 1968, its two light attack squadrons, VA-82 and VA-86, flying A-7As. *America* was followed in that regard by USS *Constellation* (CVA 64) and CVW-14's cruise on 29 May.

While USS *Hancock* continued to deploy throughout the remainder of the war with three A-4 squadrons, it was not until 1972 that all three squadrons flew the -F model. Prior to that, the air wing had been mixed with A-4C and A-4E squadrons. When the Skyhawks were on last cruise, they performed all attack roles for the carrier, with the AD having been phased out of service.

Three A-4Bs from VA-95 fly together for strikes against Vinh in October 1966. These Skyhawks flew with USS Intrepid's **'all-strike' air wing, which consisted of A-4Bs from VA-15 and two squadrons of A-1H Skyraiders. The A-4B in the forefront, piloted by Lt Sam Lev USN, carries markings from thirty bombing missions.** Capt Walter Ohlrich USN Retd

Called the 'Bonnie Dick', by those familiar with her, USS Bon Homme Richard (CVA 31) made six cruises to Vietnam, all with various models of the A-4 Skyhawk. US Navy via author

This picture of USS Enterprise (CVAN 65) marks its 1965 cruise with four A-4 squadrons. These included VAs-36, -76, -93, and -94, all assigned to CVW-9, which also had two F-4B, one A-3B and one RA-5C squadrons. US Navy via Boeing Historical Archives via Harry Gann

Enterprise's first war-cruise, four A-4 squadrons (VAs-36, -76, -93, -94) were deployed with the Air Wing 9, all of which were -C models. This was the only time during the war that four Skyhawk squadrons would be deployed on one carrier. By its next cruise in November 1966, one A-4 squadron had been replaced with an A-6A squadron and another eliminated from the air wing. USS Ranger, during its November 1967-May 1968 and November 1968-May 1969 cruises, also operated a unique combination of attack aircraft, with one A-4, one A-6, and one A-7 squadron. Ranger is believed to be the only carrier to have done this mix. USS Kitty Hawk's (CV 63) air wing carried one A-1, one A-4, and one A-6 squadron on her 1965/66 cruise.

Several of the 'Essex' class carriers were deployed as anti-submarine (ASW) carriers to provide protection against submarines deployed by the Soviets. Assigned to these air groups (called CVSGs) were typically four Skyhawks in a squadron detachment. Throughout the war, four VA and even two Marine Corps squadrons would deploy a small portion of their A-4s (in four-plane Dets) to serve in an air defence role for the ASW groups. Two Skyhawk squadrons, VSF-1 and VSF-3, were specifically formed to deploy from these CVS carriers. Both units were filled with the older A-4B models. However,

Skyhawks like these A-4Cs from VA-112 frequently tanked before and after missions. Here, an A-3 tanks the CAG-bird as two Skyhawks wait their turn. These Skyhawks flew with CVW-11 aboard USS Kitty Hawk **during its 1966–67 and 1967–68 Vietnam cruises and participated in the Navy's first strikes against the large MiG base at Kep north-east of Hanoi.** US Navy via Lt Cdr Rick Burgess USN Retd

One problem witnessed personally by a few pilots was the A-4's narrow tricycle undercarriage, which made trip-overs possible in crosswinds. US Navy via author

CVW-9 and USS Enterprise **served eight days on the line on Dixie Station during January/February 1966. Skyhawks from her four VA squadrons contributed to the nearly 1,100 combat sorties flown during that time. In this shot, three A-4s from VA-36 'Roadrunners' prepare for a mission loaded with 12 Mk 82 Snakeyes.** US Navy via Boeing Historical Archives via Harry Gann

the same. Approximately thirty to thirty-five aircraft would be launched, with four flights of four A-4s serving as the strike component and four F-8 Crusaders flying a Target CAP, or TARCAP, along the axis between the bombers and the perceived air threat. A section of A-4s flew *Iron Hand* or anti-SAM ahead of the group and on each side, with two to four F-8s flying flak suppression. Offshore an EA-1 or EA-3 would provide electronic support while a pair of KA-3s or A-4s with buddy-stores would circle as tankers. This same system was used by the big deck carriers, although F-4s replaced the F-8s and A-6s and A-7s replaced the A-4s, with Shrike-armed Corsairs filling the *Iron Hand* role. KA-6D tankers eventually replaced the A-4s and KA-3s.

Mini-alphas, consisting of four A-4s, two to four F-8s as TARCAP, and flak suppressors, were also flown against smaller targets. Most of the strikes against the Thanh Hoa Bridge in Route package IV were mini-alphas. The Thanh Hoa Bridge, called Ham Rung or 'Dragon's Jaw', was an immensely strong bridge carrying rail traffic from Hanoi south to Vinh. Built in the 1950s, it measured some 540ft (165m) long and 56ft (17m) wide and was supported on concrete piers. It was among the most heavily bombed targets of the war. Unfortunately, most of these strikes did little damage to the bridge. A total of 1,250 tons of ordnance were expended at the cost of eight aircraft, but it was not until 13 May 1972, with the introduction of the first laser-guided weapons, that the bridge was finally brought down.

Alpha strikes were launched as many as three times per day, with the biggest criticism being that they tended to occur on a regular, and predictable basis. At one point, Alphas were set for 10, 2, and 4 o'clock, making it rather easy for North Vietnamese gunners to know American intentions. A perfect example of the frequency of Alphas occurred on 21 August 1967, when five Alphas were launched from the carriers USS *Constellation*, *Oriskany*, and *Intrepid* on Yankee Station. *Constellation*'s CVW-14 struck two major targets, including the Kep airfield (a major MiG base north-east of Hanoi) and the rail yards at Duc Noi. While no A-4s were lost in that raid, three A-6s' were shot down. At the same time, *Intrepid*'s Skyhawks were hitting Port Walluc with two Alpha strikes approximately three hours apart, and *Oriskany*'s A-4s led AGM-62 Walleye attacks against the Hanoi thermal plant.

Cyclic operations were more closely associated with the strikes conducted under Operation *Rolling Thunder*, the elaborate bombing campaign against the North that began on 1 March 1965. These strikes were more flexible in nature than the Alpha strikes and involved something

Skyhawks were renowned for taking massive battle damage. One such mission was described by Capt. Otto E. Krueger which occurred while he was Air Boss aboard the USS Ticonderoga **(CVA 14) in 1968: 'Sam Chessman, CO of VA-195 aboard** Ticonderoga **returned from a strike with his A-4 "all shot up" after tangling with a SAM. He was led back to the 'Tico' by a tanker, running fuel out the holes as fast as he could take it aboard, then dropped off right on glide slope just before he landed. He was on fire. Sam shut down and got out and let the fire crews put it out. By then, the tail was about burned off. We put the plane on the hangar deck and when we got back to Subic Bay, we declared it a total loss. It had something like 250 holes in it, some as big as a baseball. But it brought him home!'**

the vast number of A-4s gave air wing commanders great flexibility.

Route Packages

In the early days of the war, confusion reigned as to which service would control what sector. Initially, a plan was conceived where each day would be divided into three-hour slots, with control over these slots alternating between the Navy and Air Force. This soon proved cumbersome, and a new method, using Route Packages (RPs), was devised.

In November 1965 a decision was made to divide North Vietnam into six geographic regions for which bombing responsibility would be given to a specific service on an alternate, weekly basis. Subsequently, this was also found confusing and it was decided to give permanent control of each RP to only one service.

RPs ranged from I in the southern part of North Vietnam to VI just north-east of Hanoi. RP I was assigned to the Air Force and ran from the Demilitarized Zone (DMZ) north to just above the 18th parallel and included the port of Dong Hoi. RP II ran north to the 19th parallel; RP III included Vinh and numerous passes through which the North Vietnamese sent supplies to the Ho Chi Minh Trail – both were under Navy control. RP IV, also under Navy control, extended to just below Hanoi and Haiphong and included the prized Thanh Hoa rail bridge and the MiG base at Quan Lang. The largest single area was encompassed within RP V, which extended north-west of Hanoi to the Laotian border and north to China, and was under Air Force control. RP VI was divided into two areas. The first, RP VI-A, which ran east from the 105 degree 30 minute line of longitude and north of the north-east rail-line, fell under Air Force control and included Hanoi, the Paul Doumer Bridge, and the large MiG bases at Kep, Hoa Lac, and Phuc Yen. RP VI-B was Navy territory and included Haiphong, Cat Bi, and Gia Lam. Virtually all of the Navy's Alpha strikes were focused against targets in RP VI-B.

Iron Hand

Operation *Iron Hand* became the Navy's answer to the surface-to-air missile, or SAM. In its early days, the air war presented many threats to the aviator, namely those from MiGs and AAA. However, on

akin to armed reconnaissance or 'road recce'. Cyclic ops were conducted on a twelve-hour on, twelve-hour off basis on a three-day rotation. Unlike the targets selected for the Alpha strikes, which were chosen in Washington by the Pentagon and those higher up, road recce targets were selected by the on-scene naval commanders, given the general target parameters. General target categories targets changed from week to week, rotating between trucks, bridges, and similar targets. Alpha strikes were generally the exception.

For most operations, aerial refuelling was a must, with tanking performed by D-704-equipped A-4s or KA-3s. Tankers flew both mission profiles and provided emergency tanking. The Skyhawk's ability to serve as a tanker proved invaluable as

5 April 1965, Soviet-built SA-2 Guideline sites were discovered being constructed around Hanoi by a Navy RF-8A photo reconnaissance bird from USS *Coral Sea*, which brought an entirely new threat to the air war. The SA-2 had been in service with the Soviets since 1958. A typical battery consisted of between four and six launchers deployed in a circle about 165ft (50m) in diameter. Located in the middle of this circle was a trailer or truck containing the radar and communications equipment.

The SA-2 featured its own early-warning VHF radar, called 'Spoon Rest', which operated in the A-band. Radar guidance was handled by a 'Fan Song' radar operating in the S-band, but changing to the L-band just before launch. This change was detectable by radar warning instruments which were later incorporated into Skyhawks and other Navy attack aircraft. A 350lb warhead tipped the SA-2, with either contact, proximity, or command detonation fusing. They were usually fired in pairs, according to standard Soviet doctrine, but larger salvos of ten to twelve were not uncommon.

More sites were also discovered by early July forming an irregular ring pattern around the Hanoi/Haiphong area. Rear-Adm Edward C. Outlaw, who temporarily replaced Adm Henry L. Miller in command of TF 77 in early 1965, wrote this in a 1971 *New York Times* article:

In the spring of 1965, a photographic reconnaissance plane returned to the flagship with photos which were immediately identified as a surface-to-air missile site. This was the first clear proof that SAM sites were under construction.[31]

Adm Outlaw then flew to Saigon to detail his plan for strikes against the sites, at which his supervisors balked.

Such a refusal was beyond my comprehension. It was feasible to have destroyed this site and others still under construction which were ultimately completed. It was not until the North Vietnamese had shot down some numbers of our aircraft that our combined air forces were permitted to strike back at these, now well established, defensive sites. Since then approximately

A deck full of Skyhawks are shown in this photograph from USS Kitty Hawk. **These A-4Cs belong to VA-112's 'Bombing Broncos', who made two Vietnam cruises with Air Wing 11.** US Navy via author

The A-4 used a bridle system for catapult launches as seen here on this 'Essex' class carrier. US Navy via author

Chance Vought's F-8 Crusader flew flak suppression missions in support of the Alpha strikes and Iron Hand missions. For this, F-8s were typically armed with full 20mm ammunition and Zuni rockets.
US Navy via author

A-4 Ordnance

Although it began its career with a nuclear mission, the Skyhawk emerged as one of the most flexible conventional platforms around. In its early days, the Skyhawk was fitted with only three pylons and could carry about 5,500lb (2,500kg) of ordnance. Other than nuclear 'shapes', A-4As typically carried iron bombs of the day, plus unguided 2¾in (6.9cm) FFAR rockets, mines, and 200 rounds of ammunition for its 20mm cannon.

Unfortunately, the Skyhawk's 20mm cannon was not as functional as pilots would have liked. Not only was the cannon given a limited supply of ammunition, but it often jammed and was not highly accurate. One A-4E pilot made the following comments about these deficiencies:

> The A-4E was a fine, fine airplane for combat, a great machine except for the guns. The 20mm wasn't much good to start with and after the *Shoe Horn* system was put in, its capacity was reduced from 150 rounds, which was bad, to seventy-five – which was ridiculous. I used the 20mm to check out buildings, see if there was anything in the building explosive in nature. I'd roll in, squirt a few rounds with the gun, and see what happened. If there was some reaction, the plan was to come around and hit the structure with a bomb or rocket. That was about the only use for a 20mm.[32]

However, events eventually dictated a new mission for the A-4. The intensification of the Cold War in the form of smaller, conventional brush-fires, and regional conflicts, rather than an all-out nuclear exchange; the Lebanon Crisis in 1958; and the rapid deployment of Fleet units to China were just a few examples. In the late 1950s, the need was identified for a more conventional platform and so Douglas sought to improve the A-4's ability to perform in that environment.

Hardpoints
The first three Skyhawk models carried only three hardpoints. The centre pylon was rated at 3,550lb (1,610kg) with the wing pylons each rated at 1,200lb (544kg). With the need to carry a fuel tank on at least the centreline mount, only two were left for weapons carriage. The A-4E added not only two additional hardpoints (rated at 500lb/227kg each), but also an up-rated engine, which allowed for even greater ordnance carriage.

Weapons
As the 1960s went on, Skyhawk ordnance expanded to include a variety of air-to-ground ordnance, including the Mk 80 series iron bombs, Snakeye retarded bombs (Mk 81 and 82 class), and Cluster Bomb Units (CBUs) with Rockeye II submunitions. The Mk 80 series utilized an Aero 1A shape with an aspect ratio of 8.3 and was developed by Douglas during the 1950s as it pursued a low-drag ordnance.

Mk 80 series
Mk 81	250lb	LDGP	Snakeye
Mk 82	500lb	LDGP	Snakeye
Mk 83	1,000lb	LDGP	–
Mk 84	2,000lb	LDGP	–

Some 90 per cent of all Navy bombs delivered during the Vietnam War were Mk 80s, with the vast majority being Mk 83s.

With the A-4B also came the ability to carry and fire the infra-red homing (heat-seeking) AIM-9 Sidewinder, something that proved important when the A-4 fulfilled the fighter air defence role aboard the anti-submarine carriers, such as USS *Intrepid* (CVS 11), USS *Yorktown* (CVS 10), and USS *Hornet* (CVS 12). The Sidewinders of the day were primarily the -D variant, which weighed about 160lb (72.5kg) and carried a 10lb (4.5kg) warhead. Effective range was between 1,000ft (305m) to a little over two miles (3km), but attacks were limited to the target's rear quarter. Skyhawk pilots also used a light-seeking variant of the AIM-9 called Focus.

Rockets have always been a mainstay Skyhawk weapon and could be carried in packs of nineteen LAU-61/A and -69/As (using the Aero 7 dispenser) or seven LAU-68/A (using the Aero 6 dispenser), 2¾in (6.9cm) FFAR and LAU-10/A Zuni 5in (12.7cm) rockets. Napalm was used by US Navy and Marine Corps forces in South Vietnam and was delivered using the Mk 77. It was rarely dropped in the North. Cluster Bombs (CBUs) were also used, but again only in South Vietnam. Armed with Mk 20 Rockeye II CBUs, Skyhawks were particularly effective against troop concentrations and anti-aircraft artillery batteries and were commonplace on flak suppression missions and on early *Iron Hand* missions.

Skyhawk pilots also used a specially-fused bomb designed to produce an air blast:

> Early in the war we also used the 36in bomb extenders, called *Daisey-cutters*. These extenders were just what the name implied; a long, 36in slender cylinder extending from the nose of the bomb. This would allow the bomb to go off right on the surface, whereas without the extenders, the bombs could and did bury themselves in the soft earth before exploding. That really increased their damage potential and made them excellent for knocking things down like buildings. But they were soon withdrawn from use by the Navy because [of] concerns about the powder.[33]

These bombs were very effective and sorely missed.

In the early days of the Vietnam War, A-4 pilots relied heavily on the same high-altitude delivery methods as had been used in Korea.

> The weapons we took to war were basic. The bombing techniques were the old pilot-computed lead with the gun-sight. We had no radar; there was ground clearance radar, but nothing to give us any help on moving targets, night work, or rendezvous or anything like that.[34]

Lt Donald D. Smith of VA-72 explains this as it pertained to the A-4:

Loaded on this VA-83 A-4E are two 2¾in. (6.9cm) rocket pods, 12 500lb Mk 82 bombs, and a 300 US gallon (1,136litre) centreline tank. US Navy via Boeing Historical Archives via Harry Gann

Multiple Carriage Bomb Racks (MCBRs) were developed by VX-5 at China Lake to enable Skyhawks to carry greater numbers of bombs. Shown here are groups of Mk 81 bombs being tested. The MCBRs were later built by Douglas and proved invaluable in Vietnam. US Navy via Lt Cdr Rick Burgess USN Retd

Our initial tactic for putting bombs on target, which of course later had to be abandoned, was a 60 degree dive angle because the only worry was the ground-fire. A 60 degree dive rolling in at 16,000ft is straight down the chute, just hanging in the straps. Of course it's not an accurate run – it's hard to correct for winds and Vietnam is a fairly windy place – but we got pretty darn good at it. We'd come in at 16,000- 22,000ft (4,877–6,706m), pull down to a roll-in at 16,000 and head in at 60 degrees on the target, pull out high and never, never get low.[35]

Later in the war, with the introduction of surface-to-air missiles, high-altitude attacks became exceedingly dangerous and pilots resorted to low-level approaches. Staying under the SAM envelope meant, however, that pilots were now in prime range for AAA and small arms fire.

The weapons and tactics we used were in a constant state of evolution during the early part of the war. By 1966, we had pretty much used up stocks of bombs left over from World War II that were being stored at Guam. These were the old 'iron fat bombs' that weren't very aerodynamic insofar as reducing drag was concerned. And this was happening at a time when McNamara was telling everyone that 'there is no bomb shortage, it's a distribution problem'.

The Mk 80s and their electronic fusing were a learning experience for us all. Many of us dropped our first on a mission; even the kids coming out hadn't trained on them because they were in such short supply. Early on we were still trying to figure out what would work best against any given target. But by '68 or '69, those parameters were set and the typical loads were established based on our experience. We started early in '65 to use retarded Snakeye MK 80 series bombs which allowed a low-level drop. With the fins open, the bomb was slowed which permitted aircraft separation from the blast.

One big plus to our strike capability with the A-4 was the introduction of MERs and TERs in the early 1965 time frame. (We first used them in early 1965 on *Ranger's* cruise.) With these we could carry three 500s on each wing and/or six on the centerline. On our 1965–66 cruise, we were carrying three 500 pounders (Mk 82s) on each wing pylon with a 300 gallon (1,136 litre) tank on the centerline. Mk 81s (250lb) were used somewhat less, although when we did, we carried six per TER. We occasionally used napalm in the south, but flights there were limited to a few warm-up hops from Dixie Station at the outset before heading north for the remainder of the cruise and Yankee Station.

Up north, especially on the second cruise, we oftentimes flew in a 'slick-wing' configuration, with a single 2,000lb bomb on the centerline and a 1,000 pounder on each wing. We didn't carry the external drop tank so we couldn't spend as much time over the target. This slick config let us get in and out real fast.[36]

As Krueger indicated, an interesting feature of the Navy's early involvement in the war was the fact that pilots of all attack communities had to rely at times on vintage ordnance:

We also used a larger 750lb bomb for a short time. These were old iron bombs left from World War II and they had a thinner skin, which meant that more explosives could be packed. A 750lb bomb from that era had the explosive force of a 1,000lb Mk-83, but with the aerodynamics of a Mk 82.'[37]

Once this passed, however, Vietnam served as a virtual testing-ground for newly developed systems.

For example, Vietnam saw the introduction of several new guided, semi-stand-off weapons such as the AGM-12 Bullpup and the AGM-62 Walleye. The Bullpup was a rocket-propelled radio-guided bomb that was originally developed with a 250lb warhead and later modified to carry a 1,000lb SAP warhead, reflecting the common knowledge that the Bullpup A did not carry enough 'punch'. Both models of the Bullpup, however, suffered from one drawback that would later lead to its abandonment as an effective attack ordnance. 'The [Bullpup] B was a lot more sophisticated than the old Bullpup, but we learned after getting into Vietnam there was little extensive application for the bomb because the pilot had to stay on a long, steady, descending path to control it to the target. In an AAA environment, that wasn't exactly the thing you wanted to do.'[38] Most people considered the Bullpup obsolete as early as the mid-1960s.

The AGM-62 Walleye was an optically-guided weapon that was introduced into combat in 1967 and scored several successful hits on key North Vietnamese targets, including the Haiphong thermal plant. The Walleye used a television camera 'gated' to remain pointed at the target area (high contrast) and could be Locked-On Before Launch (LOBL), enabling the carrying aircraft to leave the area. Initial versions of this missile carried the 825lb (374kg) linear shaped-charge warhead and possessed a range of approximately 10nm. An improved version, dubbed the Walleye II, carried an improved seeker and a larger, 2,000lb warhead.

A much-needed anti-radiation missile was also added to the Skyhawk arsenal in 1966 with the AGM-45A Shrike. The Shrike homed in on SAM radar beams and rode them into the guidance van, destroying the site. Skyhawks flying *Iron Hand* missions against North Vietnamese SAM sites typically carried two Shrikes for such missions and when the Shrike supplies were limited, carried one simply to 'listen' for North Vietnamese radars. Early Shrikes were problematic because they had a fixed gimbal and could not 'remember' site locations once they shut down. Moreover, they used a pre-tuned seeker that was matched to a particular frequency.

> One reason the Shrike did not perform well was the enemy's excellent electronic emission discipline and the use of two or more antennae. Another is that missile ranges are so short that prospective targets are obvious. The enemy ceased emitting when the attacker pointed in his direction and radiated when he turned away. Shrike should be modified to enable homing on a Fan Song radar radiating into a dummy load. . . .[39]

To combat the wide variety of frequencies, some thirteen frequency seekers were made. An extended range variant was also produced, the AGM-45B.

An improved ARM was later deployed, the AGM-78 Standard, carrying a longer range and larger warhead. The Standard was originally deployed with a modified Shrike seeker (called the Mod), but later incorporated a Maxsom wide-band seeker, justifying the Mod 1 redesignation, and subsequently AGM-78B. The Standard also used a gimballed seeker, memory circuits, and carried an impact marker for designating the sites' location for follow-on strikes. The AGM-78B had a 35nm range and travelled at near Mach 2.5 speed. A-4 pilots used the Standard to some degree, although its availability was sometimes limited due to its high cost.

Because the Skyhawk's gun was not all that it should have been, a Mk 4 gun pod was developed and was used in Vietnam by US Navy A-4s on their road recce missions and by Marine Corps pilots for close air support missions. This gun pod offered a tremendous rate of fire – 4,000 rounds per minute. A one-second burst (firing sixty-six rounds per gun) has the equivalent of a 4,000lb bomb load delivered from 1,000ft (305m). Mk 24/25 para flares were also carried by A-4s, although at first there was some trouble mounting them on the Multiple Ejector Racks (MERs)s However, as noted in the USS *Independence* Command Debrief following its 10 May 1965–13 December 1965 deployment, at least early in the war, a need was identified for an improved, or at least more reliable flare for night recce missions.

> For night operations, greater quantities and improved reliability of the Mk 24 flare are necessary. A near 50 per cent dud rate was experienced with this flare. However, it is an excellent pyrotechnic when it works; and the only one that should be used in an AAA environment, because of the delay feature and the enemy's habit of shooting out flares as well as leading the flares in an attempt to hit the aircraft.[40]

Flares were later improved to meet these complaints.

The A-4 also carried a variety of Aero 1D drop tanks – 150, 300, and 400 US gallon (568, 1,136, 1,510 litre). For most A-4E and -F missions over Vietnam, two 300 gallon wing tanks were used, taking full advantage of the extra wing stations. Special missions were also authorized using no tanks, and a single centreline-mounted 2,000lb Mk 84 or Walleye. A-4E and -F aircraft also flew many missions with a 400 gallon centreline tank and some combination of stores on the wings. A-4C missions were often flown with a single centreline tank, leaving the outboard stations available for weapons stores.

The A-4M brought new stores such as the AGM-65 Maverick capability. Skyhawks could also carry the LAU-10/A leaflet dispensers, the Aero 14/B spray tank (thought to be intended for application of defoliating chemicals), the Mk-12 smoke tank, and the LB-18/A centreline-mounted camera pod.

---

115 of our planes have been destroyed by surface-to-air missiles launched from pads which I believe could have been destroyed at a minimum risk before they became operational.[41]

Despite warnings from Navy officials about the threat these systems posed, the SA-2 sites would remain untouched because Washington feared that a strike against the sites might injure or kill Soviet advisers who were known to be training North Vietnamese crews on how to operate the new weapons. On 24 July an Air Force F-4C of the 47th Tactical Fighter Squadron based in Ubon, Thailand, was downed by an SA-2 near Hanoi. Three days later, a strike was organized against this site.

Less than a month later, on the night of 11 August, VA-23's Lt(jg) Donald H. Brown became the Navy's first SAM victim, when his A-4E flying from the carrier USS *Midway* was struck while he was on a road recce mission about 60 miles (97km) south of Hanoi. Brown's lead, Lt Cdr Francis D. Roberge's A-4 was also hit. Reports from the incident revealed that both pilots were flying at 9,000ft (2,740m) when they noticed what looked to be two glowing flares below the clouds about 15 miles (24km) ahead of their position. As the 'lights' grew closer and broke through the clouds, the two immediately recognized the threat and tried to take evasive action, accelerating with full power. Unfortunately, it was too late and Brown's plane was destroyed. Roberge's A-4, although badly damaged and on fire, made it back to *Midway* where more than fifty holes were found in its fuselage.

The SAM incident sparked an immediate, albeit unsuccessful, retaliation the next day when seventy-six *Iron Hand* strikes were launched against SAM sites. Five aircraft and two pilots were lost and another seven planes damaged with no SAMs found. 13 August 1965 became known as 'Black Friday'.

This A-4 pulls off target over Vietnam.
US Navy via author

On its second war cruise, VA-106 went with CVW-10 aboard USS Intrepid **(CVA 11). This A-4E is being manipulated with a nose-wheel steering bar on one of the carrier's catapults during operations in September 1968. An Mk 80 series iron bomb is visible on the outboard port station and an LB-18/A camera pod is attached to the front of the centreline station just above the fuel tank. These cameras were used for Bomb Damage Assessment (BDA). This provides a good view of the Charlie's extended nose and ECM antenna.** US Navy via author

During their time together on USS Oriskany (CVA 34), VA-164 'Ghost Riders' concentrated on the Shrike mission and VA-163 'Saints' focused on Walleye. This 'Ghost Rider' sits with an anti-radiation missile on stations one and five and 300 US gallon (1,126litre) tanks on stations two and four. US Navy via author

Although not seeing combat in Vietnam, A-4s from VA-64 'Black Lancers' were sent to aid the USS Liberty (AGTR 5) when she came under attack from Israeli aircraft during the 1967 Arab-Israeli war. US Navy via author

A VA-72 A-4E launches for a strike against Vietnam from the deck of USS Independence (**CVA 59**). The 'Blue Hawks' took one cruise aboard the Independence in mid-to-late 1965, then a second with Air Wing 1 aboard USS Franklin D.Roosevelt (**CVA 42**) beginning in June 1966. VA-72 transitioned back to the Bravo for two Mediterranean cruises then transitioned to the new A-7B Corsair II in January 1970. US Navy via author

Loads such as the one shown on this VA-164 'Ghost Rider' A-4C were made possible by Multiple Ejector Racks (MERs) and Triple Ejector Racks (TERs). Loaded to this A-4 are 14,250lb Mk 81 bombs. VA-164 Skyhawks later participated in the 1972 Linebacker I raids, attacking major installations in North Vietnam. US Navy via author

The Shrike Shooters of VA-164

The *Iron Hand* mission was regarded as one of the most dangerous of all missions flown by Skyhawk pilots during the Vietnam War. It took a special breed of person to go out and 'play chicken' with SAM operators, all for the good of the strike package. Capt Bob Arnold served with VA-164 of CVW-16 aboard the USS *Oriskany* (CVA 34) during its 1968/69 cruise and was one of those men who welcomed the challenge of confronting the SAM. Capt Arnold provides the following overview of Shrike operations and the tactics used by the *Iron Hand* pilots:

For the *Iron Hand* mission, we flew the A-4E, with its five stations. We'd carry a 300 lb tank on the centreline, a TER [triple ejector rack] with two five hundred pounders on the two and four stations, and our Shrike on stations one and five. We only carried two Mk 82s on the TERs because of the tank. If we wanted more maneuvrability, we'd carry single five hundreds on the inboard stations, instead of the TERs.

At the time VA-164 was designated as the *Iron Hand* squadron and VA-163, our sister, was the Walleye squadron. Now, you must remember that we had no state-side training on the Shrike or the *Iron Hand* tactics; this was all learned in the field. There were no electronic warfare ranges or the like.

We'd normally fly two sections with the Alphas; one on each side, escorted by a section of F-8s for flak suppression and in case any MiGs came up. Our job was to listen to the electronic signals generated by the different modes of the enemy radars. These modes were picked up by the Shrike's seeker and funnelled through our headsets. Each radar had a distinctive sound which allowed us to tell who was painting us.

Before the strike, we would brief on the mission with the guys from Intel and they would identify the probable SAM sites that we were to watch for. Usually, each one of us would take a site and fly a racetrack pattern around it until we found something with our seekers.

As we approached the target area we flew out in front on the strike package listening for emissions. The first radar that came up was the search radar. Next would be height finding, followed by gun control. It sort reminds you of an orchestra tuning up, with each instrument adding to the sound. The missile acquisition radar was the next mode and it created low warble. Our instruments had an enhancing device to help us distinguish this mode. A flashing light would also come on in the cockpit. As soon as one of us heard this, we'd call out 'singer low', meaning that they were about to launch at one of us.

The guidance radar sent a high pitched sound through our headsets. That meant that a SAM was in the air and we'd better start trying to find it. When we heard this sound, we'd call 'singer high'. The needles in our LABS told us which direction the signal was coming from. The vertical needle showed us the azimuth and the horizontal needles height. Once we had the needles pointed at the target, we had our fire solution and then we'd fire the Shrike. If the Shrike tracked, we'd follow-up with our two Mk 82s. This attack method was called a 'down the throat' delivery.[42]

Arnold explained that later on during that cruise, VA-164 began using a new tactic whereby the Shrike would be launched using a 'loft' technique, allowing the missile's seeker to search out its victim. Arnold explained:

... to do this, we would hang above the main strike force, listening for the tale-tell signs of the SAM radars. Before we'd launch, we study the mission and determine just when the strike aircraft would enter the SAM envelope and how long it would take them to reach the target. Then we'd calculate when our Shrikes would have to be launched to get to the radars before the SAMs could get to our planes. Just as the strike aircraft were entering this zone, we'd dive down to about 10,000ft, then pull up to 30 degrees and loft our Shrikes. This would put the missiles over the target just before the strike aircraft arrived over the target. The first time we tried this, during a raid on Phuc Yen just outside Hanoi, it worked perfect. Not a single SAM came up.'[43]

This method proved much more effective at suppressing the SAMs.

While the A-4s were the 'shooters' for the *Iron Hand* missions, the role of the F-8 must not be underplayed. Not only did the Crusader crews protect against any air threats, but they carried air-to-ground ordnance and helped suppress flak, and, probably more important, they kept an eye out for SAMs while the A-4s made their runs. Capt Arnold commented: '... we flew with F-8s as our flak suppressers and really, our extra set of eyes. Once we began our run on the site, we had our heads buried in the cockpit studying our needles. The F-8s kept watch for MiGs and SAM.[44]

The Crusaders also carried bombs and rockets that could be used against SAM sites successfully attacked by the A-4s. Once it became apparent that the MiG threat had diminished, the idea was hatched to use A-4s as escorts. Capt Arnold describes this in more detail, '... later in that cruise we did some more experimenting and tried using A-4s as our escorts. These would be armed with four 500 pounders and a centreline tank and had little trouble keeping up with us. They'd follow us in and hit the site with their bombs; it made quite a combination'.[45]

One of the problems during the war was the lack of training on newer weapons systems – many weapons were rushed to service directly from the test squadrons.

The Shrike missile was all hands on, in-the-field learning. You had to learn everything on cruise. During *Oriskany*'s 1967/68 cruise we had a former Air Force B-47 pilot who had brought with him a horde of tapes with radar modes. He used to conduct training sessions in the Ready Room, where we'd listen to the emissions recorded on the tapes. It was invaluable. Those of us who flew the *Iron Hand* can credit these tapes to saving our lives on more than one occasion.[46]

Unfortunately, that pilot was later shot down on one of the squadron's *Iron Hand* missions and it was not until this past year that his remains were returned to the United States.

On 17 October 1965, Cdr Harrison B. Southworth, Commanding Officer of VA-72 squadron, led the Navy's first successful strike against a North Vietnamese SA-2 site near Kep. Southworth described this in his own words:

USS *Independence* was assigned to destroy a SAM site that posed a threat to a large CVA 62 strike group that was to attack the large highway north of Hanoi. CVW-7 assigned the SAM site attack to VA-72 and I was tasked to plan and lead the strike. Our package consisted of four A-4Es (Cdr Harry Southworth, Lt(jg) Carl Moslener, Lt Cdr Jack Davis, Lt Dick Koffarnus) and one A-6A from VA-75 (Lt Cdr Pete Garber, Lt(jg) Ken Jones) and we used a combination of 500lb and 1,000lb low-drag bombs.

The plan for our group called for us to tag along behind and below the larger strike group until we were abeam of the valley that would lead us to the target area. The A-4s remained low until reaching a pre-established checkpoint, where we accelerated and climbed to the target area, jinking as we went.

Priority on the attack was assigned to the missile control van, usually located in the center of the site. Next were the launchers with missiles, then any missiles in the site area. Once we found the target, we made our initial run and when we left, the control van was on fire and unable to launch any more SAMs. The A-6 then attacked several of the missile

Errant bombs and missiles often lead to disaster for deck crews. This Skyhawk from USS Ranger **(CVA 61) loses a Shrike missile as the aircraft catches a wire.** US Navy via author

The addition of the AGM-45 Shrike made Iron Hand missiles much deadlier for North Vietnamese SAM operators. Shown here is an A-4E launching with two Shrikes. These were typically carried on the outboard stations. Shrikes were effective in this role, although SAM operators could avoid the missile's 145lb (44.2kg) fragmentation warhead by simply turning off their radars. Nevertheless, even if this occurred, the site had been shut down and effectively 'suppressed' for the purpose of the mission at hand. US Navy via author

Skyhawks from VA-93 and VA-94 are on USS Ranger during its 1964–65 cruise. The carrier was on Yankee Station during spring 1965 when this photo was taken, which corresponds with the timing of the strike against the Tam Da Bridge shown on page 138. Robert Olen via Lt Cdr Rick Burgess USN Retd

transporters parked nearby the SAM site and left them twisted and in flames.[47]

When the strike exited the area, Southworth reported seeing several radar vans afire, vehicles burning, and one SA-2 missile destroyed. A second SAM was snaking along the ground burning itself out.

At that time, *Iron Hand* missions were flown at altitudes below 3,500 ft (1,065m) using Snakeyes, Zuni rockets, cluster bombs, and other low-altitude ordnance to keep out of the SA-2's envelope. Of course, this opened the attacker up to a barrage of enemy AAA fire, which claimed many A-4s in the first *Iron Hand* efforts.

In 1965, the Navy, together with Douglas and Sanders Associates, began modifications to the A-4 airframe (called Project *Shoe Horn*) allowing the installation of electronic self-protection equipment, namely the Sanders AN/ALQ-51A ECM deception system and a receiver for the Magnavox AN/APR-27 SAM launch detection system. All of these were housed in the distinctive aft hump, that would later be retrofitted into a number of -E models. Wiring was also added for carriage of the wing-mounted AN/ALQ-81 ECM jamming pod, and installation of the Itek AN/APR-25 RHAW, which was subsequently replaced by the Bendix AN/APS-107 RHAW for use with the Shrike missile system. A canted refuelling rod was then added to avoid interference with the electronics. To complete the systems, a Goodyear/Tracor AN/ALE-29A chaff/flare dispenser was added near the rear of the Skyhawk.

> Project Shoehorn was retrofitting three new pieces of electronic equipment into our Skyhawks. A black box called the ALQ-51 would provide the pilot with a visual alert to any activity by the SAM-associated *Fan Song* radar. A blinking red light would indicate that the aircraft was being illuminated by a *Fan Song* in the search mode. A steady red glow would mean that the radar was locked on preparatory to fire a SAM. The second piece, the APR-27, would simultaneously generate a tone through the pilot's helmet earphones – sounding a low pitch during the search phase and increasing to a higher, more frantic pitch at lock-on. Eventually, a third component, the APR-23, would provide a visual indication, relative to the nose of the aircraft, of the direction of the threat.
>
> To help counter the SAM threat, the new gear was a step in the right direction. But without the APR-23 to determine the direction of the threat, cockpit aural and visual alerts were merely something else to promote adrenalin flow. The real problem in dealing with a SAM lay in not knowing where it was coming from.[48]

Adding immensely to the *Iron Hand* mission capabilities was AGM-45 Shrike mission, developed by the US Navy at its China Lake Weapons Center, and first fired on 18 April 1966. With its passive sensor homing head, the Sparrow-shaped AGM-45 would detect operating frequencies of various Soviet-block radars, then fly down on the radar beam and destroy the guidance equipment with its 145lb (66kg) blast fragmentation warhead. Follow-up strikes against the missiles or their launchers with Mk 80s, cluster bombs or Snakeyes, would then finish the site. AGM-45As possessed a range of about 3 miles (4.8 km). The -45Bs, however, introduced later in the war, increased the range to nearly 10 miles (15km).

The Shrike thereafter became a standard load on all *Iron Hand* missions. In some cases, Shrikes were in short supply but carried simply to allow the operator to 'listen' for SAMs. For most missions, two Shrikes were carried, with two Mk 82s on single pylons, giving the Skyhawk 'slicked up' aerodynamics. Most mid-war Shrike missions were flown by the A-4Es to take advantage of the additional weapons station and more powerful engines. This mission later evolved to the -F with its superior ECM capability. Cdr Nichols tells about this mission in *On Yankee Station*:

> An *Iron Hand* section was composed of an attack aircraft – A-4 or A-7 – packing two Shrikes, escorted by an F-4 or F-8 fighter. Within five minutes of the target, the fighters would break off as the attack craft continued on to their assigned SAM site. While the crews

would focus on their scopes as the range to the target decreased, the escorting fighters would maintain a visual guard during the run-in. Usually the VA pilot would loft both Shrikes at the same time. What was good doctrine for the SAMs was good doctrine for the Shrikes. That left the fighters, if F-8s, to follow up the Shrikes in hopes of finishing off the site.[49]

In his book, *Rolling Thunder*, John T. Smith described just how the *Iron Hand* missions meshed with Alpha strikes:

> The Navy *Iron Hand* missions were carried out by standard strike aircraft, a major Naval *Alpha Strike* involving four or eight *Iron Hand* aircraft. A-4s carrying Shrike missiles would be given specific sites to attack where it was known these sites were active and close to the route of the main strike force. They could be paired with F-8s to provide protection and to add weight to the attack on the missile sites.[50]

Without question, the Shrike and the proven *Iron Hand* tactics quickly brought Navy losses down to pre-SAM levels and better, improving odds from one aircraft lost per seventeen SAMs in 1965 to one lost per sixty SAMs by 1973. Added to the *Iron Hand* arsenal was the AGM-78 Standard ARM, a larger, longer-ranged ARM, that appeared in 1968 and was equally as effective against AAA gun-director radar.

According to Rear-Adm Paul Peck, who served as Commanding Officer of VA-94 in 1965 and later in 1967–8 as CAG-9 aboard USS *Enterprise*, although many improved anti-missile systems were later developed, the Shrike was a 'success': 'The reduction of the threat was considerable judging from the shut down of missile guidance radars when the Shrikes were in the air. Other pilots reported the same result achieved'.[51] In fact, early in the war, the 'Shrike in the air' fear was capitalized on by A-4 pilots who would launch Zuni rockets at the sites. SAM operators, so fearful of the Shrike riding their beam, would then shut down. This bluff worked for a while, but was discovered by the North Vietnamese and quickly disseminated.

One of the most distinguished *Iron Hand* pilots was Lt Cdr Mike Estocin, from VA-192 who flew A-4Cs with CVW-19 aboard USS *Ticonderoga*. Estocin was key in the development of anti-SAM and Shrike tactics. Noted for his tenacity and aggressiveness against SAM sites, Estocin was shot down during an *Iron Hand* mission against site 109 north of Haiphong on 26 April 1967 and was posthumously awarded the Medal of Honor.

A-4 Operations

Naval aviation's involvement in the Vietnam War began on 2 and 4 August 1964, when North Vietnamese P-4 PT boats attacked the destroyers USS *Turner Joy* (DD-951) and USS *Maddox* (DD-731) in the Gulf of Tonkin. *Maddox* had been patrolling near the North Vietnamese shores since mid-to-late July performing electronic surveillance, called *Desoto Patrols*. On these missions, *Maddox* was to gather intelligence on North Vietnamese radar characteristics and to evaluate navigational and hydrographic conditions in the area. Going on at the same time was Operation *Plan* 34A (OPLAN-34A), under which South Vietnamese troops conducted small raids against naval installations in North Vietnam. Indeed, one

Skyhawks from VA-144 and VA-146 aboard USS Constellation **(CVA 64) led the strikes against Hon Gai on 5 August 1964 as part of Operation** Pierce Arrow, **which were the reprisals against North Vietnamese for the 2–4 August attacks against USS** Turner Joy **(DD 951) and USS** Maddox **(DD 731)**. US Navy via author

This bomb-ridden A-4C prepares for take-off. Visible on the three stations are ten 500lb Mk 82 iron bombs. The Skyhawk appears to be from VA-36. US Navy via author

OPLAN-34A mission took place on the night of 30 July near Vinh.

Prior to the attack of 2 August, A-4Es from VA-55 and VA-56 aboard USS Ticonderoga had been providing aerial refuelling and flying escort for RF-8 Crusader and RA-3 Skywarrior reconnaissance missions into Cambodia, Laos, and South Vietnam. These flights had been generally uneventful except for an incident in May 1964, when an RF-8 from USS Kitty Hawk piloted by Lt Charles F. Klusman was shot down over Laos. Although Klusman was captured, he later escaped.

Following the North Vietnamese attacks on the two US destroyers, immediate air cover was provided by planes from the carrier USS Constellation (CVA 64), which had been recalled from port in Hong Kong. Following the initial attack on Maddox on 2 August, several of Ticonderoga's Crusaders from VF-51 and VF-53, plus one of the Air Group's A-4s, flew cover for the destroyers until relieved some time after midnight by Skyhawks from Constellation. This became known as the 'Gulf of Tonkin Incident' and is regarded as the beginning of the air war against North Vietnam.

In retaliation, President Lyndon B. Johnson immediately ordered air strikes against various PT boat bases and POL facilities. Secretary of Defense Robert S. McNamara is said to have determined the precise targets while the strikes were inbound. On 5 August at approximately 12.30 local time, a total of sixty-four sorties were launched from the carriers Ticonderoga and Constellation under Operation Pierce Arrow. Of the thirty-four launched by Ticonderoga, six F-8Es struck at the PT boat facilities near Quang Khe with Zuni rockets and 20mm cannon fire. Eight of the boats were destroyed and another twenty-one damaged. VF-51's F-8Es, together with twenty-six A-4Cs from VA-55 and VA-56, hit the POL facilities at Vinh. Covering these attacks were the new F-4B Phantom IIs of Constellation's VF-142 and VF-143, which were making their first deployment. The strike left the POL facility in near ruins, with estimates that 90 per cent of the structure was destroyed. Five of Constellation's Skyhawks also struck PT boat bases at Loc Chao and eight struck Hon Gai, the latter on the outskirts of Haiphong. In all, a total of thirty-three of the thirty-four North Vietnamese PT boats were either sunk or damaged by the strike.

However, there was a cost to the operation – one A-4C (BuNo. 149578) flown by Lt Everett J. Alvarez of VA-144 and one A-1 from VA-145 (BuNo. 139760) were shot down in the Hon Gai raid. Alvarez was captured and became the first US Navy POW, Lt(jg) Richard C. Sather, the pilot of the 'Spad', was killed. Unfortunately, President Johnson's announcement of the strikes happened to occur just as the aircraft were leaving their carriers, then some 300–400 miles (485–650km) offshore, and the North Vietnamese were waiting.

On 10 August, Congress passed the Gulf of Tonkin Resolution, which gave the President the power to take 'all necessary measures to repel armed aggression' in Vietnam until the 'peace and security of the area is reasonably assured'.

Following the incident, the carriers USS Ranger (CVA 61) and USS Kearsage (CVA 33) joined Ticonderoga and Constellation setting up patrols in what would become Yankee Station. Kearsage had been deployed primarily to guard against any Soviet or Chinese submarine incursions towards the task force. As the year witnessed an election, air activities over Vietnam were mainly reconnaissance, despite numerous and violent Viet Cong (VC) attacks around Saigon and a build-up of US air forces at bases throughout South Vietnam.

On 14 December, however, and at Adm U.S. Grant Sharp's urging, orders were given to begin Operation Barrel Roll, which consisted of armed reconnaissance flights by Navy and Air Force planes directed against the Ho Chi Minh Trail along the border of Laos. While most flights were conducted by the Air Force, Navy planes did participate when inclement weather prohibited action 'up north'. Skyhawks from the carriers USS Constellation and USS Ticonderoga participated in many of these strikes, as did those from USS Ranger and USS Bon Homme Richard. Moderate

Of all the carriers participating in Vietnam, one of the most active was USS Hancock **(CVA 19), making seven Vietnam cruises. Many of the strikes early in the war were flown by Skyhawks from the Hancock. For its last three cruises, all three A-4 squadrons flew the A-4F.** Hancock **was the last carrier to deploy with the A-4.**
US Navy via author

success was achieved by these strikes, with damage inflicted to the main road running from North Vietnam south. These raids forced trucks to travel at night.

The next major operation to involve Skyhawks took place in February 1965. As with the *Pierce Arrow* strikes of August, these too, were retaliatory, responding to the Viet Cong (VC) attack on Camp Holloway at Pleiku, near the Central Highlands of 7 February. Nine US personnel were killed and nearly 100 wounded, and ten aircraft destroyed. On 8 February, Operation *Flaming Dart I* was launched by planes from the carriers USS *Hancock*, *Ranger*, and *Coral Sea*, which were already in the Gulf of Tonkin. *Coral Sea* and *Hancock* had, in fact, been steaming towards the Philippines and had to be recalled to join *Ranger*.

In a combined launch from *Hancock* and *Coral Sea*, forty-nine aircraft, including VA-212 and VA-216 from *Hancock*, and A-4C/Es from VA-153 and VA-155 aboard *Coral Sea*, struck Vietnamese Army barracks and port facilities at Dong Hoi. Ten buildings were destroyed, two damaged, and an undetermined number left burning. The raid caused only moderate damage, but Skyhawk pilot Lt E. A. Dickson was lost when his A-4E (BuNo. 150075) took small arms fire to its port wing. *Ranger*'s strike force of thirty-four aircraft was not as fortunate with its target, as poor weather over the Vit Thu Lu barracks prevented it from completing its strike. Foreshadowing things to come, Defense Secretary McNamara refused to allow *Ranger* to divert and support those underway from *Coral Sea* and *Hancock* at Dong Hoi and instead ordered the pilots to drop their bombs harmlessly into the sea, a source of contention for many Skyhawk pilots for years to come.

Outraged at the US attack, Ho Chi Minh launched another strike, this time with VC forces destroying the American enlisted barracks at Qui Nhon, killing twenty-three and wounding another twenty-one. Johnson retaliated with a ninety-nine-plane strike on army barracks at Chanh Hoa. Again, indicative of what lay ahead, McNamara not only selected the targets, but also the aircraft that would participate, their loads, and even the fusing. Moreover, he ordered the attack to commence at 0900 local time, oblivious to local weather conditions, which were poor, restricting flight to low altitudes. Operation *Flaming Dart II* was only marginally more successful than the first operation, with twenty-three of the seventy-six buildings damaged. Again, there was a cost, as three aircraft were lost. One, an A-4C from *Coral Sea*'s VA-153 (BuNo. 149572), was lost, but the pilot survived. Another belonging to VA-155 diverted to Da Nang with stuck ordnance.

15 March marked the first US Navy involvement in Operation *Rolling Thunder* strikes, with Skyhawks from USS *Ranger* and USS *Hancock*, flying two or three missions a week, mostly interdiction by two and four plane units. *Rolling Thunder* was intended to force the North Vietnamese to capitulate in the face of bombing that began in the south and moved slowly north. The problem was, however, that it took too long and had too many restrictions. Naval aircraft had been flying tactical reconnaissance missions over North Vietnam under the code-name *Blue Tree* since *Rolling Thunder* began on 2 March. Marine aviation units also played a role in *Rolling Thunder*, but in South Vietnam. On 18 March, Skyhawks from *Coral Sea* and *Hancock* launched strikes at the supply buildings at Phu Van and the depots at Vinh Son. One week later, the same carriers struck radar sites at Bach Long Vi Island, Ha Tinh, and Mui Ron, losing one A-4E from VA-212. Its pilot, Cdr K. L. Shugart, was recovered. On 31 March,

seventy attack aircraft again hit the radar installations at Cap Mu Ron.

Road Recce

One of the more interesting Skyhawk missions involved night bombing along the Ho Chi Minh Trail. These strikes were supposed to be limited to military trucks. Since much of North Vietnam was already mobilized for war, that limitation baffled many a pilot. Later, however, this limitation was modified to allow strikes against any truck within 328ft (100m), then 984ft (300m) of roadways.

VA-153 aboard USS *Coral Sea* was one of the first squadrons involved in this mission, which generally saw sections of two A-4s flying low-level attack runs against North Vietnamese trucks. *Coral Sea*'s Skyhawks were joined in this mission by USS *Midway*'s VA-22 and VA-23. Loads for these missions included flares, Snakeyes, cluster bombs, and gun pods – 'all low-level, lay-down ordnance', as one pilot described. A-4s flying these missions would launch, refuel, then cross 'the beach' using dead-reckoning navigation or VFR. Flares would then be released and the two Skyhawks would dive down to 100–200ft (30–60m) looking for trucks to hit.

Cdr David Leue, an A-4C pilot with VA-153 aboard USS *Constellation*, commented on these tactics thus:

We took a simple tactic and made it highly successful even though our A-4Cs were severely limited fuelwise.

We carried flares and bombs, all low-level, lay-down ordnance. You could not see a truck from ten thousand feet, or dive-bomb-it; you had to get down underneath the flare and look at it. The rules were don't go low in the daytime; it sounded crazy to go low at night. But it was absolutely safer to go low at night than in the daytime, if you could overcome your fear of the hills and the dark.

Typically, I'd put my wingman at four thousand feet, lights out, and we'd always tank just before coasting in. I'd get on Route 1, [at] about five hundred feet, and rocket down the road with my wing down a little bit, and just like that I could see trucks. They'd throw a little lead, so I would jink, but the North Vietnamese were lousy shots at night.[52]

Captain Wynn Foster also flew road recce missions during his time with VA-163 aboard USS *Oriskany*:

The Navy was ill-prepared for night recce, and while the kind of mission we ended up fighting was carrying and dropping flares, the proper equipment for that mission wasn't available. [Multiple Ejector Bomb Racks] MERs which eject bombs real well were available, but they punched holes in the flares. So in 1965 the squadron [VA-163] ended up modifying the [Practice non-ejector Multiple Bomb Racks] PMBRs, which for some reason we took with us.[53]

But, as seemed to be the case throughout the war, A-4 pilots adapted to the situation and became quite adept at night operations, much to the chagrin of their A-6 night-attack brethren.

At the same time, Navy aircraft renewed their *Barrel Roll* efforts over Laos, but under a different name. Operation *Steel Tiger* designated the interdiction missions in the Laotian panhandle region south of the 18th parallel, while *Barrel Roll* still referred to missions flown in the

The A-4B, although lacking the sophistication of the later Charlie and Echo models, flew several missions in and around the Haiphong area when deployed aboard USS Intrepid **(CVA 11) in 1966.** US Navy via author

135

Skyhawk road recce missions were flown from Dixie Station during 1966 by aircraft from USS Oriskany (CVA 34). Using flares and iron bombs, aviators flew 'in country' at night, releasing their flares then bombing North Vietnamese trucks travelling down the Ho Chi Minh Trail through Laos.
US Navy via author

A load of LAU-10/A 5in (12.7cm) Zuni rockets are fired against Viet Cong forces in South Vietnam.
US Navy via author

Bullpups at the Tam Da Bridge

One of the most interesting developments of the war was the gradual shift from an all 'dumb' bomb ordnance to a mix of 'smart bombs'. One of these early smart bombs was the AGM-12 Bullpup made by Martin. Capt Otto Krueger, then a Commander flying Skyhawks with VA-94 aboard USS *Enterprise* (CVAN 65), tells about his two strikes against the Tam Da Bridge near Vinh:

> The Bullpup was a line-of-sight, rocket-propelled bomb controlled by a thumb toggle on the pilot's control stick. At launch, it would be ejected downward from the plane and initially would drop out of sight. We'd have to tug back on the knob to bring it up into view. The Bullpup had a flare on its tail that let us follow it down and control the trajectory to the target.
>
> Bullpup was a good idea, but first models were just not powerful enough. The -B, though, carried a punch and if you could get it on target you could do some real damage. The Bullpup was heavy, weighing about 2,000lb, and the sheer velocity of it would have done damage alone. But with the warhead addition, the Big Bullpup was a good weapon, in my opinion.
>
> To show how the weapons had progressed, in early 1965 we launched two-carrier Alpha strikes against the Tam Da Bridge south of Vinh. Maximum ordnance loads from two air wings missed the bridge in the morning, with the same result in the afternoon, until the final four-plane division of A-4s from VA-94 dropped several spans. About a year later they asked me to lead another strike against the bridge which had been put back into use, this time with only two planes carrying the new Bullpup 'B'. I managed to hit the bridge abutment, dropping the remaining span and putting the bridge out of commission again. The RA-5C post-strike photos showed a big hole where the abutment had been. So instead of a two carrier, max-effort Alfa strike, it was now one plane, one Bullpup, one bridge! (We saved the second Bullpup for another target.)

The RF-8 reconnaissance photo in this insert shows the Tam Ho Bridge after Captain Krueger's Bullpup attack. The damage from the first strike several months earlier (the dropped spans) can also be seen.

Capt Otto E. Krueger, then a Commander with VA-94, flew a Skyhawk like this on his strike against the Tam Da Bridge. US Navy via author

The Bullpup was hailed as the first 'stand-off' weapon, but did not fully live up to designer's claims. To properly fire the rocket, the operator had to fly a straight attack trajectory that made him quite susceptible to enemy AAA and gun-fire. US Navy via author

This photo recce BDA shot shows the damage that Krueger's Bullpup caused to the bridge. The bridge runs south (left) – north (right). The south abutment is destroyed. The 45-degree line down towards the abutment shows the flight path of Krueger's Bullpup. The downed spans (left and centre) from the initial 1965 Alpha strikes are still visible. Capt. Otto L. Krueger, USN(Ret.)

northern regions. *Steel Tiger* strikes were co-ordinated by Air Force C-130 Airborne Command and Control Center (ABCCC) aircraft. Call signs for the ABCCC in the *Steel Tiger* region were Hillsboro during the day and Moonbeam during the night.

Also in April 1965, carrier aircraft from USS *Coral Sea* and USS *Midway* conducted strikes against VC positions around the Black Mountains, supporting US ground forces in the area. It was at this time that attempts were made to establish what would eventually become an operational station off the southern coast of Vietnam. On 20 May, Dixie Station, located approximately 100 miles (160km) south-east of Cam Ranh Bay, came to life as USS *Oriskany* became the first carrier to be assigned official station duties.

December of that year saw the largest carrier strikes to date in the war, with over 100 planes from USS *Enterprise*, *Ticonderoga*, and *Kitty Hawk* striking the giant Uong Bi thermal plant 15 miles (25km) north/north-east of Haiphong. Skyhawks from *Enterprise* approached the plant from the north as A-4s from the other two carriers hit from the south causing considerable damage to the facility and marking the first major industrial site to be hit in North Vietnam. Two A-4s from *Enterprise* were lost. Reports show that the boiler house was severely damaged and that several storage tanks were left ablaze. Any hopes of this signalling a new direction for the air war were diminished, however, when a new peace offering was made, followed by a thirty-seven day bombing pause instigated by Washington.

In September, Cdr James B. Stockdale, CAG of CVW-16, was shot down by 57mm flak while leading a strike against the Thanh Hoa bridge. Stockdale, an F-8 pilot, who was on the scene at the time of the Gulf of Tonkin incident, was flying an A-4E at the time. He would become a POW and later receive the Medal of Honor for his leadership of prisoners in Hanoi.

1966 saw the air war increase with a sharp intensity after the bombing pause was lifted in early February, although most targets were limited to the southern areas of North Vietnam. Hanoi and Haiphong were absolutely off-limits. Skyhawks were also encouraged to pick up the pace of their night-time, anti-truck patrols.

Poor weather continued to hamper operations as the VC continued to expand its SAM network and move supplies south over the Ho Chi Minh Trail. During January and February, fourteen were lost, seven of which were A-4s. Also during this period, Navy planes flew nearly 1,400 sorties, the majority of which were over South Vietnam. At this time, tactics were beginning to change, as aircrews adapted to the presence of the SAM and devised new ways to counter the threat. For example, high and mid-altitude flight was prohibited in high SAM areas. Of course, this placed the pilots 'down in the weeds', which subjected them to heavy small arms and AAA fire. Also plaguing pilots was the shortage of bombs, which the Department of Defense denied.

In April 1966, the first AGM-45 Shrikes arrived in Vietnam, giving *Iron Hand* sections their first effective weapon against SA-2 sites. The first Shrike firing took place on 25 April by pilots of VA-23. At about the same time, the Alpha strike concept was put into practice, with Alpha strikes now occurring into RP VI. TF 77 pilots flew some 6,500 sorties over Vietnam in March, losing eleven aircraft, six of which were Skyhawks.

Navy strikes from the carrier USS *Kitty Hawk* hit the coal port of Cam Pha, some 35 miles (56km) from the Chinese border, dropping 50 tons (45,360kg) of ordnance on the city's rail yards, water pumping station, and coal treatment plant. Fires were started and smoke was seen billowing to 2,000ft (610m). TF 77's Commander, Rear-Admiral J. R. Reedy, stated that the Cam Pha targets had been frequently requested by the TF for major strikes: 'When the word came that Cam Pha was

The end of 1967 saw the introduction of the Chance Vought A-7 Corsair II with VA-147 'Argonauts' aboard USS Ranger **(CVA 61). The Corsair had prevailed against a souped-up Skyhawk in the 1963 LAV competition. The Corsair soon replaced the Skyhawk on all large-deck carriers and many** Essex **class carriers.** US Navy via author

now "on the list", we launched our strikes in less than 90 minutes'. Washington would later complain that pilots had struck a Polish merchant ship; the pilots contended that they had not, but that the Polish ship was shooting at them.

An interdiction campaign began against trucks, roads, and bridges south of Hanoi, and, on 18 April, A-4s struck the Uong Bi plant for a second time. Strikes against the Vinh-Ben Thuy complex that month cost the Yankee Station carriers twenty-one aircraft, including five Skyhawks. April also saw a devastating strike by eleven Skyhawks and four Crusaders from USS *Ticonderoga*'s CVW-5 attacking a major highway bridge in Hanoi that connected the city with China. Approaching from behind a ridge, the A-4s flying clean-wings and with a single 2,000lb bomb dodged at least two SAMs and AAA from 37mm guns and downed five of the bridge's twenty-four spans.

29 June saw the first attacks against POL facilities at Haiphong and Hanoi. Skyhawks from VA-55 and VA-146 aboard USS *Ranger* dropped 19 tons (11,582kg) of ordnance on the Haiphong plant while A-4s and A-6s from USS *Constellation* struck Do Son. The next day, A-4s from *Constellation* and *Hancock* struck the facilities at Bac Giamg, destroying seven POL tanks and four support buildings.

By August of 1966, the pace of strike operations had so picked up that Adm David McDonald, Chief of Naval Operations, modified the composition of navy carrier air wings to add another VA squadron, taking the number of VF units down to two. At this point, at least on the larger deck carriers, some of the A-4s and the A-1 Skyraider were being replaced by the newer A-6A Intruder. For the remainder of the year the carriers focused on a number of the POL delivery systems throughout North Vietnam, striking rail junctions at Vinh, Ninh Binh, Thanh Hoa, and Phy Ly, and also searching out and destroying depots, convoys, and barges that might be carrying supplies to the VC and North Vietnamese Army (NVA) units in the South.

September 1966 marked the beginning of a new interdiction phase against the Hanoi/Haiphong area. After analyzing traffic patterns, strikes were organized against the infamous Thanh Hoa bridge, as well as rail yards around Nin Binh and Phy Ly. All bridges south of the Thanh Hoa were subsequently destroyed.

Up to 1967, the majority of A-4 strikes were conducted with Mk 80 series bombs, napalm (only in the south), Zuni rockets, and, as of mid-1966, Shrike. For 'hard' targets, Mk 84 2,000lb bombs were used; however, Task Force Command permission was needed to use the larger bombs. For the most part, this ordnance was delivered from low altitudes to avoid the SA-2s, although opening the attacking pilots up to heavy AAA from the North Vietnamese 37, 57 and 85mm guns. The AGM-12 Bullpup, although intended as a

For part of 1968, attacks 'up north' focused on transportation systems immediately south of the Haiphong area in RP IV. Here, an Echo fires a Zuni rocket at a North Vietnamese train. Other photos in this series show that the last carriage to the right was struck by the rocket. US Navy via Boeing Historical Archives via Harry Gann

might well have had two kills. Controversy soon followed, as some accused him of saving his Zunis for MiGs that were supposed to be used as flak suppression. Nevertheless, it was a significant achievement for the Skyhawk community.

On 19 May, three Walleyes were launched against the Thanh Hoa bridge, and despite direct hits, could not destroy the structure. Again, that strike was led by Cdr Smith. Overall, the Walleyes were regarded as accurate and effective against all but the most hardened targets. An improved Walleye II, with longer range, was deployed near the war's end. Rear-Adm Thomas J. Walker, Commander of Carrier Division Three, who oversaw the Walleye's introduction into combat, commented on the impact of this weapon, stating that: '... for the first time in the history of naval warfare, a combat commander could launch one aircraft carrying one weapon with a high degree of confidence that significant damage could be inflicted on a selected target'.[54]

The next day, however, Cdr Smith was shot down when his A-4E was hit by anti-aircraft fire while attacking a heavily defended thermal power plant. Smith escaped his plane but was captured and later died in captivity. For his outstanding actions in combat and his extraordinary heroism, Cdr Smith was posthumously promoted to Captain and awarded the Navy's highest combat award, the Navy Cross.

A major follow-up strike on the Hanoi thermal plant facility was conducted in November, which Cdr Bryan W. Compton, who flew on this strike, described as follows:

> We planned to coast in from the south until we were just west of a line between Phu Ly and Hanoi and just south of the range of Hanoi's major SAM batteries. From this point, we would turn our A-4s north to Hanoi, fanning out about 25 miles from the target, which was on the north-west edge of the city. We planned for five Walleye drops to execute a simultaneous network coming from the west counter-clockwise to the south-east. We thought this approach would give each of us a chance to release the weapon on his individual aim point and still dilute the defences by the simultaneity of the attack.[55]
>
> Even though the main part of the plant was large, we were concerned that smoke and dust from the impact of the first weapon might decoy the others. We were anxious to get as close to simultaneous impact as possible. Since we were coming in essentially together, this required some careful adjustment of speed and maneuvering. We were not using any flak suppression on the strike for the final attack, so we rejected the option of dropping the weapons sequentially.[56]

Cdr Compton's plan was put into action on 21 November.

> On the morning of the strike, we were up early for our last-minute briefing. Since we were only dropping one Walleye each, we slicked up the airplanes, taking off the 400-gallon center-line auxiliary fuel tanks and the two triple ejector racks (TERs) on the inboard wing stations. Since we wanted to be topped off (attain maximum fuel state), we planned to refuel en route to our coast-in point. The only cover we had was a Target Combat Air Patrol (TARCAP) that went into our turn point south of Hanoi and two *Iron Hand* aircraft dropped off at the same basic position.[57]

All five of the Skyhawks on Compton's strike made hits on the power plant, with Compton's Walleye impacting directly through a window.

1967 was one of the most intense periods of the war. VA-113's cruise aboard USS *Enterprise* is a testament to this fact, as it flew some 2,287 combat sorties and delivered over 2,450 tons (1,493,520kg) of ordnance. That year, the eleven carriers that served with TF 77 destroyed an estimated thirty SAM sites, 187 AAA sites, 734 vehicles, 4,100 locomotives, and some 955 bridges. Another 1,586 bridges were damaged. All of this cost 133 aircraft, sixty-five of which were A-4s. That year also saw *Oriskany*'s air wing suffer tremendous losses, as its Skyhawks served 122 days 'on the line'.

After 1967, more target restrictions were lifted, but any benefits were lost in November 1968 when yet another bombing halt signalled the end of *Rolling Thunder*. In early 1968, the weather played a major role in limiting strikes, as rain, storms, and low cloud limited visual strikes to about three days per month. Nevertheless, the weather did allow A-4s from

One of VA-212's sister squadrons, a VA-216 A-4C launches from the port bow cat during operations in 1965.
US Navy via author

A 'Rampart Raider' from USS Hancock (CVA 19) departs with several Mk 83 1,000lb bombs on its centreline and two wing tanks. *Robert F. Dorr*

The Marine bases at Chu Lai, South Vietnam had to be built from scratch. Navy Seabees quickly prepared a 4,000ft (1,233m) aluminium Short Airfield for Tactical Support (SATS) and Marine A-4s began using the base within two months of arrival. This photo shows two A-4s on the runway and a third in a state of repair. *US Marines Corps via author*

Two-seat TA-4Fs flew FAC and TAC(A) missions supporting Marines on the ground as well as spotting missions for artillery and US naval gunners aboard USS New Jersey. The Skyhawk's speed, ruggedness, and warload made it a good choice for these missions. Lt Cdr Rick Burgess USN Retd

catapult system or JATO bottles. Recoveries could also be accomplished by a system of carrier-like arresting wires, called MOREST. This SATS system, in fact, had been tested earlier by the Marines during their operations at Taiwan in the late 1950s. On 31 May, just twenty-four days after they arrived, the 'Seabees' had completed a 4,000ft (1,215m) runway, some 70ft (21m) wide, complete with taxiways and parking ramps. Later this runway was extended to 8,000ft (2,438m) of matting.

On 1 June 1965, MAG-12's Commanding Officer, Col John D. Noble, made the first SATS landing with a VMA-225 A-4 brought over from Da Nang. Four more Skyhawks from VMA-311 arrived later that day and a VMA-225 A-4, led by its Commanding Officer, Lt Col Robert W. Baker, flew the base's first operational sortie that afternoon. Work continued on the facilities and they were declared fully operational in July. As a testament to its contribution to the war effort, Chu Lai logged its 100,000th A-4 mission on 7 December 1966.

A 10,000ft (3,040m) concrete runway with associated taxiways was completed in 1966, eventually eliminating the need for using the SATS or JATO. JATO had been used on occasion during extreme cross-wind conditions on the long runway, as Col John Caldas, who flew A-4Es with VMA-211 out of Chu Lai in 1966 and 1967, describes: 'We rarely used JATO at Chu Lai, but when we did it was because there was a severe cross-wind on the 8,000 ft main runway (aluminum). The cross runway, as I recall, was less than 4,000 feet. Once the concrete runway was completed, we never again used JATO there'.[58] According to Caldas, using JATO had its drawbacks, because 'if the bottles failed to ignite, we'd have bought the farm. Once you committed yourself for the take-off, there was nowhere to go, besides crossing a perimeter road that circled the inside of the air base'.

Chu Lai was the focus of a major VC effort to oust the Marines from 18–24 August. Code named Operation *Starlite*, Marine A-4s, with F-4s from Da Nang, flew around-the-clock missions in support of Marine ground units. Once the VC uprising was defeated, Chu Lai remained in US hands throughout the war.

The Marine Skyhawks' role in Vietnam was primarily one of close air support. Over the course of the war, seven Marine A-4 squadrons would operate out of the Chu Lai base, including VMAs-121, -211, -214, -223, -224, -225, and -311. Most of these Skyhawks were A-4Es, although VMA-223 did operate a few -C models for a time. Chu Lai's close proximity to targets in I Corps meant that many of the Marine strikes were only minutes away. One Marine pilot from Chu Lai commented on this '... when we operated in country, we were rarely more than 10–15 minutes from our targets. On many occasions, we'd raise the gear and climb to roll in altitudes to strike a target. This was not the case for strikes into Laos and Cambodia. Then, we were conserving our fuel'.[59] Indeed, Marine Skyhawks relied heavily on tanking from neighbouring KC-130Fs from VMGR-152 and later VMGR-352 operating out of Da Nang. According to sources, while Marine Corps Skyhawk pilots were trained on aerial refuelling with the D-704 stores, it happened seldom, at least during the early years of the war.

Marine Skyhawks at Sea

Two Marine A-4 squadrons sent detachments of A-4s to sea with Navy carriers during the war. H&MS-15 sent four Skyhawks to USS *Midway*, which were later transferred to USS *Hornet* and its CVSG-57 air group. During the squadron's two-month stint at sea, its four A-4s flew a total of 108 sorties and delivered approximately 160,000lb (72,640kg) of ordnance. VMA-223 also sent a four-plane Det. to USS *Yorktown* for the carrier's cruise with CVSG-55 (October 1964–May 1965). The H&MS-15 Det's Skyhawks were A-4Cs and those sent by VMA-223 were A-4Bs.

Tac Air Co-ordination

Control of Marine air units was initially given to the Air Force, although precise control over which squadrons were available remained with the Marines. This, in turn, ensured that some Marine assets would always remain available to support Marine units in the field and that their close air support needs were met before offering the remaining aircraft to the Air Force for tasking. Operational air control was routed through Da Nang's Tactical Air Direction Center (TADC), which, at first was composed of the Tactical Air Operations Center (TAOC) and Direct Air Support Center (DASC). These sub-units governed air surveillance and air defence, respectively. Using radar information gathered from a variety of sources, operators would manually plot aircraft movements on a large board.

In 1967 a new computer-assisted TAOC arrived, called the Marine Tactical Data System (MTDS). This was similar to that used by the Navy but significantly easier to operate. Established at Monkey Mountain near Da Nang, this unit could handle upwards of 250 aircraft tracks at any given time and eventually would grow to incorporate Air Force activity. Both the TADC and the MTDS were key in the Marines' use of the TPQ-10 blind-bombing system used by A-4s and other Marine attack jets.

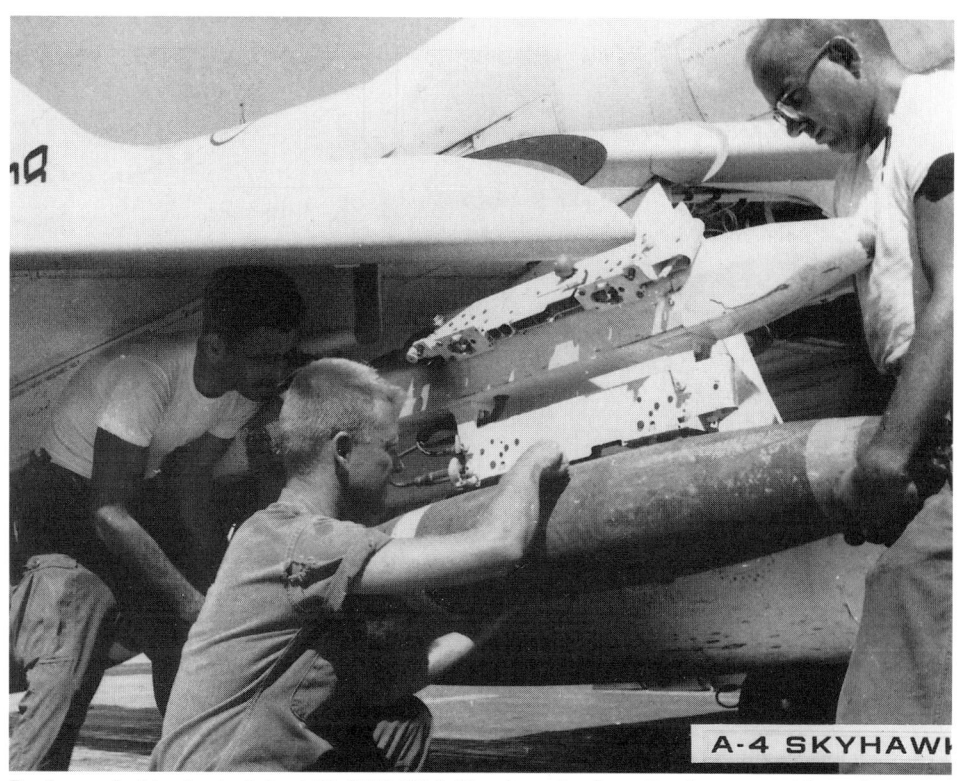

Bombs are double-checked about this VMA-225 A-4C as it readies for strikes in support of Operation Piranha **in September 1965.** US Navy via Boeing Historical Archives via Harry Gann

During 1966 and early 1967, as many as five squadrons operated from Chu Lai at any one time, with full squadrons being rotated in and out. Due to the disruption caused by the replacement of combat veterans, a new policy was adopted in 1968, whereby aircraft and crews would be rotated on an individual basis. Thus, squadrons such as VMA-211, -214, and -311 served at Chu Lai for many years. VMA-311 eventually accumulated over 54,000 combat sorties before it logged its last flight in 1972.

Colonel Caldas described some of the missions flown by Chu Lai based Marine A-4s:

> During the tour at Chu Lai most missions were in direct support of USMC units and Army outposts in the highlands. Our missions were usually two and four plane formations, controlled by airborne FACS or ground FACS. Rarely did we attack without a clearance from

Marine ground crews prepare this VMA-311 A-4E Skyhawk for the 10,000th combat sortie from Chu Lai. The original image is slightly lop-sided, but is reproduced in full here for completeness. Aerospace Publishing

This photo shows a Marine Corps A-4E with a sampling of the stores available to it by the mid-1960s. From left to right are: Zuni rocket pods, Mk 77 napalm, Mk 81 and 82 Snakeye retarded bombs, a Mk 83 1,000lb slick bomb, a 150 US gallon (567litre) drop tank, a 2,000lb Mk 84 bomb, a HiPeg gun pod, a 1,000lb Bullpup B, the smaller 250lb Bullpup A, an AGM-45 Shrike, and a Mk 20 Rockeye II cluster bomb unit. US Navy via Boeing Historical Archives via Harry Gann

A Marine Corps TA-4F armed with Zuni rockets is being towed with crew embarked and ready for a mission over South Vietnam. These two-seat Skyhawks proved invaluable in the resupply efforts during the siege of Khe Sanh in 1968 by helping co-ordinate deliveries to outlying posts. Thomas H. Idema via Robert F. Dorr

some control agency – usually in the vicinity of the targets. If a target was resilient enough to warrant continuous attacks, we'd stay on station (fuel permitting) until we were relieved. We also used radar bombing with TPQ radar. A controller would control our drops from a radar site. This was usually done at night or in conditions of bad weather.

As for TPQ, our recon or advanced ground troops would sometimes place a beacon in the field somewhere, and by triangulation our Marine support units would direct us to drop from those reference points. This was a method of area bombing. We could harass the NVA and VC by bombing their known or suspected assembly points without them ever seeing us – or we them for that matter. We usually bombed from 12 to 15 or 16,000 feet.

We also provided armed escorts for helicopter assaults – either site preparation or cover for unit inserts or med-Evacs. In major assaults, we might have three or four divisions (four aircraft) prepare concentrated attacks on an area before the troop inserts. Then maintain a presence or keep an area secure from intruding troops. In the South we did not have to worry about enemy air.

On one occasion I remember dropping leaflets in the DMZ from jury rigged drop tanks. We only did this once, to my knowledge.

On many occasions, we checked in with controllers after t/o and were advised to hold while they tried to find us a mission(s). Several times I can recall sighting what I (we) thought were VC and could not get clearance to attack. After a few minutes the possible targets would be gone into the jungle.[60]

According to Caldas, and other pilots, the Skyhawk was ' ... an ideal close air support aircraft'. Col Caldas added:

... if we had any limitation, it had to be the limited load and/or time on station available to us. We normally carried about 4,000 to 5,000 pounds of expendable ordnance. We generally used a centerline drop tank, which left us with four open wing stations. Our loads were typically (1) Mk 80-series Snakeyes and napalms (250/500 pounders and two napalm tanks); (2) rockets and bombs 12–250s or 6–500s (using 2.5 and 5 inch HVAR pods) or (3) two 1000 pounders for bunkering. [All flights carried 20mm cannon ammunition]. We sometimes used a MK 4 gun pod centerline. It wasn't too reliable.'[61]

Marine Corps strikes differed from Navy strikes in size and composition. The Navy tended to use Alpha strikes, featuring a large number of different aircraft directed at a large target such as a marshalling yard or refinery. 'That's a combined effort of fighters, ECM, flak suppressors, attack birds and post strike recon,' added Caldas.[62] Marine strikes were often in

A 1,000lb Mk 83 has just been released by this VA-23 Skyhawk during an attack on Viet Cong positions in South Vietnam. US Navy via Robert F. Dorr

A heavy load of Snakeyes on this VMA-211 A-4E meant more close air support for the Marines. Skyhawks such as this one flew hundreds of missions supporting the siege of Khe Sahn in January 1968.
Boeing Historical Archives via Harry Gann

smaller sections or flights and were oriented toward ground support.

Air operations intensified as 1967 began, with MAG-12 Skyhawks providing 24-hour support for US Marine, Army and South Vietnamese ground forces. To keep pace, A-4s at Chu Lai often sat fully loaded on the ramps with pilots on standby in what was termed 'hot pad' alert, awaiting a call to scramble.

1968's *Tet* Offensive launched by North Vietnam on 30 January saw a further increase in Skyhawk operations, as MAG-12 units provided much needed air cover for the besieged Marines at Khe Sanh. Code named Operation *Niagara*, the air effort in defence of Khe Sanh was joined by all services, with Marines performing close air support and radar-guided attacks and Air Force B-52 *Arc Light* strikes. Co-ordination of all aircraft was handled by a Tactical Air Controller (Airborne) or TAC(A), who sometimes complained that there were simply too many strike sorties hovering overhead. Indeed, reports would later show that an average of 300 sorties per day were directed at Khe Sanh and over 35,000 tons (21,336,000kg) of ordnance delivered. Some of the Khe Sanh strikes were handled with the TPQ-10 radar system, which proved particularly effective and saved many a crew from the heavy barrage of North Vietnamese AAA in the area. This system was used to control both A-4 and F-4 units.

It was during this battle that the *Super Gaggle* concept was developed, a means by which outposts were re-supplied in the hills surrounding Khe Sanh by a combination of A-4s and Marine helicopters. The first such operation took place on 24 February 1968, when twelve Skyhawks escorted a large contingency of CH-46 transports. Four UE-1E gunships also flew cover, with a single TA-4F providing the overall tactical co-ordination for the mission.

Once the aircraft and helicopters had launched, all would gather in the vicinity of Khe Sanh and await instructions from the TA-4F. When word was given, the A-4s would then charge down and 'sanitize' the area with cannon fire, rockets, and napalm, after which the CH-46s would land and unload their supplies. Amazingly, many of these unloads took no longer than five minutes to accomplish, although it certainly must have seemed longer to the crews. The UH-1E gunships would follow the CH-46s to pick up any crews that may have been shot down or become stranded.

Following the Khe Sanh defence, air control of Marine units fell under the 7th Air Force under the so-called 'single management doctrine'. Marine units now had to detail their assets' availability daily and the Air Force, not the Marines, had complete tasking control. Air Force officials claimed that the Khe Sanh operations confirmed the efficiency of such a system, but the Marines never fully accepted it, arguing that the Air Force simply did not understand the Marine air role.

Fast FAC Skyhawks

One of the interesting developments of the war occurred with the innovative use of two-seat jets as forward air control aircraft, observation, and escorts for helicopter transports. Given their range, speed, and weapons-carriage, the jets were perfect for these roles and the added set of 'eyes' further enhanced their value for low-level operations. Beginning in 1966, H&MS-13 based at Da Nang had been

VMA-223 flew sorties from Chu Lai from late 1965 until early 1968 and again from May 1968 until early 1970. Pictured here is an A-4C with its pilot. Notice the dark colouring around the 20mm cannon barrel indicating heavy use. Defense Department via Robert F. Dorr

operating the Grumman TF-9J Cougar in the Forward Air Controller (FAC) role (called Tactical Air Control (Airborne) or TAC(A)) supporting both MAG-11 and MAG-12. These FAC aircraft carried the standard 20mm ammunition and also rockets for both attack and for target designation. As the Cougars began showing their age, the two-seat TA-4F became available and Marine units seized upon the opportunity to grab a few of these for the FAC role.

Originally designed to operate as a trainer for advanced jet units in the States, these two-seaters retained the single-seat A-4s full combat operational capability. Only range was limited by the addition of the second cockpit, which was seldom a problem because of aerial refuelling. TA-4Fs served with H&MS-11 at Da Nang, and H&MS-12 and -13 at Chu Lai – and performed outstandingly in this capacity. Missions included the traditional FAC role, observation, and spotting for both Marine artillery and naval guns from USS *New Jersey* (BB 62), which patrolled off North Vietnamese shores during a portion of 1968.

The End Draws Near

Early 1969 saw Marine Skyhawks supporting Operation *Dewey Canyon* in the A Shau Valley in north-west South Vietnam, which ran from 22 January until 18 March. These operations, which were some of the most successful by Marine ground forces, aimed to infiltrate VC camps in Laos and to interdict the supply lines from North Vietnam.

Marine Skyhawk activity began to wind down in mid-1969 with President Nixon's decision to phase-out US troops in Vietnam, and in early 1970, VMA-211 and VMA-223 left Chu Lai for the US. Many of the MAGs lost combat squadrons and MAG-13, still based at Chu Lai, was down to one A-4 squadron, VMA-311. Notable also were several Marine Corps F-4 squadrons taken from Da Nang. Later that year, in July, Skyhawks from VMA-311 were transferred to MAG-11 at Da Nang where they operated against targets along the Ho Chi Minh Trail. Chu Lai was then transferred to the Army. VMA-311 A-4s also flew strikes in support of the South Vietnamese offensive, *Lam Son 719*, launched into VC staging areas in Laos during early 1971. All Marine air units had left Vietnam by mid-1971.

However, that departure soon proved premature, as the North Vietnamese launched a major invasion across the DMZ into South Vietnam on 30 March 1972. US forces again scrambled to deploy support units and air power to the region, as only two carriers and various Thailand-based Air Force units remained. As part of the effort, three Marine fighter squadrons and two VMA squadrons were ordered to return to South Vietnam. A-4Es of VMA-211 and VMA-311 deployed to Bien Hoa air base, 15 miles (25km) north-east of Saigon, arriving on 17 May. Both squadrons immediately began flying sorties

An A-4E armed with four Mk 77 napalm bombs taxies under the guidance of a plane handler prior to a mission in South Vietnam. *Boeing Historical Archives via Harry Gann*

along the Cambodian and Laotian borders attempting to interdict the flow of troops and supplies into the south. Again, Colonel Caldas flew some of these missions with VMA-311 as its Commanding Officer:

> Targets in Cambodia were usually along the 'Ho Chi Minh' Trail. Occasionally we caught them transporting equipment passing through clearings, etc. But most of the time we dropped bombs in tree lines. All drops were controlled by airborne FACS, usually in Oes [O-1 Bird Dogs] or Oys – little puddle jumpers. Sometimes we relieved pressure on combat bases under siege, using Napalm or high drag (Snakeyes) bombs – 250 or 500 pounders (113 or 227kg). This could get interesting if operating under a low overcast and running in towards the hills, where you'd be recovering on the climb out flying through the soup. We also acted as cover for insertions and extractions of Recon troops or recovery of crews from downed helicopters.
>
> VMA-211 and -311 flew only daytime strikes from Bien Hoa. We supported ARVN [South Vietnamese Army] units and occasionally teamed up with observation aircraft from the Air Cav and 20th Tactical Air Support Squadron (20th TASS-USAF) for strikes in II and IV Corps.[63]

Finally, on 28 January 1973, a division of A-4Es from VMA-311 delivered the final Skyhawk warload of the war during a mission over Cambodia. Both VMA-211 and VMA-311 left Bien Hoa for Iwakuni, Japan, on 29 January 1973. These were the last two fixed-wing squadrons to depart Vietnam.

The Vietnam War came to a close on 23 January 1973, with an armistice signed. Negotiations resulted in POWs being released by 29 March. While all air activity over the North was done, strikes continued in Laos and Cambodia until all US forces in south-east Asia were stood down on 15 August 1973. In the nine years from 5 August 1964 to August 1973, over 6.2 millions tons of ordnance was dropped over Vietnam, Laos, and Cambodia, and some 3.5 million sorties flown, during which 3,720 fixed-wing aircraft were lost, including 266 Skyhawks.

A-4 SQUADRON CARRIER DEPLOYMENTS IN VIETNAM

1964

Carrier/Air Wing	A-4 Squadrons	Variant Used	Tail Code/Modex	Deployment Dates	Days on the Line	Combat Losses
USS *Bon Homme Richard* (CVW-19)	VA-192	A-4C	NM 2xx	28 Jan 1964 to 21 Nov 1964	39	0
	VA-195	A-4C	NM 5xx			0
USS *Constellation* (CVW-14)	VA-144	A-4C	NK 4xx	05 May 1964 to 01 Feb 1965	68	1
	VA-146	A-4C	NK 6xx			0
USS *Coral Sea* (CVW-15)	VA-153	A-4C	NL 3xx	07 Dec 1964 to 01 Nov 1965	167	6
	VA-155	A-4E	NL 5xx			5
USS *Hancock* (CVW-21)	VA-212	A-4E	NP 2xx	21 Oct 1964 to 29 May 1965	82	1
	VA-216	A-4C	NP 6xx			1
USS *Ticonderoga* (CVW-5)	VA-55	A-4E	NF 5xx	14 Apr 1964 to 15 Dec 1964	61	0
	VA-56	A-4E	NF 4xx			0
USS *Kearsage* (CVSG-53)	VA-153 Det. R	A-4B	n/k	19 Jun 1964 to 16 Dec 1964	58	0
USS *Ranger* (CVW-9)	VA-93	A-4C	NG 3xx	5 Aug 1964 to 6 May 1965	103	0
	VA-94	A-4C	NG 4xx			
USS *Yorktown* (CVSG-55)	VMA-223 Det. T	A-4C	WP xx	23 Oct 1964 to 16 May 1965	57	0

1965

Carrier/Air Wing	A-4 Squadrons	Variant Used	Tail Code/Modex	Deployment Dates	Days on the Line	Combat Losses
USS *Bon Homme Richard* (CVW-19)	VA-192	A-4C	NM 2xx	21 Apr 1965 to 13 Jan 1966	136	1
	VA-195	A-4C	NM 5xx			1
USS *Enterprise* (CVW-9)	VA-36	A-4C	NG 7xx	26 Oct 1965 to 21 Jun 1966	131	4
	VA-76	A-4C	NG 5xx			3
	VA-93	A-4C	NG 3xx			0
	VA-94	A-4C	NG 4xx			4
USS *Independence* (CVW-7)	VA-72	A-4E	AG 3xx	10 May 1965 to 13 Dec 1965	100	2
	VA-86	A-4E	AG 4xx			1
USS *Kitty Hawk* (CVW-11)	VA-113	A-4C	NH 3xx	19 Oct 1965 to 13 Jun 1966	122	2
USS *Midway* (CVW-2)	VA-22	A-4C	NE 2xx	06 Mar 1965 to 23 Nov 1965	144	4
	VA-23	A-4E	NE 3xx			4
USS *Oriskany* (CVW-16)	VA-163	A-4E	AH 3xx	05 Apr 1965 to 16 Dec 1965	141	4
	VA-164	A-4E	AH4xx			2
USS *Ranger* (CVW-14)	VA-55	A-4E	NK 4xx	10 Dec 1965 to 25 Aug 1966	137	8
	VA-146	A-4C	NK 6xx			2
USS *Ticonderoga* (CVW-5)	VA-56	A-4E	NF 4xx	28 Sep 1965 to 13 May 1966	112	2
	VA-144	A-4C	NF 5xx			4
USS *Bennington* (CVSG-59)	VA-113 Det. Q	A-4B	n/k	22 May 1965 to 07 Oct 1965	34	0
USS *Hornet* (CVSG-57)	H&MS-15 Det. N	A-4C	YV 8x	12 Aug 1965 to 23 Mar 1966	80	0

1966

Carrier/Air Wing	A-4 Squadrons	Variant Used	Tail Code/Modex	Deployment Dates	Days on the Line	Combat Losses
USS *Constellation* (CVW-15)	VA-153	A-4C	NL 3xx	12 May 1966 to 03 Dec 1966	111	3
	VA-155	A-4E	NL 5xx			4
USS *Coral Sea* (CVW-2)	VA-22	A-4C	NE 2xx	29 Jul 1966 to 23 Feb 1967	109	4
	VA-23	A-4E	NE 3xx			3

Carrier/Air Wing	A-4 Squadrons	Variant Used	Tail Code/ Modex	Deployment Dates	Days on the Line	Combat Losses
USS *Hancock* (CVW-21)	VA-212	A-4E	NP 2xx	10 Nov 1965 to 01 Aug 1966	143	2
	VA-216	A-4C	NP 6xx			4
USS *Intrepid* (CVW-10)	VA-15	A-4B	AK 3xx	04 Apr 1966 to 21 Nov 1966	103	0
	VA-95	A-4B	AK 5xx			0
USS *Kitty Hawk* (CVW-11)	VA-112	A-4C	NH 4xx	05 Nov 1966 to 20 Jun 1967	149	2
	VA-144	A-4C	NH 3xx			2
USS *Oriskany* (CVW-16)	VA-163	A-4E	AH 3xx	26 May 1966 to 16 Nov 1966	87	1
	VA-164	A-4E	AH 4xx			1
USS *Roosevelt* (CVW-1)	VA-12	A-4E	AB 4xx	21 Jun 1966 to 21 Feb 1967	95	0
	VA-72	A-4E	AB 5xx			4
	VA-172	A-4C	AB 3xx			4
USS *Ticonderoga* (CVW-19)	VA-192	A-4E	NM 2xx	15 Oct 1966 to 29 May 1967	34	1
	VA-195	A-4C	NM 5xx			2

1967

Carrier/Air Wing	A-4 Squadrons	Variant Used	Tail Code/ Modex	Deployment Dates	Days on the Line	Combat Losses
USS *Bon Homme Richard* (CVW-21)	VA-76	A-4C	NP 6xx	26 Jan 1967 to 25 Aug 1967	112	4
	VA-212	A-4E	NP 2xx			6
USS *Constellation* (CVW-14)	VA-55	A-4C	NK 5xx	29 Apr 1967 to 04 Dec 1967	121	0
	VA-146	A-4C	NK 6xx			2
USS *Coral Sea* (CVW-15)	VA-153	A-4E	NL 3xx	26 Jul 1967 to 06 Apr 1968	132	2
	VA-155	A-4E	NL 5xx			3
USS *Enterprise* (CVW-9)	VA-56	A-4C	NG 4xx	19 Nov 1966 to 06 Jul 1967	132	1
	VA-113	A-4C	NG 3xx			2
USS *Forrestal* (CVW-17)	VA-46	A-4E	AA 4xx	06 Jun 1967 to 14 Sep 1967	5	0
	VA-106	A-4E	AA 3xx			0
USS *Hancock* (CVW-5)	VA-93	A-4E	NF 3xx	05 Jan 1967 to 22 Jul 1967	102	5
	VA-94	A-4C	NF 4xx			1
USS *Intrepid* (CVW-10)	VSF-3	A-4B	AK 1xx	11 May 1967 to 30 Dec 1967	103	2
	VA-15	A-4C	AK 2xx			5
	VA-34	A-4C	AK 3xx			4
USS *Oriskany* (CVW-16)	VA-163	A-4E	AH 3xx	16 Jun 1967 to 31 Jan 1968	122	10
	VA-164	A-4E	AH 4xx			10
USS *Ranger* (CVW-2)	VA-22	A-4C	NE 2xx	04 Nov 1967 to 25 May 1968	88	0
USS *Ticonderoga* (CVW-19)	VA-23	A-4F	NM 3xx	27 Dec 1967 to 17 Aug 1968	212	0
	VA-192	A-4F	NM 2xx			7
	VA-195	A-4C	NM 5xx			1

1968

Carrier/Air Wing	A-4 Squadrons	Variant Used	Tail Code/ Modex	Deployment Dates	Days on the Line	Combat Losses
USS *Bon Homme Richard* (CVW-5)	VA-93	A-4F	NF 3xx	27 Jan 1968 to 10 Oct 1968	135	4
	VA-94	A-4E	NF 4xx		0	
	VA-212	A-4F	NF 5xx			2
USS *Coral Sea* (CVW-15)	VA-153	A-4F	NL 3xx	07 Sep 1968 to 18 Apr 1969	110	0
	VA-216	A-4C	NL 6xx			3
USS *Enterprise* (CVW-9)	VA-56	A-4E	NG 4xx	03 Jan 1968 to 18 Jul 1968	100	2
	VA-113	A-4F	NG 3xx			2
USS *Hancock* (CVW-21)	VA-55	A-4F	NP 5xx	18 Jul 1968 to 03 Mar 1969	107	2
	VA-163	A-4E	NP 3xx			0
	VA-164	A-4E	NP 4xx			1

154

Carrier/Air Wing	A-4 Squadrons	Variant Used	Tail Code/ Modex	Deployment Dates	Days on the Line	Combat Losses
USS *Intrepid* (CVW-10)	VA-36	A-4C	AK 5xx	04 Jun 1968 to 08 Feb 1969	106	0
	VA-66	A-4C	AK 3xx			1
	VA-106	A-4E	AK 2xx			1
USS *Kitty Hawk* (CVW-11)	VA-112	A-4C	NH 4xx	18 Nov 1968 to 28 Jun 1968	125	1
	VA-144	A-4E	NH 3xx			3
USS *Ranger* (CVW-2)	VA-155	A-4F	N E 4xx	26 Oct 1968 to 17 May 1969	91	0

1969

Carrier/Air Wing	A-4 Squadrons	Variant Used	Tail Code/ Modex	Deployment Dates	Days on the Line	Combat Losses
USS *Bon Homme Richard* (CVW-5)	VA-22	A-4F	NF 3xx	18 Mar 1969 to 29 Oct 1969	97	0
	VA-94	A-4E	NF 4xx			0
	VA-144	A-4E	NF 5xx			1
USS *Hancock* (CVW-21)	VA-55	A-4F	NP 5xx	02 Aug 1969 to 15 Apr 1970	113	1
	VA-164	A-4F	NP 4xx			0
	VA-212	A-4F	NP 3xx			1
USS *Oriskany* (CVW-19)	VA-23	A-4F	NM 3xx	16 Apr 1969 to 17 Nov 1969	116	1
	VA-192	A-4F	NM 4xx			0
	VA-195	A-4E	NM 5xx			0
USS *Ticonderoga* (CVW-16)	VA-112	A-4C	AH 4xx	01 Feb 1969 to 11 Sep 1969	97	0

1970

Carrier/Air Wing	A-4 Squadrons	Variant Used	Tail Code/ Modex	Deployment Dates	Days on the Line	Combat Losses
USS *Bon Homme Richard* (CVW -5)	VA-22	A-4F	NF 3xx	02 Apr 1970 to 12 Nov 1970	101	0
	VA-94	A-4E	NF 4xx			0
	VA-144	A-4F	NF 5xx			0
USS *Hancock* (CVW-21)	VA-55	A-4F	NP 5xx	22 Oct 1970 to 02 Jun 1971	110	0
	VA-164	A-4F	NP 4xx			0
	VA-212	A-4F	NP 3xx			0
USS *Shangri-La* (CVW-8)	VA-12	A-4C	AJ 4xx	05 Mar 1970 to 17 Dec 1970	120	0
	VA-152	A-4E	AJ 5xx			0
	VA-172	A-4C	AJ 3xx			1

1972

Carrier/Air Wing	A-4 Squadrons	Variant Used	Tail Code/ Modex	Deployment Dates	Days on the Line	Combat Losses
USS *Hancock* (CVW-21)	VA-55	A-4F	NP 5xx	07 Jan 1972 to 03 Oct 1972	165	3
	VA-164	A-4F	NP 4xx			0
	VA-212	A-4F	NP 3xx			2

1973

Carrier/Air Wing	A-4 Squadrons	Variant Used	Tail Code/ Modex	Deployment Dates	Days on the Line	Combat Losses
USS *Hancock* (CVW-21)	VA-55	A-4F	NP 5xx	08 May 1973 to 08 Jan 1974	28	0
	VA-164	A-4F	NP 4xx			0
	VA-212	A-4F	NP 3xx			0

CHAPTER FIVE

Skyhawks in Foreign Service

Although it took over ten years and some 2,000 A-4s to be produced before any orders were placed, the A-4 Skyhawk became one of the most successful export aircraft in US history. With its low cost, high degree of reliability, and low maintenance requirements, not to mention its proven track record with US forces in Vietnam, foreign countries became interested in the Skyhawk to modernize their frontline air forces. Some have attributed this long delay to the fact that no two-seat version was available for pilot training: there may be some merit to that claim, since the export sales began about the same time as the two-seat TA-4E/F was developed.

Most foreign purchases consisted of refurbished models, with only 277, less than 10 per cent of all built, consisting of new builds. Of the foreign sales, only Australia, Israel, Kuwait and New Zealand received new builds. Argentina, Malaysia, and Singapore would receive reworked and refurbished models, with Indonesia purchasing a batch of A-4Es from Israel and Brazil buying twenty-three A-4s from Kuwait.

Certainly, the new builds offered many advantages to the US military. Building export models permitted Douglas to keep its production line open longer, thereby helping to contain manufacturing costs for the US models, such as the -F and -M. Sales of new and refurbished Skyhawks also gave US allies, such as Israel and Australia, current-generation hardware and permitted some level of standardization of weapons and stores.

At one point in 1958, Douglas identified an export aircraft, called the DA-101, based on the A4D-2. These were to come from surplus Skyhawks and were priced at $35,000. However, with the Vietnam War heating up in 1964, these A4D-2s were needed for Reserve and non-deploying Fleet squadrons. Douglas later considered a special export Skyhawk, designated CA-4E for the single-seat, and CA-4F for the two-seat variant, that offered many of the added capabilities developed over the years.

An advanced trainer version, the TCA-4F, was also offered. Based on the A-4F model but stripped of its weapons, the TCA-4F was powered by the 9,300lb (4,222kg) thrust J52-P-8A, although other options were provided, including the 12,000lb (5,448kg) thrust Rolls-Royce RB 168 Spey and the 11,650lb (5,290kg) thrust General Electric non-afterburning J79.

The following review looks at each foreign user in order of purchase, beginning with Argentina in 1965.

Argentina

Entering into a $7.1 million contract in 1965, the Argentine Air Force (Fuerza Aerea Argentine or FAA) became the first foreign buyer of the A-4, with an initial purchase of fifty surplus A-4Bs to replace their ageing Gloster Meteors and North American F-86 fighters. Argentina's Skyhawks were refurbished to the new standards at the Douglas plant in Tulsa, Oklahoma, and, following the initial flight on 31 December 1965, were delivered in two batches. The first, consisting of twenty-five A-4Bs, redesignated as A-4Ps, were delivered in June 1966. The delay resulted from initial crew training in the US.

Douglas introduced the designations CA-4E (single-seat) and CA-4F (two-seat) to identify export variants based on the US Navy A-4F. A third export designation, CTA-4F, was used for the advanced two-seat trainer variant. Douglas Aircraft Co. via Aerospace Publishing

Argentina became the first purchaser of A-4s when it bought fifty surplus A-4Bs. The photo shows these refurbished Skyhawks on the line at the Douglas plant at Tulsa. Boeing Historical Archives via Harry Gann

The second batch, also of twenty-five aircraft, was delayed until 1970 due to Congressional concerns that the sale would deplete the number of aircraft available to Naval and Marine Corps Reserve units and force them to rely on the outdated A4D-1 model. All A-4Ps relied on the 7,700lb (3,495kg) thrust J65-W-16A engine and none were fitted for Sidewinder carriage or loft bombing. These Skyhawks featured the Escapac I ejection seat with the Stencil modification and were equipped with the lift spoiler introduced in the A-4F model. Visibly, they differed from US models by the addition of a ADF aerial 'blister' on the top fuselage and a 'ring' type antenna on the tailfin

In 1971, the Argentine Naval Air Arm (Comando de Aviacion Naval Argentina or CANA) decided to equip its Navy's sole carrier, the 16,000 ton ARA 25 Veintcino De Mayo (the ex-British light carrier HMS Venerable), with Skyhawks and acquired sixteen refurbished A-4Bs, redesignated as A-4Q. These models were updated by Lockheed Martin Air Services at Ontario, California. Unlike the A-4P, this variant used the 8,400lb (3,815kg) thrust J65-W-20 engine. This variant, too, as with American models, was equipped to carry the AIM-9 Sidewinder. Having had success in operating the Skyhawk, Argentina again turned to the US in 1976 to purchase another twenty-five A-4s, this time a refurbished A-4C variant.

The A-4Ps, still called the A-4B by Argentinians, served with I and II Escuadrones from Grupo 5 de Caza of V Brigada Aera. These units were based at General Pringle's Air Base at Villa Reynolds. The A-4Cs were stationed at Commandate Espora Naval Air Station and were assigned to I Escaudrone of IV Aerea Brigada's Grupo 4 de Caza. Today, A-4s all operate with Grupo 5 de Caza, with III Escuadron operating the remaining A-4Cs, and I and II Escuadron operating the new A-4AR.

The Falklands War

The most recent test of the A-4 Skyhawk at war came in April 1982 when Argentine military forces invaded the Falkland Islands. At the outset, Argentina had a total of forty-eight Skyhawks of various models; twenty-six of these were A-4Bs, twelve were A-4Cs and ten were A-4Qs belonging to the CANA. When the invasion began, the ten A-4Qs aboard the ARA Veintcino De Mayo were ready to provide cover for advancing Argentine troops. But because British forces offered no air opposition, these Skyhawks were not called into action and were subsequently returned to their shore base for additional training.

Within days of their return, however, the carrier and its air group, as a part of Task Force 79, were back at sea to conduct further training in anticipation of battle with the British carriers HMS Hermes and HMS Invincible which it foresaw developing as early as 30 April. By 2 May, the two opposing carrier groups were only 150 miles (245km) apart and reports state that the Argentines were close to launching a strike against the British carriers using all eight Skyhawks equipped with six Mk 82 Snakeye iron bombs. One A-4 was reported to have been configured for air defence with AIM-9 Sidewinders.

This strike was apparently abandoned due to unusually light winds that hampered take-off in the maximum weight configuration, which was needed to reach the British fleet. Later that morning, the S-2E Tracker shadowing the British carrier group lost contact and, following the sinking of ARA General Belgrano by a shadowing British submarine that afternoon, the Veintcino De Mayo returned to port on 5 May. Although that battle never occurred, one wonders how it would have impacted the war effort had Argentina succeeded in damaging or sinking one of the British carriers.

Shortly after the occupation began, Grupo 4 moved its twelve A-4Cs (nine of which were operational) to San Julian; Grupo 5 moved its twelve A-4Bs to Rio Gallegos. No real combat occurred until 12 May when HMS Glasgow and HMS Brilliant were attacked by Skyhawks from Grupo 5 de Caza. Glasgow, a Type 42 destroyer, was hit, although two 500lb bombs failed to detonate and passed through the ship. Four attacking Skyhawks were lost, although Argentina considered it a success – it believed it had sunk Brilliant and damaged Glasgow. Interestingly, after this attack, Argentina re-evaluated its attack tactics and determined that it would conduct all future anti-ship attacks from abeam. Tanking would also be used for future missions.

Argentine A-4 Losses in the Falklands War

Forty-eight Skyhawks were deployed for combat operations during the conflict, with twenty-two lost. Eight losses were at the hands of British Sea Harrier pilots, seven were due to sea-launched SAMs, and four were downed by ground-fire.

Date	Aircraft	Details
9 May	A-4C/C-313	Grupo IV de Caza
9 May	A-4C/C-303	Grupo IV de Caza
12 May	A-4B/C-246	Grupo V de Caza – lost to Sea Wolf from HMS *Brilliant* near Port Stanley
12 May	A-4B/C-208	Grupo V de Caza – lost to Sea Wolf from HMS *Brilliant* near Port Stanley
12 May	A-4B/C-206	Grupo V de Caza – crashed avoiding Sea Wolf from HMS *Glasgow*
12 May	A-4B/C-248	Grupo V de Caza – mistakenly shot down by Argentine 35mm AA fire over Goose Green
21 May	A-4C/C-325	Grupo IV de Caza – lost to Sea Harrier flown by Lt Cdr Blissett over West Falkland
21 May	A-4C/C-309	Grupo IV de Caza – lost to Sea Harrier flown by Lt Cdr Thomas over West Falkland
21 May	A-4Q/A-307	III Eslla 0660 – lost to Sea Harrier flown by Lt Morrell over Falkland Sound after attack on HMS *Ardent*
21 May	A-4Q/A-314	III Eslla 0667 – lost to Sea Harrier flown by Flt Lt Leeming over Falkland Sound
21 May	A-4Q/A-312	III Eslla 0665 – damaged by Sea Harrier flown by Lt Morrell and downed by Argentine AA over Port Stanley
23 May	A-4B/C-242	Grupo V de Caza – downed by AAA/SAM over San Carlos Water
24 May	A-4C/C-305	Grupo IV de Caza – downed by AAA over St. George Bay
25 May	A-4B/C-244	Grupo V de Caza – downed by Sea Dart from HMS *Coventry* north of Pebble Island
25 May	A-4C/C-319	Grupo IV de Caza – downed by AAA and SAM over San Carlos Water
25 May	A-4C/C-304	Grupo IV de Caza – downed by Sea Dart from HMS *Coventry* north of Pebble Island
27 May	A-4B/C-215	Grupo V de Caza – downed by 40mm Bofors from HMS *Fearless*
30 May	A-4C/C-301	Grupo IV de Caza – downed by Sea Dart from HMS *Exeter* east of Falklands
30 May	A-4C/C-310	Grupo IV de Caza – downed by Sea Dart from HMS *Exeter* east of Falklands
8 June	A-4B/C-226	Grupo V de Caza – downed by Sea Harrier flown by Flt Lt Morgan over Choiseul Sound
8 June	A-4B/C-228	Grupo V de Caza – downed by Sea Harrier flown by Flt Lt Morgan over Choiseul Sound
8 June	A-4B/C-204	Grupo V de Caza – downed by Sea Harrier flown by Lt Smith over Choiseul Sound

Reproduced with the permission of Aerospace Publishing

Argentina's attacks on British shipping continued on 21 May at what is now called the Battle of San Carlos Water. There, Skyhawks damaged the frigate HMS *Argonaut* as it steamed unescorted off Fanning Head and put it out of action for the remainder of the war. Two flights of three A-4s put two 1,000lb bombs into *Argonaut*, although neither exploded.

That same day, HMS *Ardent* became the next victim, as it took hits from a Grupo 6 'Dagger' and subsequent strikes of two 500lb Mk 82 bombs from three A-4Qs from III Escuadrilla. HMS *Antelope* fell victim on 23 May to two successive flights of Grupo 5 de Caza Skyhawks.

On 21 May 1982, Argentinian Skyhawks from Grupo IV, and later, III Eslila, attacked and sunk HMS Ardent during the Falklands War. Royal Navy, SMH via Aerospace Publications

These bombs, which hit the forward and aft parts of the ship, failed to explode on impact. During the night, though, the aft bomb detonated causing a vicious fire that ultimately caused the ship to explode and break in two. Another mission was mounted by III Escuadrilla on 23 May directed against 'any suitable target in San Carlos Water'. While warships were found and attack runs made, at least one of the Skyhawks' bombs failed to release.

By this time in the war, Argentina's Grupo 4 and 5 had made several changes in their overall tactics based on lessons learned. For example, rather than launch in flights of two, flights were now launched in two groups of three, with each 'wave' a few minutes apart. In-flight refuelling was also made a part of missions, especially those to San Carlos Water. Missions were also often accompanied by a 'spare', which would then depart after conclusion of the in-flight refuelling segment.

The anti-ship campaign continued on 25 May, Argentina's National Day, with an attack on HMS *Coventry* and HMS *Broadsword*, which had been providing British units with excellent radar coverage from a picket position some 15 miles (24km) north of Pebble Island. Two flights of Grupo 5 aircraft, call-signs 'Vulcan' and 'Zeus', took off that day carrying an unusually large load of three 1,000lb bombs. This was permitted only because of the shorter range involved and the use of refuelling. In the action, *Broadsword* was hit but only lightly damaged, while *Coventry* took three direct hits, exploded, and sank in just over an hour.

On 30 May a major effort was undertaken by both the FAA and CANA to sink the British carriers. Four A-4Cs from Grupo 4 armed with two 500lb bombs each were chosen for the attack, which was to be in conjunction with an Exocet-touting Dassualt Super Etendard. The attack was ultimately unsuccessful as the Super Etendard mistook the Type 21 class frigate HMS *Avenger* for the carrier HMS *Invincible*, which was some 20 miles (33km) to the north. One of the A-4s was shot down and the remaining three missed their target. Following this, a period of calm resulted as poor weather hampered air operations and Argentine intelligence sources failed to locate any British shipping.

This came to a rather abrupt end on 8 June when five Argentine Skyhawks from Grupo 5 attacked two British landing ships unloading the Welsh Guards near Fitzroy. Perhaps lulled by a relatively long period of Argentine air inactivity, the British attempted to land a large part of its 5th Infantry Brigade at Port Pleasant. Led by Primer Teniente Cahon, Argentine Skyhawks scored three hits on RFA *Sir Galahad* and two on RFA *Sir Tristram*, although the latter bombs failed to explode. *Sir Galahad* was not so lucky and caught fire after ammunition aboard was set aflame. The ship burned for a week and eventually sunk; fifty-one were killed and sixty-four injured, the worst single-incident loss of life in the campaign for the British.

On 8 June, CANA's III Escuadrilla, down to its last two serviceable Skyhawks and unable to launch a strike since 23 May, sent these two A-4Qs against suspected British positions on Broken Island. A similar strike was conducted by two A-4Qs on 12 June, which was foiled by the presence of British Sea Harriers, and the CANA was essentially out of the war. During the war, III Escuardilla de Caza y Ataque flew thirty-four operational sorties and lost three aircraft (3-A-307, -312, -314) to combat operations.

The A-4P and A-4Q provided the bulk of Argentina's strike assets during the Falklands War.
Boeing Historical Archives via Harry Gann

Just days later, on 13 June, the FAA mounted its last attack, and its only CAS mission of the war. Two Grupo 5 Skyhawks, launched against a concentration of British troops and an HQ unit near Two Sisters, succeeded in reaching the target without interference from British Harriers. One of the A-4s dropped its warload while the other strafed with its 20mm cannon. Several vehicles and helicopters were destroyed, but only light damage was done to the overall facilities. The next day the Argentine forces on the Falklands surrendered. Interestingly, Maj-Gen Jeremy Moore, Commander of the British forces, was at the HQ unit which had been attacked at Two Sisters.

From an operational standpoint, it was clear that the Argentine Skyhawks were on their last leg, suffering from shortages of spares, battle damage, and component failure. Had the war lasted much longer it is doubtful what role the A-4s could have continued to play.

In total, 505 sorties were flown from Argentine land bases, with 149 of those by A-4Bs and 106 by A-4Cs. Of these sorties, the -Bs flew 133 operational missions (eighty-six in combat) and the

Argentina's Air Force received a considerable upgrade by purchasing thirty-six A-4M and five OA-4M Skyhawks formerly operated by the US Marine Corps. These Skyhawks have been substantially reworked with new avionics, and have been redesignated as A-4AR Fightinghawks. This photo shows four single-seat and one two-seater lined-up for testing. Conversions were performed by Lockheed Martin Aerospace Services. Denny Lombard

A-4Cs flew eighty-six operational missions (forty-one in combat). Ten A-4Bs and nine A-4 Cs were lost, most coming from Grupo 4 de Caza. In exchange for the destroyer, landing ship, and two frigates sunk, the Argentines lost twenty-two Skyhawks and fifteen pilots. Of these aircraft losses, eight were the result of Sea Harrier engagements, and seven were from shipborne SAMs. Four resulted from ground-based AAA/SAMs and one was due to friendly fire.

Despite the rather high loss rate, A-4s performed well considering everything that was stacked against them. First, those A-4Bs operating out of Rio Gallegos were approximately 482 miles (780km) from the Port Stanley area; the A-4C and A-4Q Skyhawks flying from Rio Grande were 437 miles (700km) from the theatre of operations. With a shortage of refuelling aircraft, A-4s had little time over the target and were only able to make one pass before fuel supplies dictated that they return to base. Also aggravating the situation were the older electronics and navigational equipment, plus the complete failure of some of the Argentine bombs to explode, thereby limiting the damage even when a strike resulted. Argentine Skyhawks also suffered from the lack of any real co-ordinated air plan or air control.

In December 1983, the FAA consolidated its A-4s, with Grupo 4 transferring its seven remaining -Cs to Grupo 5 de Caza and re-equipping itself with ex-Israeli Mirage IIIs. The twelve A-4Bs and four A-4Cs remaining in the mid-1990s were phased out and replaced by the newer A-4AR, based on the US Marine Corps A-4M. The last A-4Q flew in April 1988.

New Skyhawks for Argentina

In 1993, the embargo prohibiting sales of A-4 spares to Argentina was lifted and immediately negotiations began on acquiring replacements for the losses sustained in the Falklands War. Previously, Argentina had tried to purchase twenty-four ex-Israeli Skyhawks, but the US protested and was generally against any such purchases until 1993. In 1994, Argentina entered into a $208 million contract with Lockheed Martin to modify and convert thirty-six surplus A-4Ms and another five surplus OA-4Ms for the FAA. Requiring extensive avionics and airframe upgrades, this new purchase was designated as the A-4AR Fightinghawk.

Modifications to the A-4AR included incorporating an ARG-1 radar (a modified version of the Westinghouse APG-66 used by the F-16), and adding the ALR-93V(1) RWR, a Nav-attack system, the Sextant Smart HUD, a chaff and flare system, and Hands-On-Throttle-And-Stick (HOTAS) configuration. An On-Board Oxygen Generating System (OBOGS) was also added. The cockpit was further modified by adding two AlliedSignals CRT panels, a military standard 1553 electrical bus, and a state-of-the-art mission planner with a data link ground control capability. Excluded from this deal, however, was the Hughes ARBS system used by Marine Corps A-4Ms. These units were apparently removed and reinserted into the AV-8B programme.

Two dual-seat TA-4ARs were also in the deal as well as several airframes for spares and other contract provisions for service, manuals, and crew and maintenance training. Argentina plans to continue to upgrade these variants by incorporating advanced Air-to-Air Missile (AAM), laser/tv-guided weaponry, and Maverick.

The first of these improved A-4s (BuNo. 158161) flew on 17 July 1997, with Lockheed Martin test pilot Kirk Kalstad at the controls. Although the first nine A-4ARs were built in the US at Lockheed Martin's Ontario and Palmdale facilities, Lockheed opened a new factory in Cordoba, under the name of Lockheed Aircraft Argentina, South America (LAAS), where the remaining twenty-seven will be built. The first five A-4ARs were delivered on 12 December 1997 to Grupo 5 de Caza at Villa Reynolds AB. Further deliveries took place in June 1998, with the first local-built deliveries commencing on 22 July 1998. Sources say that the A-4AR will be used to enhance Argentina's air-to-air defensive role.

Argentina's Navy now flies the Dassault Super Etendard. Some discussion is presently underway for the purchase by Argentina of an additional eighteen TA-4Js for use as advanced trainers.

Australia

Australia became the next, albeit limited, purchaser, with initial deliveries of eight single-seat and two two-seat A-4s taking place in 1967. These Skyhawks, purchased at a cost of $18.5 million, were to fill the Royal Australian Navy's need for a fighter attack aircraft to replace the outdated de Havilland Sea Venoms for their 16,000 ton class HMAS Melbourne (Ex-British HMS Majestic). Australia had recently purchased fourteen Grumman S-2 Trackers and was looking to operate both as an air group from Melbourne with its small contingent of Wessex ASW helicopters.

Beginning in January 1967, pilots were sent from Australia to NAS Lemoore where they spent four months training with VA-125. These pilots, Lt Cdr John DaCosta and Lt Cdr Graham King, then returned to Australia to conduct the first RAN conversion and operational flight courses and develop the training syllabus. As Lt Cdr DaCosta, later to become Commander of VF-805 and of the air wing assigned to Melbourne, reported in a 1997 issue of the Skyhawk Association Newsletter, the time at VA-125 was well spent:

> Our A-4 RAG syllabus was entirely attack oriented and fully met our needs. Highlights were the 'Sandblower' low-level navigation exercises over much of Nevada and the weapons training deployment to NAS Fallon. At the latter place, I was snowed upon for the first time in my life, even though it was in a desert! Since there was no 'fighter' phase of the RAG syllabus, special arrangements were made for a one week A-4E/TA-4E deployment to MCAS Yuma for air-to-air gun attacks on a towed banner target, GCI (Ground Controlled Interception) training and Sidewinder firings against parachute flare targets.[64]

Although DaCosta reported that they experienced problems with the Sidewinder firings at MCAS Yuma, later live-firings resolved these with the RAN using a heat-source target towed by a drone.

Once established in Australia, the training programme took place with No. 724 Squadron over a six-month period, where new pilots flew an average of 110 hours on both the A-4G and TA-4G. It took about five flight hours before a student could fly 'solo', and about twenty-five hours before the conversion to the new aircraft was considered complete. The remaining flight time was spent in advanced training for operational flight – refuelling, tactics, bombing – and in carrier qualification. New or conversion pilots were given approximately 100 'looks' at the practice landing field at NAS Nowra before qualifications took place aboard Melbourne.

Unlike Argentina's Skyhawks, Australia's were new builds and ultimately were the equivalent of the US Navy A-4F and TA-4F, but without the aft avionics hump. Originally, the contract

This Australian A-4G sits on the deck of the RAN's sole carrier, HMAS Melbourne in July 1977. The RAN purchased sixteen A-4G and T4 A-4Gs. About half were lost to operational accidents and the remainder sold to the Royal New Zealand Air Force in the early 1980s where they were modified to the A-4G and TA-4G standards. Peter Foster

The Israeli A-4N of No. 102 'Tiger' squadron seen in 1998. This model is also based on the Marines A-4M, but features two 30mm DEFA cannons with 150 rounds each and an extended tailpipe to reduce infra-red signature. Israel bought 117 of these, with deliveries commencing in 1972 replacing A-4E losses during the Yom Kippur War. Peter Foster

MCAS Yuma. Designated as the A-4KU and TA-4KU, the Kuwaiti Skyhawks have been described by some as the most capable of all the variants.

The A-4KUs were based on the already successful A-4M being produced at that time for the US Marine Corps. For the most part, the single-seat model remained the same as its American counterpart, although certain capabilities were deleted, such as Shrike, Walleye, and the nuclear delivery. The Hughes Angle-Rate Bombing Set (ARBS) was added, however, and the Maverick capability retained. As for the TA-4KU, it was the sole two-seat variant produced with the up-rated 11,200lb (5,085kg) thrust J52-P-408 engines. It also incorporated the aft avionics package of the OA-4M used by the US Marines and retained an ordnance capability equal to that of the single-seat A-4KU.

Deliveries began in late 1976, following the A-4KU's first flight on 20 July 1976 and the TA-4KU's first flight on 14 December. McDonnell Douglas test pilot Fred Hamilton was at the controls for each flight. Nos 9 and 25 Squadrons received these Skyhawks at Ahmad al-Jabr.

Kuwait A-4s saw their 'baptism-by-fire' with the 2 August 1990 Iraqi invasion. Many A-4s were captured by the Iraqis, although twenty-four (mostly A-4KUs) escaped to Saudi Arabia where they would later fly missions as the Free Kuwait Air Force (FKAF) from Dhahran Air Base, in support of Operation *Desert Storm*. During the course of the war, FKAF A-4s flew a total of 1,361 sorties and lost only one aircraft. Standard warloads for the Kuwaiti Skyhawks included two 450 US gallon (1,703 litre) tanks on the inboard stations, and five Mk 7 dispensers for cluster bombs or Mk 82 bombs (LDGP, Snakeyes, or LDGPs with daisy-cutter fuse extenders) on TERs. Following the war and the liberation of Kuwait, the Skyhawks were replaced by F/A-18 Hornets and eventually purchased by Brazil.

Israel

Unquestionably the largest purchaser of Skyhawks was Israel, who bought a total of 355 new and used A-4s between 1966 and 1976. Interestingly, these sales almost did not take place. During the early 1960s, Israel approached the US intending to purchase a large supply of refurbished A-4Bs for their air force, the Heyl Ha' Avir. But the political climate of the day and the desire to maintain stability in the Middle East led American officials to reject the offer in 1965. Yet, one year later, the issue was back on the table following a US sale of surplus Air Force Lockheed F-104C Starfighters to Jordan, one of Israel's foes. To restore the balance of power, Israel's purchase was finalized in August 1966, but with a much more potent variant of the Skyhawk, the A-4F.

The Israel Air Defence/Air Forces (IAD/AF) operated three A-4 variants: the A-4H (a modified A-4F), the A-4N (a modified A-4M), and the TA-4H (a modified TA-4J). Of these, some 217 were new builds (ninety A-4H, 117 A-4N, ten TA-4H). Approximately forty-six A-4Es (some sources claim as many as sixty) were purchased from US Navy and Marine Corps stocks between 1967 and 1973 to replace those Skyhawks lost in Israel's wars with Syria and Egypt. Sources also claim that another seventeen TA-4Js were purchased by Israel. Given Israel's secrecy surrounding its air forces, these numbers are difficult to confirm.

The original order called for the production of forty-eight aircraft. Twenty-five TA-4s were also purchased for training, with deliveries commencing in 1969. The first single-seat flight took place on 27 October 1967 and the first two-seater flew on 15 April 1969. Jon Lane piloted both flights. This new -H model was to serve in a tactical attack role, replacing the Dassault Mirage.

The Israeli A-4H, although based on the US Navy's -F, lacked the well-recognized aft hump, but added a squared-off vertical tail with the AN/APX-46 IFF, and a drag chute for reducing landing roll-out. It also featured the DEFA 30mm cannon with 150 rounds each, which replaced the 20mm cannons used by the US. Despite the higher ammunition capacity proposed by the US (the 200 rounds of the A-4M model), the DEFA was chosen because it was believed to be more reliable and accurate, and, based on some of the reports from US pilots during Vietnam, this seems to have been a wise decision.

The A-4Es delivered by the US were later modified to reflect the lessons learned during the 1967 and 1973 wars, where a total of approximately fifty Skyhawks were lost, most to fire from ground-based SA-7 IR missiles. A lengthened tailpipe was added to reduce the Skyhawk's IR signature and a chaff/flare device installed. By moving the exhaust further back, heat emissions were moved away from the aircraft. Electronic countermeasures were also added to increase effectiveness against radar-directed SAMs. Other modifications to all Skyhawks saw the installation of dual-disc main-wheel brakes, nose-wheel steering, and the Elliot HUD system.

The Israeli Skyhawks performed well in combat, flying the majority of missions in both the 1967 and 1973 wars. In the 1967 fighting, Israeli Skyhawks downed two

Israel's initial purchases were the A-4F-derived A-4H. These models lacked the aft avionic hump, but added a brake chute and AN/APX-46 fin-tip IFF. Boeing Historical Archives via Harry Gann

The A-4N cockpit features a combination of old and new technology, having gauges and the Elliot wide-angle HUD. Boeing Historical Archives via Harry Gann

Syrian fighters; one, a MiG-17, with the 30mm cannon, and the second, a MiG-19, with 2½in (6.35cm) air-to-ground rockets. Over the course of the eighteen-day October 1973 Yom Kippur War, Israel is said to have lost upwards of fifty A-4s, although precise numbers are not available due to the security surrounding Israeli operations.

Israel continued flying the Skyhawk in an operational role until the mid-1990s, but has since relegated the A-4 to a training role. Many A-4s have been retained, however, in war storage and for possible sale to foreign countries (such as Indonesia in 1979). Israel also reportedly modified a small number of TA-4H Skyhawks to serve in the EW role, adding jammer pods and an Elta chaff system.

New Zealand

Another long-term customer has been New Zealand. In an effort to modernize its armed forces in the late 1960s, the Royal New Zealand Air Force (RNZAF) began exploring possible replacements for

Three Israeli A-4Es drop napalm during the 1973 Arab-Israeli war. Aerospace Publishing

166

In an effort to modernize its air force, New Zealand purchased fourteen A-4s in the late 1960s. Designated as the A-4K and TA-4K, the avionics hump featured only on the single-seat A-4K, but, in many cases was empty due to financial constraints that prohibited purchasing the standard electronics/avionics gear. The A-4Ks were assigned to No. 75 Squadron based at Ohakea, New Zealand. Boeing Co. via author

Royal New Zealand Air Force A-4 Losses and Other Notables

Serial No./US BuNo.	Model	First Flight	
NZ6201/157904	A-4K	10 Nov 1969	26 June 1975 – Pilot jettisoned drop tanks during night flight in Australia after problem with hydraulics.
NZ6202/157905	A-4K	14 Feb 1970	
NZ6203/157906	A-4K	19 Feb 1970	20 June 1996 – Crashed north of Ohakea due to loss of oil pressure. Pilot recovered.
NZ6204/157907	A-4K	11 Mar 1970	
NZ6205/157908	A-4K	6 Mar 1970	Prototype 'Kahu' single-seater
NZ6206/157909	A-4K	11 Mar 1970	
NZ6207/157910	A-4K	unknown	18 Oct 1974 – Crash near Ohakea caused by loss of pressure. Pilot recovered with broken leg.
NZ6208/157911	A-4K	6 Apr 1970	23 July 1992 – Fuel-feed problems caused crash on coast of North Island. Pilot recovered.
NZ6209/157912	A-4K	15 Apr 1970	
NZ6210/157913	A-4K	unknown	24 Oct 1989 – Crashed in mid-air collision with NZ6211 during aerobatics practice. Pilot was killed.
NZ6211/154903	A-4G/K	15 Jul 1967	24 Oct 1989 – Damaged in collision with NZ6210 during aerobatic practice. Repaired and returned to service 17 Nov 1990.
NZ6212/154904	A-4G/K	20 Jul 1967	29 Jan 1986 – Lost canopy in flight.
NZ6213/154905	A-4G/K	26 Jul 1967	
NZ6214/154908	A-4G/K	8 Aug 1967	Date unknown – Successfully completed a wheels-up landing after losing a wheel during a touch and go on HMAS Melbourne.
NZ6215/155052	A-4F/G/K	26 Jun 1967	26 Oct 1968 to 17 May 1969 – Deployed to Vietnam on USS Ranger with VA-155. 2 Aug 1969 to 15 Apr 1970 – Served on USS Hancock with VA-212.
NZ6216/155061	A-4F/G/K	31 Jul 1967	Same Vietnam deployment as above.
NZ6217/155063	A-4F/G/K	unknown	26 Oct 1968 to 17 May 1969 – On USS Ranger Vietnam deployment with VA-155. 2 Aug 1969 to 15 Apr 1970 – Served on USS Hancock with VA-55 during Vietnam deployment.
NZ6218/155069	A-4F/G/K	29 Jun 1967	Last A-4F built. 26 Oct 1968 to 17 May 1969 – Deployed to Vietnam with VA-155 on USS Ranger. 2 Jul 1969 – Severely damaged by a wire strike with the USN. 3 Jun 1985 – Rolled over during landing at RAAF Base Townsville while in service for RNZAF. Repaired and returned to service 29 Mar 1990.
NZ6251/157914	TA-4K	5 Dec 1969	
NZ6252/157915	TA-4K	24 Jan 1970	5 Feb 1997 – Canopy inadvertently jettisoned during flight. Repaired and returned to service 14 Jul 1997.
NZ6253/157916	TA-4K	unknown	25 Mar 1981 – Crashed in the Ruahine Ranges. Pilot killed.
NZ6254/157917	TA-4K	21 Feb 1970	23 Mar 1994 – Prototype 'Kahu' two-seat variant damaged in heavy landing. Repaired and returned to service 1 Feb 1995.
NZ6255/154911	TA-4G/K	21 Jul 1967	14 Sep 1989 – Landed wheels-up after touching down short of the runway threshold and tearing off part of the main landing gear. Repaired and returned to service 12 Mar 1990.
NZ6256/154912	TA-4G/K	16 Aug 1967	1987 – Flew RNZAF fiftieth anniversary golden colour scheme.

Examples of the vastly improved A-4K are seen here at NAS Nowra in Australia in current markings. The Kahu retrofit, initiated in the 1980s, put the A-4 on par with the F-16 in the close support/maritime interdiction role. Most of the upgrade focused on avionics and included the installation of an APG-66 derivative radar.
Calum Gibson

its Canberras and de Havilland Vampire FB5s. Under consideration was the McDonnell F-4 Phantom II, the Northrop F-5 Freedom Fighter, and an Australian version of the French Mirage. Impressed with the A-4's performance in Vietnam, though, an RNZAF team visited Douglas in April 1968 to evaluate the Skyhawk's potential as a strike platform. Impressions were favourable, and a $26 million contract was signed on 3 July 1968 for the purchase of ten single-seat and two two-seat Skyhawks, both based on the A-4F model.

Designated as the A-4K and TA-4K, the baseline A-4Fs were modified along the lines of the Israeli A-4H and US Marine Corps A-4Ms, with the addition of a 14ft (4.2m) drogue brake chute, an AN/APX-72 IFF mounted in the vertical stabiliser, modified VHF radios, and provisions for the AIM-9 Sidewinder on two of the five stations. These were painted a four-colour camouflage of shades of green, brown, and grey – the standard T.O-114 Asia Minor/SEA scheme.

The first A-4K flew on 10 November 1969, the first TA-4K on 5 December. Test pilots Walter Smith and John Lane were at the respective controls. While the remaining orders were filled, ten pilots and forty-eight maintenance staff members trained on the A-4 with VA-44 at NAS Cecil Field. Interestingly, one of the Skyhawks that New Zealand pilots trained with (BuNo. 155069) was actually purchased by them in their 1984 acquisition of A-4s from Australia. Delivery of the entire purchase was made in May 1970, with USS *Okinawa* (LPH-3) providing the transport to New Zealand. *Okinawa* arrived on 17 May, the aircraft were towed from the docks to RNZAF Whenuapai by tugs and Landrovers. The first aircraft (TA-4K NZ6254) was flown in New Zealand on 21 May; the last arrived at Ohakea from Whenuapai on 27 May and the fleet was accepted at Ohakea on 10 June. These Skyhawks were assigned to 75 Squadron at Ohakea, and went on to serve in the close air support, interdiction, anti-shipping, and limited air defence roles, with AIM-9G Sidewinder missiles. Other weapons included standard US Mk 80 series bombs and 2¾in (6.9cm) rockets, and possibly also 5in (12.7cm) Zunis.

New Zealand's initial A-4 purchase was augmented in 1984 when it acquired ten A-4Gs (eight single and two two-seat) from Australia. They arrived in July 1984. The cost of the purchase was AUS $28.2 million/NZ $40 million. These Skyhawks were immediately upgraded to the Kiwi standards by the addition of the drag chute and VHF radios. Following the sale, Australia and New Zealand reached an accord whereby a small squadron of six A-4Ks (with the newly re-established 2 Squadron) would be stationed in Australia at the Royal Australian Naval Air Station (RANAS) at Nowra, Sydney. These Skyhawks routinely train with Australian F-111s and F/A-18s. The A-4s are based at Nowra under the Nowra Agreement, which came into being in March 1991

This Kahu A-4 sits with engine running as a groundsman makes final checks.
Calum Gibson

when six A-4s and approximately fifty personnel set up there. The agreement called for 1,080 hours per annum to be flown in support of the Australian Defence Force (mainly the RAN). This largely consists of training the crews and calibrating the weapons systems of ships just out of refit and new ships such as the ANZAC frigates entering service with the RAN and RNZN. The rest of the flying time flown by the squadron (a total of 1,700 hrs per aircraft) was available for pilot conversion (all A-4 pilots graduated at Nowra, the final two in September 1999).

Initially two, later three TA-4s were based in Australia. The squadron also undertook trials work on new equipment at Nowra. In 1996, the Enhanced Nowra Agreement was signed, increasing support flying hours to 1,350 hours, including the involvement of No.75 Squadron, and valid until 30 June 2001. It has since been stated that the same agreement will continue with the F-16s (although nothing has been signed).

The New Zealand anti-nuclear policy has led to the suspension of the ANZUS agreement (by the US), and direct exercises between the US and New Zealand have not taken place since 1984. On occasion, however, RNZAF A-4s and USN/USMC aircraft have 'just happened to bump into each other' over Australia. I am informed that the Kiwis have 'won' a number of these unofficial encounters.

New Zealand A-4s often deploy to south-east Asia for exercises under the Five Power Defence Arrangement (NZ, Australia, the UK, Singapore and Malaysia). Currently, the main annual exercise is *Vanguard*, which consists of several phases. The most recent was winding-up in Malaysia at the time of the recent troubles in East Timor. Submarine exercises in 1997 included *Thai-Kiwi* (teaching the Thais maritime attack), and *Flying Fish* (air defence and anti-submarine warfare combined). In 1997, No. 75 Squadron was the only unit involved (which included RAF Tornado F.3s, Royal Navy Sea Harriers, Singaporean A-4s, F-5s and F-16s, and Malaysian F-5s, Hawks and MiG-29 'Fulcrums') to achieve a 100 per cent sortie rate.

Overseas deployments are supported by a P-3K Orion (at least) as navigation leader and SAR support. The trans-Tasman leg requires topping-up from at least one buddy-tank-equipped A-4 which

A comparison between the pre- and post-Kahu upgrade. The latter incorporates the Ferranti 4510 wide-angle HUD and Vintan airborne video recording system, plus an ALR-66 RWR pre-Kahu (top) and post-Kahu (bottom). Troy Campbell

169

The Westinghouse APG-66NZ, a specially modified variant of the radar used by US Air Force F-16s, was added to the A-4K Kahu for an enhanced maritime mode capability. Troy Campbell

then turns back. The leg from Townsville to Singapore is usually supported by RAAF 707 tankers. Sources indicate that the new F-16s will be able to make it to Townsville and then Malaysia without AAR, which is good, because they will not be able to use the drogue equipment.

Shortly after this purchase, New Zealand military officials began a sweeping review of their air force capabilities and requirements. Particular attention was given to the upgrading of their air defence and strike assets, especially in the maritime and CAS roles. In due course, consideration was given to acquiring US Air Force F-16 Fighting Falcons, US Navy F/A-18 Hornets, the F-20 Tiger Shark, and the British Aerospace Harrier Mk II. Financial constraints, however led to the eventual decision that a retrofit of the existing twenty-two A-4s could provide the same capabilities at a fraction of the cost. This retrofit, concentrating on avionics, navigation, and weapons systems, would see the A-4K's capabilities match those of the F-16 but at 1/16th of the cost.

Known as Project *Kahu* (Maori for 'Hawk'), the retrofit began in 1986 and lasted for five years. Included in this $92 million programme were the complete rewiring, re-winging, and removal of the -F's standard aft avionics hump. For air defence and ground attack, the AN/APG-66NZ (similar to the standard -66, but optimized for maritime missions) was installed and the cockpit completely redesigned to give the modern 'glass' cockpit, with HOTAS and a Ferranti 4510 wide-angle HUD. A Mil-Std 1553 digital data bus and Litton ring laser gyro were also included in the package. The Vinten airborne videotape recording system was installed to enhance surveillance, and countermeasures were enhanced by the addition of the Tracor ALE-39 chaff/flare system and the General Electric ALR-66 RWR. Weapons upgrades gave the Skyhawks an AIM-9L, Maverick, and GBU-16 laser-guided bomb delivery capability.

The original Mk 12 20mm cannons were retained. Mavericks used by New Zealand were purchased from Jordanian stocks (apparently the same batch that the US have recently discovered don't work!), AGM-65B Scene Mag TV-guided and AGM-65G IR versions. Before the *Kahu* programme began, the A-4s were repainted in 'European One' wrap-around camouflage. ILS aerials on the fin and a raked-back aerial behind the cockpit identified those aircraft that went through the programme. The humps, which had always been empty in RNZAF aircraft except for storage, were removed before the *Kahu* programme began. More recently, some of the A-4s have been repainted green.

The first *Kahu* Skyhawk flew in June 1988, with the last rejoining active service in March of 1991. Although the *Kahu* upgrade was planned to take the Skyhawk well into the 21st century, and a follow-up *Kahu II* upgrade had been proposed, plans have recently been announced for the RNZAF to purchase or lease (in two five-year batches with an option to purchase after that) twenty-eight Block 15 OCU F-16s (originally intended for sale to Pakistan) to replace the A-4s. Sources expect this move to save approximately $29 million, with the longer-ranged, anti-ship missile and FLIR planned for the *Kahu II* migrating to the F-16 programme after it enters service in mid-2002.

Kahu II was going to include a self-designating capability for the LGBs, a new anti-ship missile, and a new ejection seat. Studies into the ejection seat and a life-of-type study involving an instrumented A-4 had begun when the F-16 lease deal was announced. The Israeli Litening pod has been chosen.

The New Zealand government has high hopes of selling the A-4s to another customer. In September 1999, officials stated that consultants Ernst and Young had been contracted to begin a marketing campaign. 'More than fifteen but less than twenty' Asian and South American countries have had information forwarded to them. The Defence Minister had said in December 1998 that selling the A-4s would raise NZ$50 million, although the New Zealand Ministry of Defence expects to get much more than that. *Flight* magazine reported in late September 1999 that the Philippines were interested in them.

Singapore

Beginning in 1972, the Republic of Singapore Air Force (RSAF) purchased forty-seven refurbished A-4s (forty A-4Bs and seven TA-4s), which were redesignated as the A-4S and TA-4S respectively. Unlike the US two-seat variants, the Singapore 'T's contained two separate canopies rather than the larger single 'clam-shell' canopy seen on other TA-4s. This was the brain-child of Lockheed Martin Air Services of Ontario, California, who had been awarded the refurbishment contract.

SKYHAWKS IN FOREIGN SERVICE

Singapore's TA-4SU is one of the rarer dual-seat Skyhawks. It features two separate canopies, a creation of Lockheed Martin who handled the refurbishing. This TA-4SU is former US Navy BuNo. 142814. Singapore Super Skyhawks feature twin 30mm ADEN cannons, enhanced avionics, and the non-afterburning GE F404-GE-100D 10,800lb (4,905kg) thrust turbofan. Rate-of-climb is said to reach 18,500ft (5,460m) per minute.
Peter Foster

Central to the Singapore A-4B model upgrade was the 8,400lb (3,815kg) thrust Curtis J65-W-20 engine, which provided a 20 per cent improvement in power over the -W-16A. Also incorporated were the lift spoilers of the A-4F variant. Navigation and communications systems were modified with solid-state electronics. Also added were a drag chute and a Ferranti ISIS D-101 lead-computing optical sight. The Mk 12 cannon was replaced with a 30mm Aden cannon. Two additional wing stations and wiring for AIM-9 Sidewinder capability were also added. The arrestor hook was retained for operations on SATS-equipped airfields.

Reflecting Singapore's need for compatibility with the remaining Hawker Hunters in its air force, most of the upgrade equipment was of British, rather than American, origin. Also problematic for the RSAF was an American embargo on sophisticated electronics, that could otherwise be obtained from Britain or internally.

Eight of the A-4Bs were refurbished in the US, with the remaining thirty-two reconditioned by Lockheed Air Services, Singapore. Delivery of the initial eight conversions took place at NAS Lemoore on 14 July 1973, where RSAF pilots were undergoing training with VA-125. The TA-4S, were also conversions from -B models, with a 27in (68.6cm) plug added. Operationally, these retained that same tactical capabilities as the single-seaters.

Initially, Skyhawks were assigned to two squadrons, No. 142 'Gryphons' in 1974, and No. 143 'Phoenix' in 1975 as an advanced training unit. Both squadrons were based at Tengah. A third Skyhawk squadron, No. 145 'Hornets', would later form at Tengah, with subsequent purchases of ex-Navy A-4Cs in 1982. A few A-4s also flew with the 'Hunter' squadron, No. 141.

Singapore's experience was so positive that an additional seventy airframes were purchased in 1980 and modified to the same A-4S standards as the initial purchase. Only the 20mm cannon was retained. This purchase, however, consisted of surplus A-4Cs, with the straight refuelling probe. An additional sixteen

A trio of A-4SUs of No. 145 Squadron sit at Kuantan. Notice the camouflage extending to the fuel tanks. Also notable is the windshield wiper, a remnant of the US Navy A-4C. Peter Foster

A-4Bs were also purchased and converted into eight TA-4S.

Over the years, Singapore's Skyhawks underwent two major upgrades. The first, called Phase One, and falling under the designation A-4S-1, took place in 1986 and involved re-engining the fleet with the non-afterburning GE F404-GE-100D. Offering a 27 per cent increase in power, this engine was rated at 10,800lb (4,900kg) thrust and was considerably more fuel-efficient than its predecessor. This, in turn, brought about an increase in range and a reduction in the man-hours necessary to keep the Skyhawks flying (ten man-hours per flight hour). The A-4S-1 first flew on 19 September 1986 and a total of forty single-seaters were converted, plus ten dual-seat. Initial deliveries were to No. 143 squadron on 1 March 1989.

The up-rated engines brought an improvement to the Skyhawk's performance. Most significantly however, maximum take-off weight was increased by 8 per cent to 24,500lb (11,113kg) and payload increased by 23 per cent to 13,950lb (6,328kg). Rate-of-climb increased by a phenomenal 131 per cent to 18,500ft (5,625m) per minute and thrust to weight ratio increased from 0.75 to 1.02. The added fuel efficiency also increased endurance without external tanks from 3.5 to 4.3 hours.

The second phase of the Singapore upgrade programme began in 1985 and was more avionics-oriented and involved the incorporation of a Maverick missile interface, a monochrome head-down display with FLIR, a GEC Marconi 4150 HUD and a new HDD. The Litton LN-93 laser INS was added as was a 1553B Mil standard databus, the Bendix flight data computer and the AN/AAS-35 Pave Penny laser tracker pod. This upgrade was referenced as the A-4SU. Visibly, the A-4SU differed by the addition of a large VHF/UHF aerial behind the cockpit and on the nose-wheel door and a longer tailpipe. Production of the Super Skyhawk began in earnest in mid-1987.

Six A-4SUs were subsequently selected for the RSAF's flight demonstration team, the 'Black Knights', when it re-formed in 1989. This became the first unit to operate the improved Super Skyhawk. No. 145 became operational as an A-4SU squadron on 24 February 1992, with Nos 142 and 143 receiving them as they became available. A-4SUs may be fitted with the LAU-10 or Alkan Triple-Ejection-Racks (TERs) and can carry the SUU-23 20mm gun pods, SUU-40/A flare dispensers, AGM-65B/E Maverick, and SNEB 68mm rockets. Future upgrades under consideration include addition of laser range-finders and the GEC Avionics Atlantic FLIR for all-weather navigation and targeting.

In June and July of 1998, a small detachment of eighteen Super Skyhawks (from the disestablished No. 143 Squadron) and

One of the Skyhawks sold to Malaysia undergoing refurbishment.

Malaysia purchased several former US Navy A-4C and A-4L airframes and converted them to A-4PTM (Particular to Malaysia) standards, adding two additional wing stations (total five), an enlarged cockpit canopy (similar to the A-4M), and drag chute. Provisions were also included to carry AIM-9 Sidewinder and AGM-65 Maverick weapons. The A-4PTMs were withdrawn from active service in 1994 and replaced by the BAe Hawk Mk 208. Six Malaysian A-4s remained as fleet tankers using the D-704 buddy-store.
Peter Foster

approximately 200 maintenance personnel deployed to Cazaux Air Base in France. The pilots underwent advanced jet training, taking advantage of the good weather and excellent training facilities at Cazaux and the ACM ranges over the Atlantic. This deployment followed the signing of the French/Singapore Defense Cooperation and Status of Forces Agreement.

Indonesia

The Indonesian Armed Forces – Air Force (Tentara Nasional Indonesia – Angkaton Udara or TNI-AU) received US support in 1979 for the purchase of fourteen A-4E and two TA-4H Skyhawks from Israel at a price of $25.8 million. Israel, now looking to reduce its stocks of A-4E Skyhawks, was actively engaged in providing refurbished versions of its older aircraft to other third world nations as it modernized its own air fleet. The purchase also reflected the Indonesian decision to re-equip its armed forces with Western technology rather than the Soviet-provided equipment it had been using before 1974.

Indonesia later purchased another sixteen A-4Es directly from the US, although the refurbishing was handled by Indonesia. This $27 million contract came about in late 1981. The Skyhawks became operational in 1985 and were assigned to 11 and 12 Squadrons based at Iswahyudi (later Hasanuddin) and Pekanbaru. Both units have seen action in anti-guerrilla operations in East Timor and Papua, New Guinea.

Two TA-4Js have been under rework by SAFE Air at Woodbourne for the TN-AUI. They are 154315 and 158454 ex USN/DMAFB. It seems this is not a major upgrade but it has caused some fuss because of A-4 use over East Timor.

Malaysia

Malaysia signed a $120 million contract on 15 December 1982 for the purchase of eighty-eight Skyhawks for its air force, the Tentra Udara Diraja Malaysia (TUDM). Of these eighty-eight, fifty-four aircraft were to be single-seat and fourteen two-seat trainers, all with updated avionics and weapons systems. Despite the large purchase, only forty of these were actually intended for operational use, with the remainder relegated to spare parts cannibalization.

Twenty-five of the Skyhawks were to come from surplus Navy A-4Cs, with sixty-three from the A-4L stocks. At the time of the purchase, all of the earmarked Skyhawks were resting at Davis-Monthan AFB in Arizona with an estimated fourteen years of service life remaining. Due to problems with the US government, a temporary hold was placed on the sale, with Malaysia receiving only forty of the planned purchase. Once delivered, the TA-4PTMs were assigned numbers M32–01 – M32–06, with A-4PTMs assigned M32–07 – 40.

Modifications were carried out by Grumman Aerospace at their St Augustine plant in Florida. Redesignated as the

This VMA-214 'Blacksheep' A-4M was used for the French Navy's carrier evaluation in 1973. The Skyhawk IIs were not selected by the French, but would have given them a credible strike platform. Stephen H. Miller via Lt Cdr Rick Burgess USN Retd

A-4PTM (Particular To Malaysia), these Skyhawks would see the installation of new wiring and the addition of two new wing stations rated at 1,000lb each. This gave the A-4PTMs an appearance similar to that of the A-4E, but with greater carriage capability. Several D-704 buddy-stores were also included in the Malaysian purchase.

For the A-4Cs, aft avionics humps were added to complete the A-4L-type upgrade. From an avionics standpoint, an AN/ARN-118 TACAN was installed as was a Saab RGS-2A lead computing weapons sight, the Lear Seigler altitude heading reference system, and the AN/ARC-154 UHF radio. The A-4PTM's cockpit was also modified to A-4M standards with a 'bubble' canopy. A drag chute was added and the aircraft given AIM-9J and AGM-65A capabilities. As with the US Navy TA-4 model, the fuselage was stretched by 28in (78cm) to accommodate the TA-4PTM's second seat.

The first A-4PTM flew in April 1984, with RMAF pilots undergoing training for their soon-to-be instructor role shortly thereafter. Flight training was included in the contract. Deliveries to Malaysia commenced in 1985 and were completed in February 1986. Two squadrons were operational with the No 6 'Naga' and No.9 'Jebat' Squadrons at Kuanton. In 1994, the A-4PTM was withdrawn from service (ahead of its planned retirement in 1995) and replaced by the BAe Hawk Mk 208. Six A-4s were retained for in-flight refuelling services.

Brazil

The most recent purchaser of A-4s is Brazil, who, in September 1998, received twenty-three Skyhawks from Kuwait. Twenty of these are the single-seat A-4KU models and three are TA-4KUs. Brazil has redesignated these as the AF-1 and AF-1A for the single-seat and two-seat version respectively, and assigned the serial numbers N1001 – N1020 to the AF-1 and N1021–N1023 to the AF-1As. These are called 'Falcoes', which means 'Hawks' in Portuguese. Brazil is reported to have selected the Kuwaiti Scooters because of their relatively low flight time and excellent condition.

The particulars of the Brazilian purchase date back to December 1997, when a contract was signed totalling $83 million. Included in the package were approximately 65,000 spare parts and nineteen spare J52-P-408A engines. The Kuwaiti Skyhawks were modified (essentially overhauled) by Boeing in Kuwait and delivered to Brazil on 5 September 1998. After a three-day road trip from port to their new base at Naval Air Station Sao Pedro d'Aldeia near Rio de Janeiro, the Skyhawks were commissioned as 1 Esquadro de Avioes de Interceptacao e Ataque (Fighter/Attack Squadron One or VFA-1). They were then officially inducted into the Brazilian Navy on 2 October and will be kept in storage until the flight crews complete their training with VT-7 at NAS Meridian. These A-4s became operational in September 1999.

When operational, these Skyhawks will operate from the 19,890 ton carrier *Minas Gerais* (A-11), formerly the British HMS *Vengeance*. Interestingly, this carrier was built in 1945 and holds the distinction of being the oldest carrier in active service. Current plans are for some level of upgrade to these Skyhawks in the early 2000s.

Other Foreign Sales Considered, But Not Fulfilled

Several other countries considered the A-4, but for various reasons did not proceed to purchase. One of these was France, who initially evaluated the A-4M for its carriers *Foch* and *Clemenceau* in September 1972. Both carriers were approximately the same size as the US Navy's 'Essex' class, which had successfully operated the Skyhawk off of Vietnam. Catapult incompatibility problems soon developed and the tests were cancelled. Rather than fix the problem by strengthening and extending the French catapults, a decision was made to purchase the Dassault Super Etendard. Some, however, speculate that the true reason for the decision not to procure the Skyhawks was political, in that the French were already operating US-built F-8 Crusaders and the presence of two foreign aircraft types on a French carrier would do little for the morale of the French aviation business.

Brazil and Columbia, both of whom wanted to upgrade their ageing air forces with the new A-4M, also made inquiries during the mid-to-late 1960s. Both gestures were quashed, however, by US concerns over possible instability that might be created in the region as a result of the introduction of the newer generation airframes.

Douglas also offered the A-4 to various NATO countries, including Greece, the Netherlands, Italy, and Belgium, to fill the role of a close air support/reconnaissance aircraft. The Indian Navy was also a potential buyer. Some of these countries, namely Belgium, and the Netherlands would eventually purchase the F-16 Fighting Falcon.

At the time of writing, Bolivia was also considering a purchase of eighteen TA-4Js for its air force, with the ultimate goal of having twelve operational trainers.

US A-4 Variant Summary (continued)

	A-4A	A-4B	A-4C	A-4E	A-4F	TA-4F	TA-4J	A-4L	A-4M ††
EJECTION SEAT	ESCAPAC 1	ESCAPAC 1 STENCEL MOD	ESCAPAC 1 STENCEL MOD	ESCAPAC 1 STENCEL MOD	ESCAPAC 1C 3	ESCAPAC 1C-3	ESCAPAC 1C-3 1F-3	ESCAPAC 1 STENCEL MOD	ESCAPAC 1C-3 1F-3
NOSEWHEEL STEERING	NO	NO	NO	NO	YES	YES	YES	NO	YES
SPOILERS	NO	NO	NO	NO†	YES	YES	YES	YES	YES
DRAG CHUTE	NO	NO	NO	NO	NO	NO	NO	NO	YES
COMMUNICATIONS	RT-355/ ASQ-17 (AN/ARC-27A)	RT-355/ ASQ-17 (AN/ARC-27A)	RT-355/* ASQ-17 (AN/ARC-27A)	RT-355/* ASQ-17 (AN/ARC-27A)	AN/ARC-51A AN/ARR-69	AN/ARC 51A AN/ARR-69	AN/ARC-51A AN/ARR-69	AN/ARC-51A AN/ARR-69	AN/ARC-51A AN/ARR-69 AN/ARR-114 (VHF-FM)
RADAR IDENTIFICATION (IFF)	RT-354/ (AN/APX-6B) ASQ-17	RT-354/ (AN/APX-6B) ASQ-17	RT-354/* (AN/APX-6B) ASQ-17	RT-354/ (AN/APX-6B)* ASQ-17	AN/APX-64(V)	AN/APX-64(V)	AN/APX-64(V) AN/APX-72	AN/APX-64(V)	AN/APX-72(V)
APC AN/ASN-54	NO	NO	YES	YES	YES	PROVISIONS ONLY	PROVISIONS ONLY	YES	PROVISIONS ONLY
DOPPLER AN/APN-153	NO	NO	NO	SOME	YES	YES	PROVISIONS ONLY	NO	PROVISIONS ONLY
TACAN	AN/ARN-21D	AN/ARN-21D	AN/ARN-21D*	AN/ARN-21D* (EARLY A-4E) ARN-52(V)	AN/ARN-52(V)	AN/ARN-52(V)	AN/ARN-52(V) AN/ARN-84	AN/ARN-52(V)	AN/ARN-52(V) AN/ARN-84
ADF	AM-1260/ ASQ-17 (AN-ARA-25)	AM 1260/ ASQ-17 (AN/ARA-25)	AM-1260/* ASQ-17 (AN/ARA-25)	AM 1260/* ASQ-17 (AN/ARA-25)	AN/ARA-50	AN/ARA-50	AN/ARA-50	AN/ARA-50	AN/ARA-50
ILS	NO	NO	NO	NO	AN/ARA-63	NO	NO	NO	NO
JATO	NO	NO	SOME PROVISIONS ONLY	SOME PROVISIONS ONLY	PARTIAL PROVISIONS	PARTIAL PROVISIONS	PARTIAL PROVISIONS	SOME PROVISIONS ONLY	COMPLETE PROVISIONS
RADAR ALTIMETER	NO	AN APN-141	AN/APN-141	AN/APN-141	AN/APN-141	AN/APN-141	AN/APN-141	AN/APN-141	AN/APN-141 AN/APN 194
AIMS	NO	NO	PROVISIONS* AFC-482	PROVISIONS* AFC-482	PARTIAL PROVISIONS	PARTIAL PROVISIONS	PARTIAL PROVISIONS	PROVISIONS AFC-482	PROVISIONS ONLY
ECM	NO	NO	PROVISIONS ONLY	PROVISIONS ONLY	PROVISIONS ONLY	SOME	NO	PROVISIONS ONLY	PROVISIONS ONLY
SPECIAL WEAPON	YES	YES	YES	YES	YES	YES	NO	YES	YES
SIDEWINDER	NO	NO	SOME AFC-203A	NO	TWO STATION BY AFC	NO	NO	SOME AFC-203A	NO
BULLPUP	NO	PROVISIONS ONLY	PROVISIONS ONLY	PROVISIONS ONLY	PROVISIONS ONLY	PROVISIONS ONLY	NO	PROVISIONS ONLY	PROVISIONS ONLY
GCBS	NO	SOME PROVISIONS ONLY	PROVISIONS ONLY	PROVISIONS ONLY	PROVISIONS ONLY	PROVISIONS ONLY	NO	PROVISIONS ONLY	YES
SHRIKE	NO	NO	LIMITED SHRIKE	YES	YES	YES	PROVISIONS ONLY	YES	YES
WALLEYE	NO	NO	NO	PROVISIONS ONLY	PROVISIONS ONLY	PROVISIONS ONLY/SOME	NO	PROVISIONS ONLY	PROVISIONS ONLY
GUNS	20 MM 200 RDS	20MM 200RDS	20 MM 200 RDS	20 MM 200 RDS	20 MM 200 RDS	20 MM 200 RDS	20MM 200 RDS	20MM 200 RDS	20MM 400 RDS

* AFC 482 UPDATES A-4C/E AVIONICS TO A-4F CONFIGURATIONS
† AFC 442 INC SPOILERS †† The OA-4M was similar except for certain communications gear: ARC-159, KY-28 secure voice. ††† Only the A4-A had single aileron all subsequent modules were tandems.

Foreign A-4 Variant Summary

	TA-4G	A-4H	TA-4H	A-4K	TA-4K	A-4N	A-4P ARG AF	A-4Q ARG Navy	A-4G
Engine	J52-P-8A, 8B	J52-P-8A, 8B	J52-P-8A, 8B	J52-P-8A, 8B	J52-P-8A, 8B	J52-P-408	J-65-W-20	J-65-W-20	J52-P-8A, 8B
Thrust	9,300	9,300	9,300	9,300	9,300	11,200	8,400	8,400	9,300
Fuselage									
Fueling Probe	YES	YES	YES	YES	YES	YES	YES	YES	YES
Air Refueling	YES	YES	YES	YES	YES	YES	NO	NO	YES
Intake Ducts	SEPARATED	SEPARATED	SEPARATED	SEPARATED	SEPARATED	SEPARATED	FLUSH	FLUSH	SEPARATED
Upper Avionics Compartment	NO	PROVISIONS ONLY	NO	YES	NO	YES	NO	NO	PROVISIONS ONLY
AFCS	YES	YES	YES	YES	YES	YES	NO	NO	YES
RADAR	AN/APG-53A	AN/APG-53A	AN/APG-53A	AN/APG-53A	AN/APG-53A	AN/APQ-145	NO	NO	AN/APG-53A
VIDEO IP-936/AXQ	NO	NO	NO	NO		PROV. ONLY	NO	NO	NO
NAVIGATION COMPUTER	AN/ASN-41	AN/ASN-41	AN/ASN-41	AN/ANS-41	AN/ASN-41	AN/ASN-41	AN/ASN-19A	AN/ASN-19A	AN/ASN-41
LABS	PROV. ONLY (WIRING)	PROV. ONLY (WIRING)	PROV. ONLY (WIRING)	PROV. ONLY	PROV. ONLY	NO	NO	NO	PROV. ONLY (WIRING)
CP-741/A	NO	NO	NO	PROV. ONLY	PROV. ONLY	NO	NO	NO	NO
OXYGEN SYSTEM	10 LITRE	HI PRESSURE GASEOUS	HI PRESSURE GASEOUS	10 LITRE	10 LITRE	10 LITRE	5 LITRE	5 LITRE	10 LITRE
EXTENDABLE CONTROL STICK	NO	NO	NO	NO	NO	NO	YES	YES	NO
FUEL GAUGING									
Fuselage	1 PROBE	1 PROBE	1 PROBE	1 PROBE	1 PROBE	1 PROBE	1 PROBE	1 PROBE	1 PROBE
Wing	6 PROBE	6 PROBE	6 PROBE	6 PROBE	6 PROBE	6 PROBE	2 PROBE	2 PROBE	6 PROBE
Drop Tanks	YES	YES	YES	YES	YES	YES	YES	YES	YES
FUSELAGE FUEL CELL CAPACITY	700lb	1600lb	700lb	1600lb	700lb	1600lb	1600lb	1600lb	1600lb
ELEVATOR †††	POWERED	POWERED	POWERED	POWERED	POWERED	POWERED	POWERED	POWERED	POWERED
STABILIZER TRIM									
12 Degrees Noseup 1 degree Nosedown	NO	NO	NO	NO	NO	NO	NO	NO	NO
11 Degrees Noseup 1 Degree Nosedown	NO	NO	NO	NO	NO	NO	YES	YES	NO
12¼ Degrees Noseup 1 Degree Nosedown	YES	YES	YES	YES	YES	YES	NO	NO	YES
WING STATIONS	5	5	5	5	5	5	3	3	5
EJECTION SEAT	ESCAPAC 1C-3	ESCAPAC 1C-3	ESCAPAC 1C-3	ESCAPAC 1C-3	ESCAPAC 1C-3	ESCAPAC 1C-3	ESCAPAC 1 STENCEL MOD	ESCAPAC 1 STENCEL MOD	ESCAPAC 1C-3
NOSEWHEEL STEERING	YES	YES	YES	YES	YES	YES	NO	NO	YES
SPOILERS	YES	YES	YES	YES	YES	YES	YES	YES	YES
DRAG CHUTE	NO	YES	YES	YES	YES	YES	NO	NO	NO
COMMUNICATIONS	AN/ARC-51A AN/ARR-69	DUAL AN/ARC-51A AN/ARR-69	DUAL AN/ARC-51A AN/ARR-69	AN/ARC-51A AN/ARC-115 (VHF-AM) AN/ARR-69	AN/ARC-51A AN/ARC-115 (VHF-AM) AN/ARR-69	DUAL AN/ARC-51A AN/ARR-69	ARC-109 UHF 618M-2D VHF	ARC-109 UHF 618M-2D VHF	AN/ARC-51A AN/ARR-69
RADAR IDENTIFICATION (IFF)	AN/APX-64(V)	AN/APX-46	AN/APX-46	AN/APX-72(V)	AN/APX-72(V)	AN/APX-72(V)	AN APX-72	AN APX-72	AN/APX-64(V)
APC AN/ASN-54	NO	NO	NO	NO	NO	NO	NO	NO	NO
DOPPLER AN/APN-153	YES	YES	YES	YES	YES	YES	NO	NO	YES
TACAN	AN/ARN-52(V)	NO	NO	AN/ARN-52(V)	AN/ARN-52(V)	NO	AN/ARN-21D	AN/ARN-21D	AN/ARN-52(V)

Foreign A-4 Variant Summary (continued)

	TA-4G	A-4H	TA-4H	A-4K	TA-4K	A-4N	A-4P ARG AF	A-4Q ARG Navy	A-4G
ADF	AN/ARA-50	AN/ARA-50	AN/ARA-50	AN/ARA-50	AN/ARA-50	AN/ARA-50	DFA-73	DF-203	AN/ARA-50
ILS	NO	NO	NO	NO	NO	NO	51RV-1	51RV-1	NO
JATO	PARTIAL PROVISIONS	PARTIAL PROVISIONS	PARTIAL PROVISIONS	PARTIAL PROVISIONS	PARTIAL PROVISIONS	PARTIAL PROVISIONS	NO	NO	PARTIAL PROVISIONS
RADAR ALTIMETER	AN/APN-141	AN/APN-141	AN/APN-141	AN/APN-141	AN/APN-141	AN/APN-194	PROVISIONS ONLY	PROVISIONS ONLY	AN/APN-114
AIMS	NO	NO	NO	NO	NO	PROVISIONS EXCEPT KIT/T SEC	NO	NO	NO
ECM	NO	NO	NO	PROVISIONS ONLY	NO	PROVISIONS ONLY	NO	NO	NO
SPECIAL WEAPON	NO	NO	NO	NO	NO	NO	NO	NO	NO
SIDEWINDER	FOUR STATIONS	FOUR STATIONS	FOUR STATIONS	TWO STATIONS	NO	FOUR STATIONS	PROVISIONS ONLY	PROVISIONS ONLY	FOUR STATIONS
BULLPUP	PROVISIONS ONLY	NO	NO	PROVISIONS ONLY	PROVISIONS ONLY	PROVISIONS ONLY	NO	NO	PROVISIONS ONLY
GCBS	NO	NO	NO	NO	NO	NO	NO	NO	NO
SHRIKE	NO	NO	NO	PROVISIONS ONLY	PROVISIONS ONLY	YES	NO	NO	NO
WALLEYE	NO	NO	NO	NO	NO	YES	NO	NO	NO
GUNS	20MM 200RDS	20MM 200RDS 30MM 300RDS	20MM 200 RDS	20MM 200 RDS	20MM 200 RDS	30MM 300 RDS	20 MM 200 RDS	20 MM 200 RDS	20MM 200 RDS

* AFC 482 UPDATES A-4C/E AVIONICS TO A-4F CONFIGURATION
† AFC 442 INC SPOILERS †† The OA-4M was similar except for the following communications gear: ††† Only the -A had single aileron all subsequent modules were tandems.

APPENDIX III

A-4 Production History

A-4 Skyhawks were manufactured by Douglas Aircraft Company (a division of McDonnell Douglas, now Boeing) at the El Segundo and Long Beach, California plants. A total of 2,960 A-4s were built in seventeen different models over a production span of twenty-five years. Of those 2,960, 555 were produced as two-seat models, and 277 were original-builds for foreign countries. The list below is a best estimate based on numerous Douglas and Grumman documents, and lists compiled by others.

US NAVY AND MARINE CORPS PRODUCTION

Model	Number	Bureau Numbers
XA4D-1	1	137812
A4D-1 (later redesignated A-4A)	19	137813 to 137831
	52	139919 to 139970
	94	142142 to 142235
	165	
A4D-2 (later redesignated A-4B)	60	142082 to 142141
	8	142416 to 142423
	280	142674 to 142953
	194	144868 to 145061
	542	
A4D-3		145147 to 145156 cancelled
A4D-2N (later redesignated A-4C)	85	145062 to 145146
	0	146460 to 146693 cancelled
	181	147669 to 147849
	14	148304 to 148317
	178	148435 to 148612
	160	149487 to 149646
	20	150581 to 150600
	638	
A4D-4 (cancelled)		
A4D-5 (later redesignated A-4E)	2	148613 to 148614
	20	149647 to 149666
	180	149959 to 150138
	180	151022 to 151201
	0	151202 to 151261 cancelled
	118	151984 to 152101
	500	

A4D-6 (VAL competition proposal – cancelled)

A-4 PRODUCTION HISTORY

Model	Number	Bureau Numbers
A-4F	1	152101 (converted from A-4E)
	46	154172 to 154217
	100	154970 to 155069
	146 + 1 conversion	
TA-4E (later converted to TA-4Fs)	2	152102 to 152103
TA-4F	33	152846 to 152878
	31	153660 to 153690
	73	153459 to 153531
	57	154287 to 154343
	44	154614 to 154657
	1	155071
	241 + 2 conversions	
TA-4J (159 TA-4Js were converted from TA-4Fs – *see below*)	1	155070
	48	155072 to 155119
	60	156891 to 156950
	75	158073 to 158147
	75	158453 to 158527
	12	158712 to 158723
	6	159090 to 159104
	277	

TA-4J conversions from TA-4F
(These TA-4Fs were modified to the TA-4J configuration by removal of much of the weapons-orientated system.)

152103, 152847–850, 152853–855, 152858–859, 152861–864, 152867–868, 152870–872, 152875, 152878, 153409, 153460–469, 153471, 153473–479, 153482, 153486, 153490, 153492, 153495–498, 153500, 153502, 153512–513, 153515–518, 153521–522, 153524–526, 153528, 153530, 153661–664, 153667, 153669–672, 153674–681, 153683–685, 153687–690, 154287–293, 154295–300, 154303, 154305, 154310, 154312–315, 154317–319, 154322–323, 154327, 154330, 154332, 154338, 154341–343, 154614–619, 154626, 154631–632, 154634–636, 154649–650, 154653, 154656–657, 155072–095

A-4L (100 conversions from A-4Cs)

145065, 145076, 145077, 145078, 145092, 145101, 145103, 145114, 145117, 145119, 145121, 145122, 145128, 145133, 145141, 147669, 147671, 147690, 147703, 147706, 147708, 147717, 147723, 147727, 147736, 147750, 147754, 147761, 147768, 147772, 147780, 147782, 147787, 147793, 147796, 147798, 147802, 147807, 147815, 147825, 147827, 147836, 147843, 148306, 148307, 148316, 148436, 148446, 148453, 148479, 148487, 148490, 148498, 148505, 148530, 148538, 148555, 148578, 148581, 148586, 148588, 148600, 148602, 148611, 149497, 149500, 149502, 149506, 149508, 149516, 149518, 149531, 149532, 149536, 149539, 149540, 149551, 149555, 149556, 149569, 149573, 149579, 149583, 149591, 149593, 149595, 149604, 149607, 149608, 149620, 149623, 149626, 149630, 149633, 149635, 149640, 149646, 150586, 150593, 150598

A-4 PRODUCTION HISTORY

Model	Number	Bureau Numbers
A-4M	2	155042, 155049 (converted from A-4Fs)
	49	158148 to 158196
	24	158412 to 158435
	20	159470 to 159489
	4	159490 to 159493
	13	159778 to 159790
	24	160022 to 160045
	24	160241 to 160264
	158 + 2 conversions	

OA-4M (23 conversions from TA-4Fs)

152856, 152874, 153507, 153510, 153527, 153529, 153531, 154294, 154306, 154307, 154328, 154333, 154335, 154336, 154340, 154623, 154624, 154628, 154630, 154633, 154638, 154645, 154651

A-4A to TA-4A (known redesignations)

137813, 142149

A-4Bs to TA-4B (known redesignations)

142103, 142111–113, 142116, 142118, 142121–122, 142125, 142131, 142141, 142220, 142676, 142679, 142682–683, 142687, 142709, 142717, 142726, 142735, 142741, 142745–746, 142764, 142768, 142772, 142777, 142783, 142788, 142790, 142800, 142807, 142809, 142815, 142818–819, 142821, 142825, 142829, 142833–834, 142837 (from NA-4B to TA-4B), 142842, 142849, 142865, 142868–869, 142873–874, 142876–877, 142879, 142881, 142890, 142892, 142895, 142897, 142900, 142905, 142908, 142913, 142920, 142922, 142929–930, 142934, 142937, 142942, 142946, 142948, 142953, 144870, 144872, 144874–875, 144878, 144882, 144884, 144889, 144894, 144901, 144903, 144913–915, 144917–919, 144924–926, 144929–930, 144932–933, 144937, 144940, 144943, 144947–948, 144954, 144956, 144964, 144966–967, 144972, 144974, 144983, 144985–986, 144988, 144994–996, 145000–001, 145004, 145008, 145010, 145012–013, 145022, 154024–025, 145029–031, 145033, 145035, 145038, 145047, 145050, 145057, 145059, 145061

Model	Number	Bureau Numbers
EA-4F Electronic Aggressors	4	152852, 152869, 153481, 154655
A-4C proposed for US Army	2	148483, 148490
Blue Angels	8	Initial A-4Fs: 154176, 154177, 154179, 154975, 154983, 154984, 154986, 155029
	10	Replacements: 154202, 154973, 155033, 155056, 154172, 154180, 154211, 154217, 154992, 155000
		TA-4J: 158722
		Temporary: 153667, 153477, 158107

Miscellaneous BuNos

NA-4B 142837; NA-4C 145062/145063; NA-4E 148613/148614/150050; NA-4F 152101; YA-4F 150050; NTA-4F 152102, 155049, NTA-4J 154332; NA-4M 155042, 155049.

183

APPENDIX IV

A-4 Squadrons US Navy

FLEET SQUADRONS

VA-12	Flying Ubangis	
VA-15	Valions	
VA-22	Fighting Redcocks	
VA-23	Black Knights	
VA-34	Blue Blasters	
VA-36	Road Runners	
VA-43	Challengers	I-RAG
VA-44	Hornets	EC-RAG
VA-45	Blackbirds	I-RAG
VA-46	Clansmen	
VA-55	War Horses	
VA-56	Champions	
VA-64	Black Lancers	
VA-66	Waldomen	
VA-72	Blue Hawks	
VA-76	Fighting Spirits	
VA-81	Sunliners	
VA-83	Rampagers	
VA-86	Sidewinders	
VA-93	Blue Blazers	
VA-94	Mighty Shrikes	
VA-95	Green Lizards	
VA-106	Gladiators	
VA-112	Bombing Broncos	
VA-113	Stingers	
VA-125	Rough Raiders	WC RAG
VA-126	Bandits	I-RAG
VA-127	Royal Blues	I-RAG
VA-133	Blue Knights	
VA-134	Scorpions	
VA-144	Roadrunners	
VA-146	Blue Diamonds	
VA-152	Mavericks	
VA-153	Blue Tail Flies	
VA-155	Silver Foxes	
VA-163	Saints	
VA-164	Ghost Riders	
VA-172	Blue Bolts	
VA-192	Golden Dragons	
VA-195	Dambusters	
VA-212	Rampart Raiders	
VA-216	Black Diamonds	

RESERVE SQUADRONS

VA-203	Blue Dolpins
VA-204	Terci Pelos
VA-205	Green Falcons
VA-209	Air Barons
VA-210	
VA-303	Golden Hawks
VA-202	
VA-304	Firebirds
VA-305	Lobos
VA-776	
VA-831	
VA-873	
VA-876	
VSF-76	Saints
VSF-86	Gators

ANTI-SUBMARINE FIGHTER SQUADRONS

VSF-1	Warhawks
VSF-3	Chessmen

TRAINING COMMAND SQUADRONS

CNATRA Chief of Naval Training

TW-1 (Training Wing One)
VT-7   Eagles

TW-2   (Training Wing Two)
VT-21   Fighting Redhawks
VT-22   Golden Eagles
VT-23   Professionals

TW-3 (Training Wing Three)
VT-24   Bobcats
VT-25   Cougars

TW-6 (Training Wing Six)
VT-4
VT-86   Sabre Hawks
NAS Pensacola, 'F', '23X'

COMPOSITE SQUADRONS

VC-1	Unique Antiquers/Blue Ali
VC-2	Usus Ubiques/Blue Falcons
VC-5	Checkertails
VC-7	Tally-Hoers
VC-8	Fireballers
VC-10	Proud Pelicans (at Gitmo)
VC-12	Fighting Omars
VC-13	Saints

ADVERSARY SQUADRONS

VF-43	Challengers
VF-126	Fighting Seahawks
VF-127	Desert Bogies
VFC-12	Fighting Omars
VFC-13	Saints
VF-101KW	Grim Reapers
VF-171KW	

FLIGHT DEMONSTRATION TEAM

'Blue Angels'

ELECTRONIC AGGRESSORS

VAQ-33   Firebirds

OTHER

RVAH-3   Sea Dragons, Albany, GA

RAW (RESERVE AIR WING)

RAW-67	NAS Atlanta, GA	'7B'
RAW-70	NAS Dallas, TX	'7D'
RAW-74	NAS Jacksonville, FL	'6F'
RAW-81	NAS Minneapolis, MN	'7E'
RAW-82	NAS New Orleans	'7X'
RAW-87	NAS Alameda, CA	'6G'

US Marine Corps

REGULAR		**RESERVE SQUADRONS**		**HEADQUARTER/MAINTENANCE SQUADRONS/MALS**	
VMA-112	Cowboys	VMA-121	Green Knights		
VMA-113		VMA-124	Bantam Bombers	H&MS-11	
VMA-211	Wake Island Avengers	VMA-131	Diamondbacks	H&MS-12	Outlaws
VMA-212	Devil Cats	VMA-133	Dragons	H&MS-13	
VMA-214	Black Sheep	VMA-134	Skyhawks	H&MS-15	Angels
VMA-223	Bulldogs	VMA-142	Flying Gators	H&MS-24	
VMA-224	Bengals			H&MS-31	Aggressors
VMA-225	Vikings	**TRAINING SQUADRONS**		H&MS-32	Bulldogs
VMA-242				H&MS-33	
VMA-311	Tomcats	VMT/VMAT-102	Hawks	H&MS-37	
VMA-322	Game Cocks	VMT/VMAT-103		H&MS-42	
VMA-324	Vagabonds	VMT/VMAT-203		H&MS-49	
VMA-331	Bumblebees				
VMA-332					
VMA-343	disestablished before converted to A-4				
VMA-533					
VMA-543					